NIGELLA 2

1. lets about shopping — making presents ✓
2. Favourites pedro criminez ✓
3. Use sherry it'll work.
4. Godfather crystalized ginger what kind of present is this ✓
5. Undercooked Jacket potato ✓ too cold batz ✓ FIGHT
6. wappers biscuits — set fine. ✓
7. I love leftovers.... ✓

HOUSE GEST

1. Quiet toilet seat. ✓
2. I am boss, I am in charge ✗

DAN HOUSE GEST

SPORT

1. Lineker looks like Trophy ✓
2. Young Sperponality of the year ✓
3. Bradley wiggins ✓
   over come
   Gold in Athens
   Double gold in beijing) Fight
4. Nobby styles — Hang alive. ✓

WALLEND

1. Honk -
HOUSE G

1. Victori

Fight!

Fight!

by Harry Hill

HODDERstudio

First published in Great Britain in 2021 by Hodder Studio
An Hachette UK company

1

p.188 image © Trinity Mirror / Mirrorpix / Alamy Stock Photo; p.223
image © Alan Davidson / Shutterstock; p.288 © Sky UK Ltd.

Colour plate section picture credits: Harry Hill Late Show © Chris Floyd; Harry Hill
and Simon Cowell © David Fisher / Shutterstock; Harry Hill and Paul Hollywood
© Sky UK Ltd; Harry Hill and Lord Robert Winston © Christopher Baines.

A CIP catalogue record for this title is available from the British Library

Hardback ISBN 9781529381504
Trade Paperback ISBN 9781529381511
eBook ISBN 9781529381528

Typeset in Minion Pro by Hewer Text UK Ltd, Edinburgh
Printed and bound in Great Britain by Clays Ltd, Elcograf S.p.A.

Hodder & Stoughton policy is to use papers that are natural, renewable and recyclable
products and made from wood grown in sustainable forests. The logging and manufacturing
processes are expected to conform to the environmental regulations of the country of origin.

Hodder & Stoughton Ltd
Carmelite House
50 Victoria Embankment
London EC4Y 0DZ

www.hodder-studio.com

This book is dedicated To The Unknown Comedian; anyone who has ever picked up a microphone and tried to get a laugh.

CHAPTER 1
BIG IN THE SEVENTIES

'I was in the garden today playing with my stepladder – not my real ladder, my stepladder. Never got on with my stepladder . . .'

'What have I done?!' I wailed into the dark night.

I was twenty-six years old and lying in a cold sweat and close to tears in a bunk bed in a rented flat in Edinburgh. It was August 1990. I'd given up my job as a junior hospital doctor only days before to become a comedy writer and performer and I'd just seen a review of the play I'd written and was starring in. It was short, pithy and to the point.

The show is a dud and deserves only box office failure.

Could my career in show business have got off to a worse start? The reviewer was one Hayden Murphy – a notoriously tough crowd. That same year, he'd slagged off The Rubber Bishops, a very funny double act, one half of which was a little-known comic called Bill Bailey. After the play's two-week run was up, I licked my wounds and went home to a bedroom in my mum's house in the Kent village I'd grown up in and attempted to write a stand-up act. It was the same bedroom that I'd slept in the night after my first success in show business – 1974's Cub Panto, *Aladdin*.

Cubs were massive in Kent in the seventies. We wore green skinny-rib jumpers, grey shorts, little green tags in the tops of our socks and a sort of ladies scarf round our necks secured by a napkin ring known as a woggle. In other words, we were pretty damn cool.

1

Was there a better place to learn about the world than at Cubs? I doubt it. We learnt all the stuff that every eleven-year-old boy needed to survive on the mean streets of rural Kent.

That meant a lot of knots.

Need to know how best to join two pieces of rope together of different thicknesses? Look no further than the sheet bend! Need a non-slip loop at the end of a rope? Try the bowline! Perhaps you're looking to secure your horse to a horizontal pole? Then the round turn and two and a half hitches is the knot for you! Oh yes, I knew that if I could get my knots right, the world would lay itself at my feet.

And it wasn't just knots!

Watch in astonishment as I start a fire by rubbing two sticks together – although if that doesn't work, watch Akela do it using paraffin and a couple of Swan Vestas.

Ahh, Akela! Although named after the she-wolf from Kipling's *The Jungle Book,* by day she went under the name of Mrs Harmer – Stephen's mum – who would also, on occasion, pop round to our house and cut my hair for 50p.

The seventies have been much maligned since so many of its stars have fallen to Operation Yew Tree, but from my point of view, as a kid growing up, they were fantastic! It's easy to look back on that time before mobile phones and twenty-four-hour screen fun, with rose-tinted spectacles – so I will.

No one spent their day glued to their phone – because the phone was glued to the wall. If you were a kid, making a phone call was a special occasion, and you never, never, ever used the phone before six in the evening unless you wanted to send your family into financial ruin. Young mothers had been forced on the game for less! No, if you wanted to find out whether your friend could come out to play, you walked the half-mile up the road to his house and knocked on the door. If you were in a hurry, you might take the spacehopper, but beware – if it sprung a puncture, you had no way of getting home.

Go on, call me 'Joe 90'. I would!

If there was no reply, you went round the back. If there was still no sign, you either left a note on his door and moved on to your second-best friend's house, or sat on the front step for a bit in the hope that he'd turn up.

If no friends could be roused, you'd walk home with one foot on the kerb and one in the gutter, up and down, up and down, to cheer yourself up. Mum told me it was dangerous, but when something was that much fun, I was happy to take my chances.

But then again, the seventies were a time when we took our road safety advice from Tufty the squirrel – not an animal known for its instinctive understanding of traffic flow, but with hundreds of his companions killed on the roads every year, we knew that he spoke from the heart.

You had to be careful on the roads in the seventies, because most of the people driving the cars had been drinking. No one wore a seat belt either; you sat on your mum's lap in the front, four kids on the back seat and one loose in the boot. There were no speed cameras – speed limits were seen purely as a 'guideline'. I remember my dad explaining to me how to work out how fast you could go: 'You just add ten,' he said. So a limit of thirty miles an hour meant you could go at forty, fifty meant sixty, and seventy meant eighty.

Unless, of course, you'd had a drink, in which case you simply *subtracted* ten and used the back routes where possible. If you were stopped by the police, you merely claimed that you'd got the amount you were allowed to drink whilst you were driving mixed up with the amount you were allowed to take through customs. 'I've only had one litre of spirits, Officer! Or was it two bottles of fortified wine?'

It didn't really matter, though. In rural Kent, at that time, the fuzz were probably pissed too.

The seventies! When men were men and had aftershaves to match. Brut! Pagan Man! And Hai Karate!

Men and women smelt different back then – men smelt of beer, sweat, Brylcreem, violence, fear and anxiety – all carefully dressed with a top note of pine. As for women, they smelt strongly of powder – some sort of scented powder that they put on their faces and inside their bras and pants – according to my friend Patrick. And when the powder met the aftershave – well, presumably it formed some sort of paste . . .

It was a golden time for sport too – the wrestler Shirley 'Big Daddy' Crabtree, the boxer Joe Bugner, and the world's strongest man Geoff Capes held sway. Yes, the strongest man in the whole world was British!

OK, when you look at them now they look like out-of-shape middle-aged men like our dads, but that just made their achievements all the more attainable. If we ate enough pies, we too might develop a rock-hard stomach like Big Daddy. Believe me, you didn't want to be under that when it fell on you in his famous 'splashdown' manoeuvre. Big Daddy! The only man to take a pot belly and turn it into a deadly weapon.

The seventies! When an energy drink was a pint of bitter, or if you were really up against it – a pint of mild! No one bought bottled water – the idea was laughable. There were only two types of water in Kent in the seventies: hot water and cold water, and they both came from a tap.

And the food? What other decade would have come up with Dream Topping and Angel Delight? By-products of the petrochemical industry. We ate Ski yoghurts for pudding, even though no one we knew had ever actually been skiing or really understood how it worked.

This is before saturated fat was seen as a bad thing. With money short, my mum had to buy the economy range of sausages and hamburgers, which had a fat content so high that if you turned your back on the frying pan for more than a couple of minutes, by the time you turned back the fat had escaped and they were like two pound coins going for a swim.

The music of the seventies helped us all stay upbeat. It was cheap, tinny, feel-good pop – 'Yummy Yummy Yummy', 'Chirpy Chirpy Cheep Cheep', 'Knock Three Times' – no one really knew what they were about, but it didn't matter so long as our toes were tapping.

There was only one really sad song – 'Seasons In The Sun' by Terry Jacks; the story of a young man dying of some indeterminate illness, made all the more poignant for me because my sister told me it was based on a true story.

That poor boy, dying – so sad, especially when all the birds were singing in the sky.

Even more tragic was that Terry looked so well when he sang it on *Top of the Pops*. Ain't life cruel?[*]

The music was good and on the whole, life was good too. In fact, pretty much all you had to remember, if you were a boy in the

---

[*] Terry is alive and well and living in Canada.

seventies, was not to cry – if you cried, it was game over. Back then, you didn't 'share' your anxieties with your friends, you bottled them up and turned them into anger.

Your parents weren't your friends – you loved them, but they were figures of authority – you certainly didn't expect them to entertain you 24/7. Once a year you'd go to a model village or have a birthday treat to the cinema, but the rest of the time you were on your own. In the seventies, we parented ourselves. Once you hit sixteen, your mum and dad made your life at home so embarrassing, you were desperate to leave it at the first opportunity.

No one lived with their parents past the age of twenty-five unless they'd suffered some sort of medical condition.

I grew up on a big sixties housing estate in the commuter village of Staplehurst, just one hour from Charing Cross. My parents split when I was about six, and me, my three sisters and brother stayed with my mum and new stepfather 'Pop'. We saw my dad every other weekend, for odd weeks here and there and during the holidays.

It's not like now, where everyone's parents have been divorced two or three times each; in the seventies you stayed together until your children grew up or died. I found the whole thing more than a little confusing, worrying and frankly embarrassing. I had no idea how to explain it away to my friends. Irrationally, there was a certain amount of shame attached to it too. Don't get me wrong, I could see how much happier my mum was, and I got on well with my new stepdad. But when you're a kid, you just want to be like everyone else, to fit in, to be normal.

Our end of terrace houses backed onto fields, and after school, at weekends and holidays that's where you'd find me and my fellow Cubs Adam and Patrick and sometimes Peter and Hugo – building camps, fishing for newts, trying to start fires and if you got a fire started, how about throwing in a couple of light bulbs, or better still, an aerosol can or anything with, *Do not expose to direct heat,* written on it?

Oh, how times have changed! These days it's all about *protecting* the environment – back then, us boys were out to destroy it. We'd spend our days building traps for small mammals, killing wasps with a rolled-up copy of *Whizzer and Chips*, or simply lying down on our fronts with a magnifying glass, frying ants. No doubt a way of letting out all that anger that we'd built up from not crying.

Carry On Camping. Left to right: Hugo, Adam, me, Patrick.

When the Cub panto turned up, it was big news. *Aladdin* – the tale of a simple Chinese boy and his struggle to escape from the ghetto. Adam landed the title role – although with his ginger hair and a complexion that burnt under bright lights, he wasn't an obvious choice to play a kid from East Asia. Aladdin lived with his tragically widowed mother – that was me: Widow Twanky. Dress, wig and full face of make-up aged twelve.

I can't remember much of what I did. I know at one point I had to get a member of the audience up and press them to sing 'Puff The Magic Dragon', then my little brother came on in a green body stocking as Puff and stood staring at the front row. One of the highlights was me screaming for some reason and jumping into Aladdin's arms, then he'd carry me off.

What I do remember very clearly was that I really enjoyed making the audience laugh, and I couldn't understand why the rest of the cast weren't as funny as me. I had an instinctive feel for where the laughs were and how to make the most of them.

I was singled out for a special mention in the local paper, the *Kent Messenger*: 'The undoubted star of the show was eleven-year-old Matthew Hall . . .' It didn't hurt that the reporter, Ron, lived opposite us and one of my sisters was best friends with his daughter Claire. An early lesson in show business – it's not *what* you know, it's *who* you know.

It's only recently that I've finally worked out what it was that I so enjoyed about that experience.

It was a feeling of power.

When you're a kid, you have no choices. You get pushed around, told what to do, what to wear, what's good for you . . . but on that night, for the first time in my young life, I felt in control – in charge of a room full of people. They were laughing because I was making them laugh, and what's more, I found it easy.

If I got that ability from anyone, it was from my mum, Jan. She and Pop were big names in the Staplehurst Amateur Dramatics Society – or SADS for short.

Who can forget their lively revue *Up Staplehurst!** – a biting satire of village life, where Pop dressed up variously as a punk rocker and the local vicar – or their annual panto, when nine times out of ten, he would play the dame and my mum would play the fairy godmother. For a teenage boy, watching his parents horsing around in front of

---

* It had an opening song, which I remember to this day: 'Up Staplehurst – don't wanna shout about it, Up Staplehurst – there ain't no doubt about it, it's the place to be . . .'

the entire village, it should have made me cringe, but I loved it. They both had natural comic timing, could sing and dance a bit, and my mum even had her own tap shoes. I thought they were really funny.

Jan may have been a fairly common name, but there was really only one Jan you needed to know in Staplehurst in the mid-seventies. Like Elvis or Madonna, if you said 'Jan', everyone knew who you were talking about. She knew everyone, and everyone knew her. As a small boy walking down to Liptons supermarket with her, we would have to stop every twenty yards to talk to someone she knew. It would take forever because she'd always have a story. I noticed that at the start of the trip the story would be loose and rambling, but by the time we got to Daphne on the till, she'd have honed it down to just the highlights, complete with a snappy punchline so that it ran almost like a routine. She'd do impressions of the people in the story and she'd mostly leave her public laughing. And me? I was Jan's son, famous by association.

At school I had a natural flair for English and art. Sport, however, was a bit of a black hole. What I didn't understand was why, just because I was a boy, I was expected to like it.

Of course, it doesn't help if you're wearing glasses – even the ones with the flexible wire bits that curl round your ears to keep them on. Yes, OK, I could have taken the glasses off, but then everything would have looked like an impressionist painting.

To be honest, the ball very rarely came my way – it doesn't when you're that crap at sport. When the only goal you ever scored is an own one.

These days, being a geek is considered cool. Who would have predicted that? The rise of the geeks? Certainly not me. 'Joe 90' they used to call me after the animatronic TV puppet, or 'Gogglebox'.

My poor eyesight had been picked up in a routine school eye test when I was eight, and it was already surprisingly ropey*, although I had no idea until I was handed my first pair of glasses. I remember walking out of the opticians and just being amazed at how sharp everything looked – I could see all kinds of stuff I'd never seen before. It was like having bionic eyes!

I can't tell you how thrilled I was with my new superpower. Until the next day at school someone called me 'Four Eyes'.

'Here, let's have a go!' shouted another, snatching them off my face and putting them on. Everyone laughed, and I laughed too, out of embarrassment. Then everyone wanted a try, pulling faces and pointing out how funny they looked wearing my glasses. After that I only wore them in lessons if I needed to read the blackboard – never in break or out of school, even though I loved wearing them.

I know, I know, it's not exactly *Twelve Years a Slave,* is it?! Well, I'm afraid as hardships go, for me, in Kent in the seventies that's as bad as it got (if you ignore the hosepipe ban in 1976)! What can I tell you? I was a happy kid – deal with it.

* -6.5 for any optician readers.

CHAPTER 2
SQUARE PEG

'Did you hear about the Irish English family? They thought Irish jokes were funny!'

It barely needs to be said that what we laughed at in the seventies and eighties is very different to what we find funny now. Back then everything was allowed* – fat jokes, sexist jokes, racist jokes, homophobic jokes and the most popular of all . . . Irish jokes!

Irish jokes were based on the idea that all the people who came from the country that produced Oscar Wilde, James Joyce, Samuel Beckett, C.S. Lewis, George Bernard Shaw, William Butler Yeats and 1970 Eurovision Song Contest winner Dana were thick. They were even funnier if told by someone who were themselves Irish – like Frank Carson or Jimmy Cricket. Jokes like 'Did you hear about the Irish woodworm? He was found dead in a brick!'

Or my favourite at the time: 'Did you hear about the Irish Sea Scout? His tent sank!'

They always started with that enquiry 'Did you hear about . . .?' Well, of course we hadn't!

We all found them hilarious, even though it transpired that my great grandparents were in fact Irish.

'Mum,' I asked one day, 'aren't we partly Irish?'

---

* I say 'allowed', but of course it was just another form of bullying. Deep down I knew it was wrong, but my excuse for laughing at that sort of horrible, lazy stuff is that I was a kid and didn't know any better. I'm yet to hear a good defence of it from the grown-ups of the time.

'Yes,' she said with a smile. 'There's a family rumour that we're related to the founder of the IRA, Michael Collins!'

'So doesn't that make us a bit thick too?'

'No!' she said, and I breathed a sigh of relief.

I guess if you grew up in Victorian times, the most important thing in your house was the fireplace – I imagine you'd all crowd round it, read Dickens and do a spot of needlepoint. In the seventies, without doubt the focal point of our house was the telly. All the chairs faced towards it.

Before the internet and mobile phones, if you lived in a village in Kent, it was your only window on the world, and when it was good, it was fantastic! At its best, it became a brilliant beacon that drew us in and held us all; the whole family, all seven of us, wedged into a three-piece suite the colour of mud.

Every Saturday night we'd be glued to Bruce Forsythe's *Generation Game*. Bruce didn't tell gags exactly – he gently took the piss out of punters, knowing just how far to push it.

I think Bruce Forsythe may well be the first modern TV comic, the first to really use the medium and exploit it; he used the camera – the sideways glance, where he'd turn and look directly at us at home with a look that said, 'I've got a right one here!'* Bruce would make a fool of the public and to take the curse off, he'd make a fool of himself too, and we loved him for it.

When I watch clips of those shows now, I'm aware that he's deliberately feeding them the wrong lines or getting his leg caught up in a bit of scenery, but at the time I believed it was all a happy accident – which, of course, was his great gift.

I spent the day with him once, recording a song for my ill-fated

---

* Ring a bell? Yeah, I got that sideways look to camera off Bruce. He got it off Laurel and Hardy. Nothing's new in comedy, but that's just between us, right?

album of comedy songs *Funny Times.*[*] A gentle soul with impeccable manners, he was in his eighties then, but even at that great age, he was absolutely on top of it. He didn't just phone it in, he wanted to make sure he'd nailed it as best he could. That attention to detail is what made him what he was.

I met him a few times over the years and what impressed me even more than his professionalism was the way he always remembered my wife's name and asked after her. The last time I saw him – at his book launch – he chatted about how he'd played golf with the old king of the music halls and one of his all-time favourites, Max Miller.

Morecambe and Wise were another childhood television thrill. What they did was nothing short of beautiful. The breakfast routine to the striptease music – well, it doesn't get much better than that. Apart from Eric's brilliant comic timing and irrepressible energy, what they had in spades was warmth. They looked like just the sort of people you wanted to hang out with.

The Two Ronnies was another favourite. Not a double act in the variety sense, like Eric and Ernie – there was no straight man – they were both funny but in a different way. Barker was the better actor – he seemed to really inhabit his characters – and Corbett just had funny bones. My favourite bit of that show was when he sat in his chair and told a long shaggy-dog story; I'd watch Ronnie C and try to remember the gag so I could tell it the next day in the playground.

There's a whole generation of young comics who are suspicious of TV and have no particular desire to do it. They figure why bother when they can make a killing online, have complete control over their stuff and not have to filter it through some commissioner who feels like it's his or her job to suggest changes and insert their own lame gags.

What I say to them is that what television has over YouTube and

---

[*] What do you mean, 'Never heard of it!' I'll have you know it sold 1300 copies!

TikTok and all those streaming channels is that it's beamed into people's houses. Which means people can stumble on things that they weren't necessarily looking for and be surprised by them. TV doesn't necessarily feed you stuff that's been chosen for you by some algorithm based on what you already like.[*]

'You like those trackpants? Here's some more trackpants that you might like!'

Don't get me wrong, sometimes it's nice being sent stuff that the algorithm has chosen, but if that's your only experience, you end up with a wardrobe full of trackpants. That's how I discovered *The Office* and Adam Curtis documentaries, and that's how, aged fourteen, I stumbled on Spike Milligan and his *Q* series on BBC Two.

As I hit fourteen and the hormones kicked in, I started to want something more from my telly. I'd sit there, crammed into the sofa with my brother and three sisters watching Little and Large on *Summertime Special,* thinking, *Is this it?* Even Syd and Eddie didn't look like their hearts were in it.[†] Or *Are You Being Served?*, with its jokes about Mrs Slocombe's pussy. I'd sit there thinking, *Am I the only person who's worked out they're doing the same joke every week?* If I could see the gags coming a mile off, why couldn't everybody else?

It was the mediocrity – the lack of ambition that I found so disappointing. The low bar that they were all aiming for and hitting reliably time after time. Surely there was something better than this? Then I found it: Spike Milligan. There he was in a fright wig held on

---

[*] Actually it feeds you stuff that's generally been chosen for you by white middle-class Oxbridge graduates – but don't get me started on that!

[†] I broached this gently with Eddie Large some time later, and he agreed that at that time they were incredibly thinly spread. 'We thought the bubble would burst any minute!' he said. 'So we didn't want to turn any work down.' Eventually, it burst anyway, which is how I managed to book Little and Large on a small-time show on Channel 4.

with a chin strap, a luggage label attached to his jacket and playing Gershwin's 'Rhapsody in Blue' on a baguette. It felt like he was speaking to me.

I know that sounds slightly psychotic, but I actually thought he was saying, 'You could be doing this!'

His name appeared in the credits as the writer, too and I wanted to know more. Back then, before Google, the only way you could get any information about anything was the public library. Staplehurst, where I lived, had a really good one, even if you did have to walk past the village's two punk rockers to get in.

I had four tickets, which meant I could take out four books. I always had four books out, and if I needed more, I'd borrow my mum's tickets. So I went to the library and looked up Spike Milligan – I took out a copy of something called *The Goon Show Scripts*. I read it and loved it – even before I ever heard it.

Spike revolutionised TV comedy. He saw the potential in the form and deconstructed it. Everything that came after him just repeats, in some form or another, what he did. He got there first and it turned out he'd done the same thing with radio comedy some thirty years earlier.

If Spike was my Elvis, then Monty Python were my Beatles. They came along, took what Spike had done, smoothed out some of the rough edges and put five brains on it instead of just one, so it's a lot more consistent. I loved Python too, but what you got with Milligan's stuff, flawed as it is at times, is one person's wonky view. The words 'comedy genius' are bandied about a lot,* but he's probably the only true one, and Christ, did he suffer for it.

---

* One year in Edinburgh so many comics had the word 'genius' on their posters that Sean Lock quipped wryly that really the Fringe ought to be renamed 'The Festival Of Geniuses'.

CHAPTER 3
BIG SCHOOL

'I was a slow developer – I had to have one of my testicles brought down . . . from Derby!'

Rural life was great when I was nine, but as a teenager it became stultifyingly dull. There was nothing to do! The fields at the back of our house had lost their attraction. Girls had taken over, but I was too shy to talk to them, let alone try my luck. I hung around with a bunch of other boys like me who never had any success with girls either. Well, that's not strictly true – Patrick was a bit more advanced. I remember looking for him one lunch break and couldn't find him anywhere. 'Where were you at break?' I said when I caught up with him on the bus home.

'Making love,' he said. He was thirteen and thought he was Omar Sharif.

At eleven, we'd been sent to the big comprehensive school, a five-mile coach ride away in Cranbrook. It was huge – some 1200 pupils, and it was exciting! There were older kids – girls with faces full of make-up and sporting their own twists on the school uniform, and troublemakers who answered back – there was petty vandalism, graffiti and there were fights.

'BUNDLE!' The cry would go up, and everyone would run towards where the fight was taking place – usually on the playing fields. I remember running to one and coming up level with Patrick who said, 'It's a bitch fight!'

'A bitch fight?' I said, a little startled at his language. 'What's that?'

'Two girls!' he said with a raised eyebrow. 'And apparently they're down to their bras!'

They were usually very short-lived, these fights, because at the same time that we were running, the teacher on playground duty was also running to break it up.

I was there the time that Mr Berman*, the moustachioed art teacher who must have been all of five foot two, got laid out. I'd managed to get to the fight pretty quickly and had a prime position ringside to watch two burly sixth-formers holding onto each other, trying to land a punch and get the other over onto his back.

'Break it up, lads!' said Mr B, pushing through the throng to confront them. The boys ignored him, so he put a hand on one of their shoulders to get their attention, and the boy swung round and punched him smack on the nose. Mr Berman teetered backward slightly, then fell forward onto his face – KO'd! When you're twelve, it doesn't get much better than that.

In class, we were 'streamed' according to our academic ability. I was put in the top stream with Patrick and Adam, then after two years most of the top stream were hived off to the grammar school up the road.

I passed all the tests and was all set to join my friends at the grammar. Then one evening, Pop got home from work and threw us a curve ball.

'We're moving to Hong Kong!' he said.

Yeah, I know.

Hong Kong, in the seventies, was like a music-hall joke, like Timbuktu; the sort of place that comics would name as somewhere that was impossibly remote as a punchline to their jokes. It was a byword for cheap plastic toys.

'My wife is so cheap she's got *Made in Hong Kong* tattooed on her bottom!'

We didn't know anything about it! What the climate was, what

---

* 'Berman the German' we called him, even though he wasn't German and looked more Portuguese.

they ate, what it looked like, what language they spoke . . . My sister actually thought it was where King Kong lived. No one in the village had ever been to Hong Kong, and I wouldn't be surprised if, at that time, we were the first people to go there from Kent.

The only Chinese people we knew ran the Chinese Takeaway in the village and they very much kept themselves to themselves.[*]

Hong flamin' Kong?! You're having a laugh, aren't you? We'd never even been to the Isle of Wight! I didn't even have a passport! It just seemed completely bloody mad!

So, I burst into tears.

'Apparently they have their summer in the winter and their winter in the summer,' said Patrick the next day as I broke the news to him. *That's all I need!* I thought. *Wonky seasons.*

According to my mum, it was a brilliant career break for Pop and a chance for them to pay off some of their mortgage.

She was right. In Hong Kong, we were immediately better off. We went from living in a rather cramped end-of-terrace house to living on the fourteenth floor of a brand new block of flats – really fancy flats too. We all got our own room – no more doubling up – and my mum was given a blank cheque to go out and buy all new furniture. This must have been like winning the pools for a couple who, up until then, had had to be incredibly careful with money. We'd had the same three-piece suite for – well – I only remember one and we'd always had it.

I got all new stuff, a new bed, a new desk, plus with a bit more cash sloshing about, we all got presents; sweeteners to get us to look more kindly at the opportunities presented by our new life. Mine was a portable record player.

There was a swimming pool at the base of the flats that me and the rest of us Hall kids pretty much ruled. There was a squash court and

---

[*] Mind you, their chips were nice! 'Chinese Chips' they were billed as on the menu and were basically chips with a lot of salt on them.

a table-tennis table – it was like a holiday camp! It would have been great if I'd had Adam and Patrick there, but I had no friends in Hong Kong and no one much to share it with.

It's a bit like staying in a fancy hotel on your own on a business trip – it's no fun if you're on your tod. I'd always much rather stay in a crap hotel with my wife than in a swanky one on my own. Better still, a swanky one with my wife!

Rather than seeing our move to East Asia as an opportunity to immerse ourselves in a new culture, my mum's attitude was more about trying to build a little corner of Staplehurst there. To minimise the shock to our fragile systems, she stuck to her tried-and-tested menus. We were in Hong Kong for two years and never had a Chinese meal all the time we were there.

Me and two of the sisters were enrolled in a big international school on Hong Kong Island.

Now, back in Kent, if ever a new boy arrived at the school, we would have been falling over ourselves to get to know him, because it very rarely happened. It was a special occasion. New blood! The headmaster would even announce it in assembly. Someone would be allocated to look after him and show him the ropes.

In Hong Kong – because most of the families there were expats and on short contracts, kids were coming and going all the time. Every term there'd be a new intake. So, I was nothing special. Subsequently, no one was interested in being my friend and after a couple of months I gave up trying to make any.

It didn't matter so much in the lessons – you had to sit next to someone. It was the breaks that were tough. Especially that long lunch hour. I would eat my lunch on my own, then just try to look busy, which involved walking around the school, pretending that I was going somewhere or was on some sort of errand, with one eye on my watch, praying that the bell would go for the start of afternoon lessons and, better still, home time.

If only it had been cool to be a geek in 1979 . . .

It was horrible.

This is how it's going to be! I thought to myself. *You're on your own.*

So, I adjusted my expectations and lived inside my head.

I had some good teachers, one in particular stood out.

Mr Gillingham, the history teacher. What was exciting about him was that although he taught history by day, in the evenings he read the news on Hong Kong TV.

All you really need from a teacher is for them to communicate their enthusiasm for their subject – which is exactly what he did. If you can see they're excited about it – you might be too.

In one lesson, he got us all to do a talk. I did mine about child labour in Victorian times – all that stuff about kids being sent up chimneys to give them a good clean.

It seemed to go over well. Then, as the class filed out, Mr Gillingham kept me behind.

'Matthew, can I have a word?' I assumed I was in some sort of trouble.

'Did you notice how the class paid special attention when you were doing your talk?' he asked. Since he mentioned it, I suppose they had been quieter during mine than in some of the others.

'You have a real talent to communicate with people,' he said, then added the caveat, '. . . make sure you never misuse it.'

Misuse it? I thought as I wandered off for another circuit of the school. *Misuse it?*

Immediately, I started to think of ways that I could.

Eventually I did make a couple of friends – I wore them down, by being funny. I noticed that jokes were a useful currency. Everyone likes the funny kid, it makes them subtly more attractive, and slowly but surely, I reeled 'em in.

When Pop broke the news that it was time to return to Kent, I didn't want to go back. I'd only just cracked it in Hong Kong!

All the time I'd been there, I'd written to Adam and Patrick back home. The TV shows we got were mainly American or Australian, so all my references were off-kilter. Fortunately, Patrick kept me abreast of the cultural scene in the UK – explaining that the big thing was ELO – the Electric Light Orchestra.

They're like the Beatles – only better – and everyone is really into them, he wrote and suggested I get hold of a copy of their new LP, *Discovery*, without delay. 'Xanadu' with Olivia Newton-John was also 'really strong' too, apparently.

Fashion-wise, he explained that the order of the day was double denim. If I couldn't get hold of bell-bottoms (fortunately, I could!), flared denim jeans would do. Ideally, your denim jacket should have some sort of emblem embroidered on the pockets, and it was important when wearing the jacket to turn the cuffs up.

And that's how I arrived on the scene in Kent in 1980 at the height of New Wave. Whilst everyone else was in sharp suits and sporting short spiky hair, there I was looking like a fifteen-year-old Jeff Lynne.

Despite being two years behind fashion-wise, when I started back at the grammar school, everyone wanted to know me. I was the tanned, exotic kid from Hong Kong!

I was the new boy and got all the attention that came with it. After my first term back, my older sister, who was in the year above, told me, 'The rumour is you're a bit of a wit!'

Roll over, Oscar Wilde!

If you're looking for action . . .

It was at the grammar that I was introduced to the funniest person I've ever met – Robert Mills. If you'd asked anyone in my year at school who the most likely person to become a comedian in later life was, they would all have said Robert. He'd been at the comp and was in the same class as Adam. I'd heard about him because he wrote and drew his own comics – which we all passed around. So I was intrigued by him; he sounded like someone I needed to meet.

At the new school, we found ourselves in the same French class.

He was down the front wise-cracking, and I was up the back being dry and sarcastic. We hit it off straightaway. The problem I had was that some of my other friends didn't like him. He was loud and a bit eccentric in his dress sense. When we got into the sixth form, we were allowed to wear our 'own clothes' – not that any of us would have been seen dead in those clothes outside of school. Pop took me into Maidstone and together we picked out a pair of brown cords, a mustard-coloured jacket and a brown tie. Yeah, I know, check out my threads! Rob turned up in burgundy cords, a burgundy jacket and a red bow tie. I rest my case.

But we had a connection, an easy shorthand. We found the same things funny. Part of me wanted to be him – outrageous and larger than life.

Before long, we were running the joke page in the school magazine. 'Pavey's Punchlines' we called it, after the new headmaster.

Generally, I'd come up with the jokes and Rob would draw them.

We even had a page banned. It had been my idea – a double-page spread of a cut-out-and-keep paper doll of Mr Pavey in his underpants with various options for how to dress him.

'We can't print that!' laughed the teacher in charge of overseeing the mag. 'He'll hit the roof.'

So, although he didn't let us include it in the main magazine, he did let us print off some copies for ourselves, which we then circulated widely.

That's as racy as my secondary school education got, I'm afraid. On the whole, my time at the grammar was pretty unremarkable. If I'd known all those years ago I'd be including it in a book, I might have made a bit more effort to spice it up. I'd have got myself expelled for taking on the system or got myself touched up by one of the teachers, but I was too busy trying to get three science A-Levels so I could go to medical school.

CHAPTER 4
BOMB MAKER

'My nan's got false teeth – so how can I believe a single word that she tells me?'

My interest in science was largely a by-product of pyromania. From about the age of ten, I loved to play with matches, and as a cover for this, I started to collect matchbox labels. It was a perfectly acceptable hobby – like stamp collecting – the difference being that inside the matchboxes were matches. I'd empty the matches out, soak the label off and stick it in a book, then I'd scrape the heads off the matches and turn that powder into a powerful propellant.

For instance, I'd pack a load of it into a cardboard tube, mount it on the roof of one of my Matchbox cars with some Sellotape and set fire to the end. A big jet of flame would shoot out, scorching the lino and sending the car skidding ten or twelve feet across the floor. Then the tube and the car would catch fire and the wheels would melt.

It was a lot of effort for such a small result – of course, these days I could video it on my phone and play it back endlessly in slow motion or upload it to Instagram. In the seventies, we lived in the moment!

Another time I set fire to my bedroom curtains whilst testing a prototype flame thrower – a syringe full of lighter fuel squirted through a lit candle.

I had an old book that belonged to my dad when he was a boy – *Chemistry Experiments for Girls and Boys*. I remember him telling me how he'd been involved in one experiment in his friend's garage

I was a complicated teenager . . .

and how it had exploded and his friend had ended up losing an eye. Well, he didn't lose it – they knew where it was – it was stuck to the ceiling of the garage. So I got a chemistry set for my birthday and off I went.

It turned out that I wasn't the only amateur arsonist in the village. Adam and Patrick were more than happy to join in and together we set up SCI – Staplehurst Chemical Industries –manufacturing and selling a variety of homemade explosives.

These days we would probably be serving a prison sentence for those activities, but back then it was seen as the sort of dangerous stuff that was perfectly normal for boys to get involved in.

I remember Patrick once got hold of a .22 rifle bullet – but as we didn't have a rifle we had no way of firing it. So, we put it in a vice in his dad's shed and took it in turns to hit it with a hammer. Nothing.

Undeterred, we suspended it by a piece of wire over a bowl of burning methylated spirits, ran out of the shed and took cover behind a wheelbarrow – still nothing. We were lucky neither of us were killed.

These were all preliminary experiments.

What we were after was a bona fide explosion.

These days all you'd need to do would be to google 'How do I blow up my shed?' but back then, you just couldn't find any information about it whatsoever. Then Patrick chanced upon a recipe for gunpowder in a library book about Guy Fawkes.

It turned out that the recipe was incredibly simple. You only needed just three ingredients: charcoal – easy, we could get that, we could even make it ourselves; sulphur – again, you could buy that from the local chemists; and lastly something called saltpetre – which we found out had the chemical name potassium nitrate. But you couldn't get that anywhere, and the reason for that was that if kids like us got hold of it, we would try to make gunpowder.

'I'll write to my auntie,' said Patrick 'see if she can get us some.'

Patrick's auntie was a chemistry teacher in a secondary school somewhere up north.

Sure enough, a couple of weeks later, Patrick received a brown paper package containing a large jar of potassium nitrate.

We could not believe our luck! Here we go, boys – this was it!

Although we knew the ingredients of gunpowder, we didn't know the ratio of the individual ingredients – was it mainly sulphur and charcoal and a dash of potassium nitrate? Or was it mainly potassium nitrate with a soupçon of sulphur and a pinch of charcoal? We spent the summer holidays between junior and secondary school refining the formula, doing various experiments until we got it right.

We never did quite manage an explosion. What we didn't know was that for something to go bang, it needed to be contained – that the explosion was the rapid release of combustible gases. If you just put a teaspoon of gunpowder on a spoon and set fire to it, it just burns very brightly, very quickly and produces a hell of a lot of smoke that brings your mum knocking on your bedroom door asking what you're up to. No, the trick to creating a bang is to detonate the gunpowder within a sealed container. Fortunately for the world of show business, we never worked that out.

By the time we got to secondary school, we had an extensive list of wares. Smoke bombs – 5p; stink bombs – 10p; disappearing ink – 15p.* By Christmas, we were able to launch our first firework – 'The Venetian Spray' – which was basically one of those green cardboard pods you got when you bought a roll of paper caps for your cap gun, packed full of SCI's secret-formula gunpowder plus a pinch of copper sulphate. When you lit the fuse (a twist of paper soaked in potassium nitrate), a blue flame an inch high shot out of the hole in the top. We only ever sold one, which was just as well because they were a devil to put together – plus they were a bit of a loss leader, as the price of the caps was higher than what we were selling the Venetian Sprays for. No, the bulk of our business was the smoke bombs – which, I have to say, were highly effective. With one SCI smoke bomb, you could fill a large front room with smoke in a matter of minutes – Rob's mum banned him from ever buying anything from us after he let off a smoke bomb and she couldn't shift the smell out of her soft furnishings.

Patrick handled sales, me and Adam were at the business end, mixing and assembling the goods back at SCI HQ – his shed.

With business booming, pretty soon we took on a marketing director – twelve-year-old Neil Tottman. His mum's typewriter had a

---

* In the end, this last product was discontinued after one boy's mum hit the roof when the disappearing ink didn't in fact disappear – we'd always known that might be a potential problem, so we gave him his money back and a free smoke bomb as a gesture of goodwill.

slightly more modern font and he started producing letter heads and order forms.

Then it all came crashing down. An uncharacteristically downcast Patrick came to us one break and confessed that whilst he'd been taking orders and handing over the goods, most of the time he hadn't actually been taking any money off our customers. He'd let them have the stuff 'on tick', a promise to pay later – but once the kids had got their grubby hands on them, it was clear that they had no intention of paying up.

'Sorry, but the pressure just got to me,' he said, stifling a sob. He did the decent thing and tendered his resignation, which we accepted, but so he wouldn't feel so bad about it, we resigned as well and divvied up the SCI cash reserves.

Our total takings? One pound and twelve and a half pence! Which was odd as we didn't have anything on the order form for half a pence. Still, not to be sniffed at – more than enough for a couple of Lemonade Sparkles and a chocolate tool each.

So that early apparent interest in chemistry and science in general somehow morphed into the idea of me becoming a doctor – which Mum, in particular, was thrilled about. To be honest, though, I was conflicted. Inside, and not communicated to anyone but Rob, I knew I wanted to be a comedy writer or possibly a comedian, but I couldn't work out how on earth you became one.

I'd seen various interviews with established comics like Spike Milligan, Peter Sellers and Tommy Cooper, and it seemed that the way they'd all got into it was through entertaining the troops in the Second World War.

I became the only sixteen-year-old praying for World War Three so that I could be fast-tracked to stardom!

Monty Python had got together at Cambridge University, but none of my teachers were suggesting I was smart enough for that.

Danger! Young scientist at work. (Photo: Robert Mills)

I was struggling in physics and chemistry – what I was naturally really good at were art and English – why wasn't I doing those? As my A-Levels approached, my physics teacher had shaken his head and told my parents that there was 'absolutely no chance' of me getting a good enough grade to do medicine and suggested I should consider chiropody instead.

I'm an awkward bastard and don't like to take no for an answer. I was also quite certain that I didn't want to spend my days fiddling with other people's feet. As soon as that teacher told me I couldn't make it as a doctor, I decided to make sure I would be one.

You could say I became a doctor out of spite.

PROCTER & GAMBLE LIMITED

P.O. BOX 1EE · GOSFORTH · NEWCASTLE UPON TYNE · NE99 1EE   TELEPHONE GOSFORTH 857141   TELEX 53-320

27th February, 1981

Matthew Hall,
77, Bathurst Road,
Staplehurst,
Tonbridge,
Kent.

Dear Matthew,

FAIRY HOUSEHOLD SOAP - CARVING COMPETITION

Congratulations! Your entry to our Fairy Household Soap
Carving Competition has won a Third Prize in the 12-16 Years age category.

No doubt you will remember that this entitles you to
£10 and a cheque for this amount is enclosed with our compliments.

Thank you very much for your interest and for taking
part in the Competition.

Best wishes,

Yours sincerely,

p.p.G.L.Brown

COMPANY REGISTERED IN ENGLAND · REG. NO. 83758 · REGISTERED OFFICE HEDLEY HOUSE ST. NICHOLAS AVE. GOSFORTH NEWCASTLE UPON TYNE NE99 1EE

Oddball. Show me another sixteen-year-old who was carving soap!

CHAPTER 5
FUNNY BONES

'My nan was a victim of the health cutbacks. They had to turn off her ventilator – because they needed the plug for something else. We couldn't have toast in the morning and Nana!'

The only advice I remember getting off my mum when I left home for St George's Hospital Medical School in Tooting was 'Get to know your local butcher and he'll sort out the best cuts of meat for you.'

Sure enough, in my first week I wandered up Tooting High Street and walked into the first butcher's shop I came to.

'Hi!' I said brightly. 'My name's Matthew and I've just started at St George's!'

The butcher looked back at me, nodded and grunted a greeting.

Undeterred, I pressed on. '. . . And I'll be coming in here quite a lot!' I said, thinking it was a good idea to dangle the carrot of regular custom.

The butcher opened his mouth slightly as if he was about to say something, but then changed his mind.

'So, I was wondering what your best cuts are today?' I said.

'Pork chop!' he said.

'Great!' I said. 'I'll take one!'

He leant under the glass counter and I swear he picked the biggest, heaviest pork chop he could find. The pig that gave that up must have been some kind of mutant.

I've forgotten how much it cost me, but I remember it being a small fortune. I never went back, and a humble country boy lost his faith in humanity that day.

*   *   *

Tooting in the eighties was not in great shape – this is long before gentrification arrived. You'd emerge from Tooting Broadway Tube station to be confronted by a statue of King Edward VII, his face encrusted with pigeon crap. So, to help me cope with this culture shock and with being away from my rosy rural home, I employed a technique used by repressed teenagers since the dawn of time. I got drunk.

The bar served cheap subsidised booze, the hospital canteen sold cheap subsidised food and if you were still hungry, when the bar stopped serving there was Starburger and Big Hamburger on Tooting Broadway, which never seemed to shut.

It was always a tricky choice, that. Starburger felt like it was probably more hygienic – the tables looked like they were occasionally wiped down – but then Big Hamburger did offer exactly that – a very big hamburger, even if the chips had been reheated time and time again.* The marvellous thing about my new lifestyle was that it was all paid for by the taxpayer! I was on a full grant! What a great time to be in higher education.

On my first night away from home, I was up at the medical school bar ordering a pint when I turned round to see a very short boy with ginger hair and a moustache. We got chatting and hit it off straightaway. He was very funny and as it turned out he too had a deep love of ELO and Monty Python. 'Can I get you a drink?' I asked.

'I'll have a snowball!' he said with a grin.

A snowball? I thought. *In October?* His name was Matt Bradstock-Smith, he'd clearly only ever been a Christmas drinker, and he was to play a big part in what we shall call my early success.

For some reason, there's a strong tradition of revues at London's medical schools, and St George's was no different. It had a thriving drama society, which me and Matt were keen to get involved in and ideally take

---

* This was years before Heston Blumenthal invented the triple-cooked chip! Sorry, Heston, Big Hamburger got there first.

over. Matt had no desire to write, but he was very good at organising people. I wrote a lot of stuff for those shows, of varying quality. One sketch featured me dressed as a pancreas chatting to someone else dressed as a kidney; another was set in an operating theatre where a shark had somehow got in because it had 'smelt the blood'.

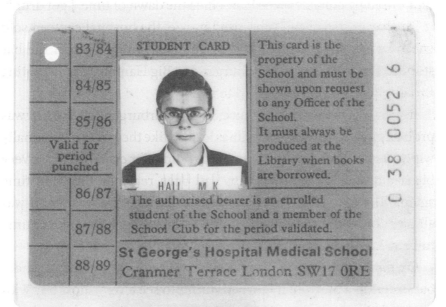

The name's Hall, M. K. Hall.

By the third year, I was writing the lion's share of the show and Matt was directing it. I was just about keeping up with my coursework but really all I was thinking about was Christmas and the medical school revue.

One year I did a solo spot. A four-minute mug's guide to anatomy. I brought on a skeleton in a carrier bag and held up the various bones and made gags about them. 'The skull – tap it, unwrap it!' I said as I took the top off. It was a big hit, but I knew that it was the humour of familiarity. It's the difference between making your friends laugh and making an audience of strangers laugh; of being a comedian rather than just a funny person. So the following year, I wrote a bit that had nothing to do with medicine – in fact, I'm not sure what it was doing in the revue at all. It was a joke cookery lesson: 'How To Cook Your Old Action Man'. I came on with a white carrier bag on my head as a chef, with my old Action Man – 'Roll in flour . . . and when you've done that, dust yourself off . . .' The great thing about it was that it had a really strong punchline. 'Cook it in the oven. Here's one I made earlier . . .' I'd say and produce a roast chicken. That got a good laugh. 'Yeah,' I'd say, 'it does tend to swell up a bit – but then so would you if you didn't have an arsehole!'

The third year was when medical school got really interesting – when we finally got to meet the patients.

We worked in groups of four students attached to a consultant specialising in a different discipline – in surgery, medicine, obstetrics and gynaecology, psychiatry, etc. These 'firms' would last for a couple of months, then you'd move on to the next one.

For the most part I really enjoyed it, particularly psychiatry – this was before care in the community was launched and so a lot of severely mentally ill people were treated in 'mental hospitals'. The one I was attached to was Springfield Hospital near Tooting Bec – a huge Victorian Gothic building set in a couple of acres of gardens. On my first day, I walked up the steps to the imposing front door to see a man with no trousers on pissing back down the steps.

'Welcome to Springfield Hospital!' he said with a smirk.

I was working for Dr E, a psychiatrist who was like a cross between Basil Fawlty and Laurence Llewelyn-Bowen. Camp and caustic. He had what today would be considered a rather old-fashioned attitude to mental health.

We had one patient suffering with schizophrenia who was convinced he was a train.

'Any improvement?' asked Dr E.

'I'm afraid not,' said the charge nurse.

'Right, well, you'd better ask him to choo-choo his way in to see us,' he said.

Another time we had a lady who was convinced that the Archbishop of Canterbury was listening in to her conversations through the electric plug sockets. The consultant told her, '*You* think the archbishop is monitoring you, but *I* think you're quite mad and that if you take the medication I've prescribed, fairly soon you will start to agree with me.'

Appalling in retrospect, but as students, we really were not in a position to challenge him. Besides, that was a perfectly legitimate view at that time. I remember chatting to the lady with the archbishop delusion as she sat waiting to go home some weeks later, apparently cured.

'So how do you feel about it now?' I asked as we sat by the window, looking out over the grounds.

'Well, I feel a bit silly,' she said humbly. 'My mind was clearly unbalanced.'

'So you accept that the stuff you were saying about people spying on you wasn't actually happening?'

'Oh yes!' She nodded. 'Of course! It was silly of me, I don't know what came over me.'

'That's good to know,' I said, happy that for all Dr E's bluntness, the treatment had worked.

'Mind you,' she said, leaning forward towards the window. 'You see that man over there?'

She pointed to a distant figure in the grounds.

'He's listening in on us – and he'll report it back to the archbishop and then he'll blow cold air through the plug sockets later and that's how I'll know.'

'Your car's here!' said the charge nurse, and off she went.

There was another patient, a woman with severe and intractable depression. It was decided that it might be partly caused by her family dynamics.

All four of her kids were grown up and still living at home, but none of them lifted a finger around the house to help her. And her husband was a lorry driver who'd turn up at odd hours and expect his dinner to be on the table. She'd been treated as a dogsbody all her life, and it seemed she had finally had enough.

So Dr E, the social workers and the nurses got the family in, and we all sat round in a big circle with the patient and talked it through. After a long hour and a half session, where everyone had talked through the issues – various family members accepting some responsibility and agreeing to improve their behaviour and a couple of her kids saying they'd planned to move out – we finished up. Then the lorry driver husband piped up.

'You know what I think the problem is?' he said.

'No,' replied Dr E dryly. 'What do you think the problem is?'

'Well,' he said sagely. 'I'm a Libra and she's a Taurus!'

'Thank you, Mystic Meg,' muttered Dr E as we all filed out.

To pass the four-week obstetrics course, you had to deliver a minimum of ten babies and get a midwife to sign a form each time to verify it. When I say 'deliver', any woman who has given birth will tell you that nine times out of ten, the only person delivering the baby is the woman in labour – most of the time all the midwife or the doctor does is catch it, wipe its face, roll it up in a towel and hand it back to her.

We only had a month to score our ten babies and competition on the obstetrics ward was fierce – partly between the student doctors but also with the student midwives. To increase the chances of us hitting our quota, we were farmed out to regional hospitals. I ended up in Hereford.

Essentially, what it involved was sitting with a pregnant woman and usually her partner for hours on end making small talk as the labour progressed – you didn't ever really want to leave your expectant mother unmarked for fear of missing out on the valuable birth and risking someone else claiming it. As anyone who has had a baby will tell you, it usually all happens in the last twenty minutes, sometimes it's even quicker – a couple of times the baby was born before I'd even got my rubber gloves on.

In those last stages, I found that as the midwife instructed the woman to 'Push!' I would also push – so that at the end of the labour, the woman would be holding a baby and I'd be nursing a splitting headache.

Sitting with a couple for all that time meant you really got to know them; you built up a rapport and hopefully they started to trust you so that when the time came, they were happy for you to be the first person to touch their precious offspring.

Well, that's what's supposed to happen.

I was once sat with a very nice couple from the Midlands – I'd put the hours in getting to know them, I'd talked to them at length about how many babies I'd delivered and how it was a 'perfectly natural process'. I went through the birth plan with them, the pain relief options and all that malarkey – in my experience, the more detailed the birth plan, the more what actually happened deviated from it. You'd get the earth-mother type with plans for a birthing pool and whale music, but they'd be the ones screaming for an epidural. That's easy for me to say, of course – I'm a man.

Anyway, the hours went by and things started to hot up in the delivery suite – so my new friend was started on gas and air. As you know I'm sure, it's a mix of nitrous oxide and oxygen. (Nitrous oxide is the so-called 'hippy crack' that's contained in those little silver bombs you see discarded in parks.) In small quantities it gives you moderate pain relief and a mild state of euphoria, but if you have too much, the oxygen bit leads to hyperventilation and you momentarily stop breathing. I know that now. Unfortunately, I didn't know it back in 1987.

The expectant mother grabbed the gas-and-air nozzle, took a deep toke, stopped breathing and collapsed back on the pillow, still clutching the nozzle with her eyes wide open – looking to me – and her husband – like she'd croaked.

'What's happened to her doctor?!' the husband shouted, stepping forward, grabbing her by the shoulders and giving her a shake. I'd like to tell you that my training kicked in immediately, that I took her vital signs and reassured her partner as she gently started breathing again. Sadly, that wasn't my course of action. I took one look at her and thought, *Well, her husband's tried shaking her – and that hasn't worked!* And I ran out into the corridor and screamed, 'HELP!' at the top of my voice.

By the time I walked back into the room, she was awake, breathing normally and wondering what the fuss was all about. Her husband, however, was looking at me like he wanted to see my qualifications. Put it this way, when the baby was born, they didn't call it Matthew.

In 1984, my old mate Rob from grammar school had come to London to study graphics at Chelsea School of Art. It was around that time that we went to our first alternative cabaret night. Note the name – it was alternative *cabaret* in those early days, not *comedy*. I think the press turned it into comedy because it was easier to understand, but when it started, it was a lot more varied than just stand-up comics. There were, for instance, a lot of poets. A helluva lot of poets. Most of them terrible and doing a subpar version of Roger McGough.

My first experience of it was in a club called Cynics and Idealists, which was held in a room above The Roebuck pub on Tottenham Court Road. It was a dark room, lit only by a couple of wall lamps, and there were no microphones. On the bill that night was Eugene Cheese – described as 'bizarre comic'; P.E. Murray – 'sharp poet'; Steve Godfrey – 'Bluesy singer'; and Ivor Dembina, who was labelled

simply as 'stand-up comic'. I know this because I kept the leaflet.*
There were maybe ten people in the audience and one of them was
Felix Dexter – one of the very few black comics on the circuit in the
eighties and nineties – who got up and also did a few minutes, as did
another poet – a bloke in an anorak who looked like he still lived
with his mum.

That night the poetry was very serious, the stand-up hit-and-miss,
and I don't remember the blues. Eugene did a bit of audience
participation – party games, really. He'd get someone up to help him
out, and that night it was me. It wasn't a great night – I didn't come
away particularly inspired by the content, but what was clear to me
was that it might be possible to take those few steps from being in the
audience to being on stage.

It was time to form The Hall Brothers.

People at parties would occasionally say to me and Rob, 'You two
ought to be in a double act,' and a couple of times we said we were –
even though we weren't.

We'd done a bit of busking – I'd taught myself to play the guitar as
a sop for not having a girlfriend. I'd sit in my room on the outskirts
of Tooting, asking the world how many roads you had to walk down
before you could call yourself a man, and occasionally I'd extol the
virtues of Norwegian wood.

The two of us did have an easy rapport and were funny together in
a soft way, but to be a double act, we needed material.

Rob was in a flat share in Balham and I was in Tooting, so we'd
meet at a pub aptly called The Hope, opposite Wandsworth Common,
with a pad of paper and a pen. Four pints later, we'd be drunk and I'd

---

* Eugene and Ivor went on to be really important figures on the nascent alt-cab
scene – not so much as comics, but as gatekeepers. They started up landmark clubs
– the Red Rose in Ivor's case, and in Eugene's, the Chuckle Club.

have three or four pages of unusable scribbles. Eventually, we did come up with a few bits of repartee. It was all a bit dodgy Derek and Clive. But we looked great.

Some of those 'unusable scribbles'. Actually, that's Rob's handwriting – it must have been my night off.

For our opening we had a record player on stage connected to an extension lead so that when our name was announced, we'd flick the plug socket on and the record player would start up playing whatever record was on the turntable. After about twenty seconds of that, we'd run on and Rob would kick the record player off the stage. I know! We were angry young men and we didn't care who knew about it!

Then we'd launch into the theme song from the *Summertime Special* that I'd so despised growing up, 'Come on down to the Summertime Special!'

Essentially, we were a double act in search of an act. Despite that, and full of the naivety and enthusiasm of youth, we got hold of a copy of *Time Out* and turned to the comedy section. We called the numbers that were listed for the venues and most went straight to answer machines.

All except one, which belonged to a man called Malcolm.

'Oh hello, I'm one half of an exciting new double act called The Hall Brothers, and I'm calling about an open spot,' I said.

'Can you make this Sunday?' said Malcolm, getting straight to the point.

'You bet!' I snapped back, not quite believing what he'd just said.

'You'll be on about ten, but if you get here early, you can watch the show. Oy, oy!'

I called Rob straightaway and told him the exciting news.

'I've got us a gig!' I gushed. 'And it's this Sunday!'

The bloke I'd talked to was none other than Malcolm Hardee and his gig was at a mock Tudor pub on the bypass that leads down to the Blackwall Tunnel, which is how it got its name – the Tunnel Club.

That name probably means nothing to you – just as it didn't to me when Malcolm booked us – but if you ask any comic from the early days of the alternative comedy scene, a wry smile will form upon their lips! Sunday Night at the Tunnel Palladium was probably the toughest club there was south of Watford, and Malcolm was its ringmaster. You'll find Malcolm's name in virtually every modern comic's memoir, not for his act – because that was a mess of stock lines and indecent exposure – but because he gave so many of us our first bit of stage time.

He was a true anarchist, had no respect for conventions or institutions or, on occasion, the law! He looked harmless enough – like just another oddball with his thick pebble glasses smeared with greasy fingerprints, a stained and crumpled suit and invariably a fag in his mouth – but if you spent any time with him, he had a real sense of danger. He was rarely sober whenever I met him, and it wasn't always booze that was making him cross-eyed.

But for all that, he went on to run a really successful club until his untimely death in 2005, aged fifty-five – untimely in the sense that knowing his lifestyle, it probably should have happened years earlier.

Malcolm championed underdogs; he booked acts that no one else would book, knowing that they'd probably die on stage just to amuse himself. He loved to subvert and sabotage the known order. So if you phoned up for an open spot, he'd put you on at the first opportunity.

By the time me and Rob played the Tunnel, it was on its last legs. It had been raided by the police a couple of weeks earlier, and the writing was on the wall.

'How many mics do you need?' said Malcolm as we arrived, fresh-faced and full of hope.

'We don't use mics!' we announced proudly in unison.

Malcolm smiled. 'You might want to tonight.'

It was cabaret-style seating – tables with gingham tablecloths and candles, and a stage maybe eighteen inches off the floor with a backdrop that was painted like a cack-handed fairground tunnel of love. Rob, using his newly developed graphic design skills, had put together a flyer with a photo of The Hall Brothers on it along with details of how to get in touch with us for any future bookings, and before the show, we walked round the sticky floor, placing them on all the tables.

We sat in the audience for the first bit. It didn't seem too bad. One of my favourites, Bob Mills, was on and was very funny. Malcolm was filthy. Then it was our turn.

Malcolm's standard introduction for open spots was, 'The next act might be good, might be shit, I don't know . . .'

I don't remember how he introduced us that night. What I do remember is that there was so much shouting and noise from the crowd that I could hardly hear what Rob was saying and he was standing right next to me.

We had no idea how to deal with hecklers, so we just ploughed on, desperately trying to get through it.

Almost immediately the crowd took Rob's flyers from their tables, screwed them up or pressed them into paper planes and threw them at us.

We had a sketch about David Attenborough that involved me rolling an orange off the stage. No sooner had I rolled it off than it came straight back at me, hitting me in the chest with such force that it temporarily winded me. Then the sound man turned our mics down and the music up, and we were left there talking to ourselves until eventually we realised that our time was up.

I'm not sure how Rob felt, but I was furious! How dare they not give us a fair hearing!

The crowd had clearly only meant it as a bit of sport, because they were perfectly pleasant to us in person as we stood at the bar afterwards to get much needed pints.

We sat and watched a bit of the rest of the show – a young Sean Hughes was booed off and then Malcolm got an oven-ready chicken, unzipped his flies and put his flaccid penis inside it.

I was shocked. Dangerous wasn't the word – this felt illegal! I remember thinking, *Any minute now, the police are going to turn up and we're all going to be arrested. I'll get a criminal record and get booted out of medical school!*

We had to make the last train back from Maze Hill, so we downed our pints and headed off.

So complete was The Hall Brothers' humiliation that we didn't do another gig for a whole year.

THE HALL

BROTHERS

01 767 5319

'01 – if you're outside London!' A rare Hall
Brothers flyer that survived the Tunnel Club.

HOW TO BE A COMEDIAN: LESSON NO.1 - HECKLERS

If you're thinking about a career as a stand-up comic, one thing you need to know is that everyone – and I mean *everyone* – will have an opinion about your act.

I remember once answering the front door to a window cleaner.

'Hello!' he said, then he recognised me. 'Oh! You're that bloke off the telly!'

'Yes, that's right,' I said.

'Hmm, yeah I like some of it . . .' he said, '. . . but that clip show you do, *You've Been Framed* – I can't stand that!'

Heckled in my own home! How are you supposed to react to that?

What I should have done is let him clean the windows and then gone round, giving him a critique on each window in turn – 'Yeah I like how you've cleaned that window, but that one's a bit crap . . .'

I didn't though. I just smiled and filled his bucket up with water. I even made him a cup of tea halfway through, but you get my point.

What's the worst heckle I've ever had? Well, that's probably being chased down the road next to the Hackney Empire by a bloke wielding a broken bottle, threatening to kill me. I'd been competing in the Hackney Empire New Act of The Year competition. The heats were held in the pub next door to the theatre, and I was on with, amongst others, a guitar act called Helen Austin. I think there was a bit of needle between the regulars at the pub and the crowd who had come for the comedy. The regulars felt like a perfectly good night's drinking was being ruined by, let's face it, a bunch of students who thought they were funny.

I was on stage and struggling, and this bloke heckled me. I came back at him with a four-letter word, and to my surprise, it worked – there was a bit of muttering, but he shut up. Helen, who was driving, had offered me a lift back into town, and as we were walking to the car, he charged at me from nowhere waving an empty beer bottle. He smashed the end off it on the kerb and staggered towards me, waving it in my face. Well, it would have been in my face if I hadn't dodged behind a parked car. He chased me round the car a couple of times, all the time I was shouting to Helen, 'Get in the car and drive it towards me with the door open!'

She stashed the guitar and when she got level, I ran round the other side of her Ford Fiesta and jumped in.

'I was right about you!' I shouted out of the window at the bloke with the bottle as we sped off down Mare Street, 'You are a c***!'

Actually, I made that last bit up – that's what I should have said, but honestly I was too scared to say anything. I'd never been threatened with physical violence. It just didn't happen in my part of Kent.

Some comics are brilliant at dealing with hecklers. I remember gigging one night at the Comedy Store with my old friend Sean Lock. He was going well, until out of the blue some bum up the back shouts, 'You're not funny!' Sean stops and pauses just for a beat, just long enough to establish who's boss, to let the guy know he's not hurt by it or in any way on the ropes. At this point, me and all the other comics on the bill are leaning forward slightly, craning to hear what he's got up his sleeve. 'Not funny?' he said. 'So all these people laughing . . . that's a coincidence, is it?'

Beautiful.

But as far as heckles go, I've never heard a funny one.

There are the stories, of course – Jim Tavaré opening with a set up for a gag that went, 'I'm a schizophrenic . . .' And before he could deliver the punchline, a voice shouts out, 'Both of you fuck off then!'

Or Jo Brand when she used to be billed as The Sea Monster saying, 'You're a nice little crowd!'

And someone coming straight back with 'So are you!'

The public, the press, *civilians*, if you will, love the idea of hecklers. 'I bet you get lots of hecklers, do you? What's the best heckle you've ever had? I bet you've got some great heckle put-down lines.'

The fact is, if the rest of the room is with you, it doesn't matter what you say – you'll get the laugh and the heckler will shut up. And if you're dying and the rest of the room hates you . . . it doesn't matter what you say either, you're toast.

Hecklers aren't really that common. Most places, you don't get heckled. Most of the time the audience want to be entertained and want you to do well. It's worth remembering that when you're starting out.

When I gave up my job as a doctor for a life in show business, one of the first things I did was buy a copy of *The Stage*. In the back pages, there was an advert offering '100 Heckle Put-Downs For Every Occasion'.

This felt like a must-have for any comic starting out, so I wrote out a cheque and sent a stamped and addressed envelope to a P.O. Box up north.

What came back was a bunch of roughly photocopied sheets held together with staples, which did indeed offer me a put-down for every occasion – sort of.

The occasions were quite specific – like 'Man with moustache gets up to go to the toilet' or 'Effeminate man gets up to got to the toilet' or 'Man with much younger woman arrives late' and stuff like that. Stock lines basically that invariably started with 'Hey!' As in, 'Hey! You have some great thoughts. Let them work their way up to your mouth!' and 'Hey! You have a lot of get-up-and-go. Please do!' and 'Hey! I like you – you've got the sort of FACE I'd like to shake hands with!'

I couldn't see how these were going to turn round a hostile room above a pub in Camden, so I rapidly binned them.

The first time I ever got heckled, I was dying and some wit shouted, 'Fuck off!'

So as quick as a flash I countered with, 'No, *you* fuck off!'

Yeah, not exactly inspired.

The problem was, having a whimsical persona, as soon as I lost my cool, the game was up. I needed to find a line that Harry Hill would use – not Matthew Hall. In the end, the put-down I came up with was 'You may heckle me now, but I'm safe in the knowledge that when I get home, I've got a lovely chicken in the oven. Yum! Yum!'

It kept the persona going, and if the audience were with me, it usually did the trick. How did I come up with it? Well, just before going out to do the gig, I had roasted a chicken and was really looking forward to getting home and eating it. Simple as that! When I did get home that night before I ate it, I thanked that chicken. Best chicken ever.

By the way, if you are in a situation where a man with a moustache gets up to go to the toilet, then try 'Is that a moustache or have your eyebrows come down for a drink?' And I wish you the best of luck.

1. Mum's new baby
2. Rain + Raindrops
3. Belongings in carrier bags
4. Nan on Oz
5. Knickerbocker Glory
6. What is NHS Nº
   No can not see Dr
   Leave sample at front desk
7. Tape.

Post Card

8. Fleshy Cactus.
9. Fish Rainbow
10. Wizard of Oz.
11. Canoeing.
12. Careers advice
13. Des O'connor
14. Dog + Biscuits
15. Lordy miss Clawdy

An old set list. Note the hole in the top where I'd
hang it on the choke button of my 1954 Austin A30
so I could practise as I was driving to the gig.

CHAPTER 6
COUNT ME EDIN'

'My dad used to like my mum to get dressed up as a nurse and then go out and work . . . as a nurse.'

As I progressed through medical school, the feeling that I wanted to be a comedy writer and performer didn't go away. If anything, it got stronger, and the once-a-year medical school revues and occasional gigs with Rob weren't enough to satisfy it.

So I said to Matt Bradstock-Smith that we should be doing a summer show as well. Luckily he'd been voted in as the head of the medical school drama society and had the cheque book at his disposal. I wrote these new shows, Matt directed them and the drama club paid for them. Then in 1989, I had the idea that we should write something and take it up to the Edinburgh Fringe. At this point, none of us had even been to Edinburgh. We'd only read about it in the papers and seen bits of it on highlights shows on BBC2.

I did some research, and it turned out that there wasn't any quality control, you didn't have to show them a script or anything, all you had to do was pay your fee to the Fringe Club, hire one of the venues on their list and, hey presto, you were going to the Fringe!

We picked a venue called Theatre West End, which was basically a long, thin room attached to St John's Church – the big one at the far end of Prince's Street. I booked us rooms in a rather faceless block of flats about a mile away. Rob, who by now was at the Royal College Of Art studying graphics, designed a poster, so all we had to do was write the thing.

BBC tv
BRITISH BROADCASTING CORPORATION
TELEVISION CENTRE WOOD LANE LONDON W12 7RJ
TELEPHONE 01-743 8000 TELEX: 266781
TELEGRAMS AND CABLES: TELECASTS LONDON TELEX

Reference: 35/IB/GK   12 August 1988

Dear Matthew Hall,

Thank you for letting us see your sketches which were
passed to us by the Radio Light Entertainment Script
Editor.

These have now been carefully read and considered but
I regret that they have not been recommended for
production.

I am returning them herewith.

Yours sincerely,

(IRENE BASTERFIELD)
Television Script Unit

Matthew Hall
10 Gambole Road
LONDON
SW17

Early rejection. God knows I was a trier.

For that, I teamed up with an art school friend of Rob's called Andrew Collins. You may know Andrew as one half of Radio 1's Collins and Maconie. He's now the movie critic for the *Radio Times*. The show was called *President Kennedy's Big Night Out*, and if I could tell you what it was about I would – but to be honest, I'm still not sure.

It was set in Dallas, just after President Kennedy had been shot, and featured a student nurse friend of ours called Sue who played Jackie Kennedy but with her native Welsh accent. I played lounge singer Val Demure – loosely based on Tony Christie – and Rob played a plastic surgeon called Dr Herbert Datta, who performed operations to turn people into teddy bears. What I can tell you is that on its opening night it was an hour and forty minutes long. Pretty much all shows in Edinburgh come in at about an hour. We didn't know that and had booked a two-hour slot.

We'd done the show once before at the medical school and it had gone OK. Me and Andy didn't do any re-writes or tweaking, we just took it up to Edinburgh wholesale as it was.

Rob drove us up in his old Vauxhall Viva – a car that always smelt strongly of petrol – and we promptly broke down on the North Circular, before we'd even left London.

We rather grandly called our company Renaissance Comedy Associates – which has got my fingerprints all over it. I think it was a reference to Kenneth Branagh's outfit at that time – Renaissance Theatre. The show was billed as 'a hilarious new comedy' and cost you £2.50 to get in.

Matt was very pleased with himself because he'd got a new computer which, when connected up to his keyboard, meant that with one click, the tunes pretty much played themselves. All he had to do was stand there. To me, this seemed like an accident waiting to happen.

Sure enough, on our opening night in Edinburgh, whilst we were setting up, I noticed Matt crouching over his computer, sweating even more than usual. I mean, he was always a big sweater, but from his red face and bad language I knew something was up, and I had a pretty good idea what it might be too.

'The mouse is fucked!' he squealed as he fiddled with the computer mouse. 'It'll only go from side to side!'

'Give it here,' I said and had a go myself. He was right. For some reason, however you moved the mouse, the little cursor would only go left or right.

'What does that mean?' I said.

'If I can't get it onto the next page, it won't play!' he said, frantically banging the mouse on the tabletop.

'Won't play the first song?' I asked.

'Won't play any fucking thing!' he shouted, his hands shaking as he lit up another fag.

'Can't you take over and play the keyboard like you would normally?' I said, thinking that we didn't necessarily need all the bells and whistles – all we really needed was some backing.

'I don't know the fucking songs!' he yelped – he hadn't bothered to learn them because he wasn't going to have to play them.

There was no time to discuss it further; the audience – all fifteen of them – were in and we had to start the show.

The first few lines went well – and then I had to come on and sing a song called, excitingly enough, 'Kitchen Units'. Matt's keyboard was stuck on some sort of swirling church-organ setting and I could make out neither melody nor beat.

'Shall we start, Wayne?' I said, turning to him – bravely staying in character.

We'd decided to have a follow spot, but because the stage was so long and narrow if you were sat anywhere other than smack bang in the middle, it was like staring into a lighthouse and completely blinded half the audience. After about twenty minutes, the crowd became restless, after thirty, one of them was asleep. Rather foolishly, we had a long sequence that was set in complete darkness – with just our voices being heard – like a radio play in the middle of a show. We thought we were being awfully clever and terribly experimental. As soon as the lights went out people started to leave. When they came back on again, two thirds of the audience had walked out.

'Cut the end song!' hissed Matt.

So we just stopped the show there!

The next day we cut thirty minutes – including the blackout – Matt got his mouse fixed, and it went much better.

We were only up there for a week – the unfashionable third one – but it was fantastically exciting. We saw a lot of shows too. One in particular sticks in my mind and when you hear how it opened, you'll understand why. It was called *Taboo* and started with a man naked from the waist down, walking on in a straitjacket. Tied to his penis was a piece of string, which lead to a skateboard, on which was a tape player that was playing something that to my untrained ear sounded like an opera by Wagner. As he walked, the string dragged the skateboard with him.

If that's not entertainment, I don't know what is.

We got a reasonable review in *The Times*: 'Silliness and bizarre logic make for an entertaining spoof on investigative stories about the assassination of JFK'. If you say so, mate!

We even won an award. Not for the show, Rob's eye-catching poster won first prize in the best poster of the Fringe competition – and four hundred and fifty pounds, which he magnanimously kept to himself.*

I came back to London having learnt something rather special: I now knew how to put on a show at the Edinburgh Festival.

---

* I'm sorry to bring this up after all this time, but it still grates.

President
Kennedy's

Big
Night
Out

An hilarious new comedy
written by Matthew Hall and Andrew Collins

Theatre West End

St. John's Church, Prince's Street, Edinburgh.
Mon 28th Aug to Sat 2nd Sept 2nd 1989
Show starts 9.45pm prompt
Tickets £2.50 (£2 conc)
available from TWE Box Office or Fringe Office
A Renaissance Comedy Associates Production

CHAPTER 7
CYNIC AND IDEALIST

'My old dad used to say to me, "Always fight fire with fire," and that's why he was thrown out of the fire brigade.'

Despite the rigours of life as a medical student, when we could afford it, Rob and I went to see comedians.

We saw all the best new comics as they arrived. A favourite was the original Meccano Club, which was upstairs at the Camden Head on Upper Street in Islington and run by performance poet James Macabre. It was there that we saw Jo Brand, in her Sea Monster days.

Jo was a knock-out star from the get-go. She came on in black, with red Dr Martens boots, thick black eyeliner, a shock of red lipstick and black, back-combed hair like a crow had crash-landed on her head, and she delivered hilariously withering one-liners. She was kind of scary and scarily brilliant in equal measure.

We saw Julian Clary when he was The Joan Collins Fan Club – accompanied by his whippet, Fanny the Wonder Dog; Jeremy Hardy in his cardigan; and our all-time favourite double act Fiasco Job-Job, made up of Arthur Smith and his mate Phil Nice.

There were a few double acts around back then, including The Oblivion Boys, with Mark Arden and Stephen Frost – made famous by the Carling Black Label ads – and Mullarkey and Myers, with Neil Mullarkey and Mike Myers. (When Myers left for *Wayne's World*, *Austin Powers* and *Shrek*, Nick Hancock took his place and they became Mullarkey and Hancock.)

Then there was the marvellous John Hegley. John was the first of the really funny alternative comic poets – in London, anyway. A fellow glasses wearer, I loved the way he celebrated that. He had one poem 'Eddie Don't Like Furniture', which involved the audience being divided up into three parts that were roughly two equal halves and a third part was just one person. Hegley handed that person a piece of paper with their lines on it and they had to stand up at a given moment and say, 'Ner-Ner'. That night it was me. Here's the proof – I kept the piece of paper. By the way, if you give Eddie some furniture, he'll return it yer.

I remember one night at Eugene Cheese's Chuckle Club in Victoria, sitting with Rob a couple of rows from the tiny stage as Jack Dee did his tight twenty.[*] I looked round at the crowd – who were all doubled up with laughter – and I distinctly remember thinking, *However funny I am, I'll never be as funny as this!*

After Jack was Lee Evans. What a night.

---

[*] A 'Tight Twenty' is what us comics call our usual twenty-minute club set.

The gig that made the biggest impression on me at that time was a New Variety gig at the Old White Horse in Brixton. Those nights were run by Roland and Claire Muldoon whose outfit CAST* was set up with the express intention of putting on diverse bills and not just white male middle-class stand-ups – which is what most of us were.

The bill that night at the Old White Horse was Stewart Lee in the first half and Kevin McAleer in the second. I've still got the handbill, which says there were two other acts on – but I don't remember them. Stewart with his sarcasm, perfectly tooled one-liners and shaggy-dog stories that relied almost solely on repetition and comic timing to get laughs was an inspiration. He looked great too. Slim, in a dark suit and tie, with a floppy quiff of black hair. When I first saw him, I wanted to be him, simple as that!

Kevin McAleer might well be the most original comic I've ever seen. He had two acts – one purely verbal where he'd take something like an episode of *Kojak* and tell you what happened in it, as if he were explaining it to someone who'd never heard of it before. There's no point in me trying to quote bits to you – it looks like nothing on the page; only *he* could make it funny – the sign of a true original. It's something about his use of language and the rhythmic way he does his routines that render them hilarious. His other act, the one that everyone who saw it talks about, was his slide show. He would stand in semi-darkness and show a series of unrelated slides. He'd talk about them, making up the scenarios that had led to the photos being taken and pointing out things in them that you hadn't noticed. Sound familiar? If you swap the slides for video clips, that's pretty much what I did on *TV Burp* for ten years.

* (Cartoon Archetypical Slogan Theatre)

It's no exaggeration to say that when I staggered out of the Old White Horse at close to midnight, my comedy horizons had shifted.*

The Hall Brothers did a few more gigs over the next couple of years – to varying levels of disinterest.

Our problem was that we weren't really a proper double act; there was no onstage relationship as such, we just divvied up the lines between us. After a while, we resurrected my old Action Man cookery sketch – the one I'd done solo at the medical school revue. That never failed to get a good reaction. Plus, there was the added benefit that at the end of it we had a cold chicken, which Rob and I would eat on the Tube on the way home. Half a chicken each, no sides, bit weird. We played the Banana Club in Balham – 'Not particularly impressed,' said Andy, who booked it. Another was a club called the Fruit 'n' Nut, where we got paid a pound each on the understanding that we gave the compère a lift home, but it was a struggle.

We briefly re-branded ourselves as The HB Nutters, but it was the act that needed changing – not the name. The truth was we liked the *idea* of being a double act more than actually being one.

We both had girlfriends by then, and so meeting up to thrash out some scripts got harder. It's tough getting a double act right. You have to find the time to write together, to rehearse and at the end of it, you have to split the money straight down the middle.

That's why there are so few of them around – well, there's only really one proper double act left: Vic and Bob.

---

* It's easy for old stagers like me to get all dewy-eyed for the old days, but with acts like John Kearns, Sara Pascoe, Mawaan Rizwan, Holly Burn, Nick Helm, Judi Love, Mat Ewins, Mo Omar and many, many more, the live comedy scene is every bit as exciting and original as it ever was. Get out there, go see it!

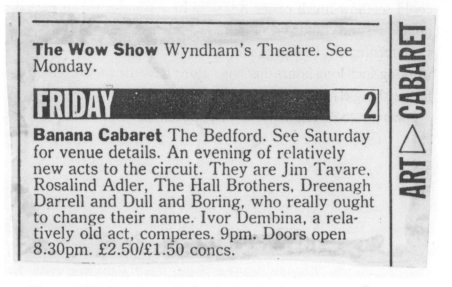

The Wow Show Wyndham's Theatre. See Monday.

FRIDAY 2

Banana Cabaret The Bedford. See Saturday for venue details. An evening of relatively new acts to the circuit. They are Jim Tavare, Rosalind Adler, The Hall Brothers, Dreenagh Darrell and Dull and Boring, who really ought to change their name. Ivor Dembina, a relatively old act, comperes. 9pm. Doors open 8.30pm. £2.50/£1.50 concs.

ART △ CABARET

Name in Lights: A rare listing in London's *Time Out Magazine*.

We had one last booking in the diary – at Bunjies, a tiny subterranean vegetarian café off Charing Cross Road. Rob called me the day before and said he was ill and couldn't do it. It seemed to me that to cancel it was a wasted opportunity. So, I decided I'd have a go on my own.

That year I'd done a sketch in the med school revue where I came on and did a sort of geek character. I had a couple of good gags and finished on a song on my ukulele. When I'd done it for the medical school it had gone down a storm, so I figured I'd try that.

I was nervous, but I got more laughs in that five minutes than I'd got in all those gigs with Rob. It was just so much easier not having to rely on someone else. Jack Dee was also on the bill that night at Bunjies and as I came off, he nodded to me.

'What did you think?' I gushed, my face flushed with excitement.

'Yeah, you did OK,' he said in that slightly snarling, distant manner of his.

It wasn't a ringing endorsement – but it was enough for me. I could see how much easier it was to be a stand-up than part of a double act and couldn't wait to have another go.

Unfortunately, I'd just qualified as a doctor and was about to start working such long hours that I just didn't have the time or the energy for anything else.

I was not to do another stand-up gig for over two years.*

---

* I know, it's all terribly dramatic, isn't it?

CHAPTER 8
DEEP BREATH

'The left side of the brain is responsible for speech, which is incredibly important, but then it would say that, wouldn't it?'

Let's get one thing straight: I was never a neurosurgeon. Every time that gets quoted somewhere, my old friends from medical school roll around on the floor laughing. Some joker put it on Wikipedia and because I rather like the idea, I've never bothered to change it. Not that I couldn't operate on your brain if you wanted me to. If you need a brain operation, I'm happy to have a go, I just can't guarantee the results.

As a medical student, and then as a doctor, you have the privilege of seeing people in their extremes – people who are desperately ill, people who are dying, people who have lost all reason, people being told good news ('It's a boy!') and being told the worst ('You've got two weeks to live . . .') and everything in between. If you think the TV show *24 Hours in A&E* is pretty harrowing, you might want to skip this chapter, or have a drink ready for when it's over.

My first job was working for a very shy man, a professor, whose whole raison d'être was something called calcium blockers, which I'm reliably informed are used to lower your blood pressure. I don't know whether you've tried to look enthusiastic about calcium blockers every day for three months, but it's not easy – particularly if you'd missed the lecture about calcium blockers because you were rehearsing your new play. Mainly I just nodded and worked my way down the list of chores he set me: get the blood tests, locate the X-rays and write the patient up for calcium blockers.

Doctor Hall will see you now . . .

**Excerpt from the diary of Dr Matthew Hall,
3 September 1988**

Mistakes so far . . . only been here two days but have made many mistakes.

Not taking temperatures.

Diagnosing heart attack in normal woman.

Told off for daydreaming during aortic aneurysm operation just when surgeon burst a vein.

Back then, us doctors were treated like gods. This was before audit came in; no one's results were checked, there were very few protocols and the public just trusted the men (largely) and women in white coats.

Before the internet, when people couldn't google what was wrong with them or ask Alexa, there'd be a notable frisson when a doctor in a white coat walked into a room. The oracle had arrived!

Suddenly, I found that people would take what I said completely at face value. I remember a visitor asked me if it was OK to smoke in the corridor.

'How many do you smoke a day?' I demanded.

'Er, about twenty?' he said.

'Hmm, well, you need to cut down,' I snapped. 'I need you to promise me you'll have quit completely by the end of the year.'

'Yes, Doctor!' he said, almost jumping to attention.

On the whole, your patients did exactly what you told them to do – it wasn't necessarily good for them, but it was much easier for us doctors!

As a junior doctor doing general surgery, one of my jobs was to examine the patients when they arrived and send them for tests to make sure they were fit for their operations. I might have seven or eight patients I had to see and getting them 'clerked' was a big part of my job and keeping my boss happy.

I once had two patients who needed specific tests – one with a bowel condition who needed a barium enema, the other was having their thyroid gland removed and so needed to have an X-ray of their neck. I filled out the forms and sent them off. Later that day, I bumped into the patient with the bowel condition.

'Did you have your X-ray?' I said breezily.

'Yes, Doc,' he replied, 'but tell me, why did I need an X-ray of my neck?'

'Of your what?'

'My neck?'

I'd sent him for the wrong test.

'It's just something we like to do in some patients!' I flannelled. He swallowed that, and I ran to the ward station.

'Where's Mrs J?' I spluttered.

'Here I am!' said a voice from behind me. It was Mrs J.

'Everything OK?' I asked nervously.

'Yes, although I do have a question . . .' she said with a puzzled look on her face.

'Yes?' I asked, knowing perfectly well what was coming next.

'I wasn't sure why I had to have a barium enema?'

'Just being thorough, Mrs J – we don't want to miss anything, do we?'

She went away more than happy, thoroughly impressed by my diligence.

Another potential obstacle to getting my work done and getting home was the consent form. It wasn't like these days where you genuinely want your patient to know and understand the risks of whatever procedure you're subjecting them to. Back then we just wanted to get the form signed – even if it meant guiding the patient's hand over the piece of paper yourself. I would run down the potential risks and side effects of the procedure lickety-split, like the terms and conditions in one of those mortgage adverts.

'Hang on a sec, Doc,' they might say. 'Did you say there's a risk of losing my leg?'

'Well . . .' I'd reply, reassuringly pressing my biro into their hand. 'In theory, yes, but I can assure you, it won't happen to you!'

Appalling!

I did have a tricky situation with one patient, though. He was a Lebanese man who, as far as I was concerned, had been admitted for the repair of bilateral hernias – you know those rather uncomfortable lumps in the groin, that usually occur in men and are caused by a little loop of bowel escaping through a tear in the wall of the abdomen. So I gave him the spiel and handed him the form to sign. Unusually, he took out his reading glasses and started to scrutinise it.

'I'm sure it's all fine, Doctor . . .' he said, looking up. 'But just one thing . . . What is a bilateral orchidectomy?'

'Removal of the testicles,' I said. 'Castration, if you like . . .'

'Hmm, so why am I having that too?'

'Eh?' I said, snatching the consent form back off him. I looked at it and sure enough in addition to both hernias he was down to have his balls off.

'I thought it was just the hernias, I don't understand'? he said, which I suppose was a reasonable enough query.

I had no idea why my consultant was planning to convert this man into a eunuch – but I was in a hurry.

'I'm sure he's got a very good reason!' I bluffed. My Lebanese friend hesitated, but reluctantly signed the form.

In the end, the mistake was spotted by the anaesthetist, and the patient left the hospital as much a man as when he'd arrived. But it just shows you the power we doctors had back then. If a man in a white coat demanded your wedding tackle, you signed on the dotted line and handed over the goods.

My houseman* passed me a note once that said, *Mrs B thinks she's going to die and wants to talk to you.*

I knew the patient well and knew that she was in hospital with a very minor ailment and certainly wasn't going to die – and I was very busy. 'Tell her I'll talk to her later!' I said. I was busy all day and didn't get to the ward until early evening, by which time, sadly, Mrs B had been found dead in the doctor's office with the telephone still in her hand.

'Maybe she was trying to call you?' said my houseman, rather judgementally. The riddle was cleared up when some twenty minutes later a pizza delivery boy turned up with a thirteen-inch margherita and a litre of Diet Coke for a Mrs B.

And if you're wondering, yes we did. Well, it would have been a shame to waste it!

*　　*　　*

---

* My houseman at that time was in fact a woman. We were all called housemen back then, regardless of what gender we identified as. It's sexist but that's what we were called so, if it's OK with you, I'll stick with the nomenclature of yesteryear. After Houseman you progressed to Senior Houseman (S.H.O.) then Registrar, Senior Registrar and then if you'd worked hard enough, passed your post grad exams and generally kept your nose clean, Consultant.

I guess my lowest point as a doctor, and I'm afraid this will shock you, was when I was running across the car park of Ashford Hospital at two in the morning to a cardiac arrest, thinking, *I hope the patient is dead when I get there.*

That probably needs a bit of unpacking.

A few words about cardiac arrests first.

If you're the medical SHO, as I was, and you're on call, you're automatically on the cardiac arrest response unit or in hospital slang, the 'crash team'.

When someone's heart stops beating – or more accurately when someone notices it's stopped beating – your bleep will make a different sound to the one it normally makes, usually a series of rapid bleeps. Really it should have played the chords from the shower scene in *Psycho*, but the people who made the bleeps weren't necessarily known for their sense of humour.

So it makes this alarming noise, and a number comes up on its little LCD display, which tells you which ward you have to run to, to try and tempt someone back from that long black corridor with the bright white light at the end, where the Angel Gabriel stands, waving a helium balloon with *Welcome To Heaven* on it.

At two in the morning, it makes you fall out of bed. After the first few times that's happened, you automatically start pulling your shoes on before you've even opened your eyes, and then you run.

You run like your life depends on it, even though, in fact, someone else's does.

As soon as someone's heart stops beating, their chances of survival fall off exponentially with the amount of time that passes.

Minutes, seconds even, make a big difference.

So you run, and if you were as unfit as I was that can be quite a shock to the system.

When they built St George's Hospital, where I trained, it was the largest teaching hospital in Europe. Some geek worked out that the distance between the two furthest points was about a mile. A mile of corridors and stairs. When they opened the new wing, they only had one crash team on call for the whole hospital – so if your arrest bleep went off whilst you were in the old wing and you were needed in the new wing, you really had to leg it if you didn't want your patient to peg it.

I knew a girl who was so out of shape that en route to a cardiac arrest, she had to stop to throw up in the corridor – now that's not something you ever see on *Holby*.

You can get a crash call at any time of day. Cardiac arrests do not respect lunch breaks – coincidentally neither did the hospital administrators when I was practising. We junior doctors didn't get a lunch break – you grabbed it when you could and hopefully it coincided with the canteen opening times.*

I was on call once and dropped by the canteen. I loaded up my plate with 'Sausage Lyonnaise', one of their specialties,† and was at the till when my cardiac arrest bleep went off. I looked at the bleep . . . and then I looked at the sausages . . . and then I looked at the lady on the till.

'Poor you!' she said with a sympathetic wince.

I sighed, grabbed a sausage off the plate, turned and ran.

I don't know whether you've ever tried eating a sausage and running at the same time, well it turns out you can't. And it doesn't look good turning up to a cardiac arrest holding a warm sausage either.

If you are called to a cardiac arrest during the day – and you aren't clutching a sausage and you aren't heaving into a nearby bin – it can

---

* This was before the days of a Costa coffee in every hospital lobby. If you missed the canteen, your only option was a coin-operated sandwich dispenser – yum, yum!

† It would turn up on the menu at least twice a week – maybe the chef originally hailed from the French town of Lyon. If he did, then he'd really worked on his accent because he sounded like he was straight out of Dagenham. I suspect it was a way to repurpose all the bangers he had left over from breakfast. Anyway, it was delicious – particularly with their big, soggy chips.

look terribly glamorous. Just like that old Hero aftershave advert. You know, that one with the Bonnie Tyler track on it? 'I need a hero!' she rasps as some swarthy, lantern-jawed hunk in a white coat rushes across a car park to save some damsel in distress – although these days he'd be more likely to be running to top up his pay-and-display ticket.

Just like that advert, old ladies would swoon as I cantered down the corridor, stethoscope trailing behind me. Passers-by would shout encouragement, 'Go on, Doc! Sort him out!'

Hospital porters, physiotherapists, pharmacists and even hospital administrators on their long lunch breaks would wave you on, full of admiration for your dedication. 'Just look at him go!'

Not quite the Thursday-night Covid clap, but you get the idea.

So look, the last thing I want to do is to put any of you off having a cardiac arrest, but honestly? They seldom work out well. Not in my hands, they didn't, anyway.

As the SHO, I'd usually be the first on the scene – the registrar tended to feel that he or she had earned the right to walk briskly, rather than jog, and the houseman would usually hang back for fear of being the first to arrive and being out of his or her depth.

The responsibility doesn't get any higher than at a cardiac arrest – what you do in those few minutes makes the difference between life, death and occasionally something in between.

Cardiac resuscitation is basically a series of steps, a flow diagram, if you like. You try the first step, and if that doesn't work you go to the second one and so on.

The first one, when I was doing it anyway, was the 'precordial thump'. So, if you're sitting next to someone at one of my gigs and the person next to you is laughing so hard they collapse,[*]

---

[*] It happened! At St Alban's Arena during the Hooves tour, an ambulance arrived ten minutes into the second half and the patient was stretchered off from the dress circle!

you need to basically punch them as hard as you can on the chest.*

However, that punch only works at the exact moment that the heart stops beating. It's pointless trying it any later than that – although it does look good to bystanders. Really, if you do it at any other time, it's just assault. All the time I was working, I never gave anyone a precordial thump – I was just never there in time.

The most urgent item on your list is to start CPR – chest compressions – and get some air into your patient's lungs. If you don't do that, even if you get your patient's heart pumping again, there won't be much point – the brain, starved of oxygen, starts dying as soon as the heart's squeaked out its last batch of blood.

There's certainly a knack to CPR – and it's never how it looks on the TV shows. You've really got to lean on that chest, otherwise it doesn't compress the heart enough for it to be effective. My registrar at the time used to reckon that unless you broke a couple of the patient's ribs, you weren't doing it right.

So you've got air going into the lungs, you've got oxygenated blood circulating to the brain – now for the fun bit. It's time to break out the Kerdunker! You've all seen defibrillators on the telly – it looks like a couple of electric irons connected to a tape deck.

'Clear!' you shout, then you announce what you've turned it up to. 'Two hundred and forty joules!'

Kerdunk!

The idea is that the shock makes the heart muscle contract to remind it what it's supposed to be doing. It's a fairly blunt instrument and also makes the patient's chest and shoulder muscles contract. The patient appears to nonchalantly shrug his shoulders like, 'Whatever!'

---

* Look, don't do any of this, it's thirty-odd years since I practised – if you want to know how to resuscitate someone, properly go on a course or join the St John's Ambulance.

If I'm honest, I could count on the fingers of one foot the number of times the Kerdunker brought someone back. But now and then, much to my surprise, it did work – and it was a fantastic feeling – because it's like magic!

One minute your patient (and it's nearly always a man and usually a smoker) is lying blue and gurgling with his eyes rolled up into the top of his head then, kerdunk! He's sitting up asking for his cup of tea, *Daily Mail* and where his horse came in the two thirty at Haydock Park, completely oblivious to the peril he was in just moments before. Most of the time they'd never even thank me! They'd look at me like, 'What are you doing here? I didn't call for a doctor!'

My registrar at the time noticed that it was really only ever the nurses who got the thank-yous – and more importantly, the *gifts*: the boxes of Milk Tray and occasional bottles of sherry – even though nine times out of ten, it was us doctors who had instigated their treatment. So, we came up with a strategy to try and turn that around.

'It's because they don't understand what we've done for them,' he reasoned. From that moment on, whenever I successfully resuscitated someone, I would lean over them and as their eyes focused on my face I'd say, 'My name is Doctor Matthew Hall – and I've just saved your life!' And it worked! The first time I tried it, I got a big box of crystallised fruit. Result!

I know what you're thinking. If the feeling of bringing someone back to life was so great why was I wishing death on that patient as I was running to meet him at two in the morning? Well, it was based on a simple, if rather heartless, calculation.

If I was successful, if I was able to cheat death, and my patient got to light up another Rothmans and collect his winnings, I would then have to *stabilise* him.

You don't need to know the details – which is handy because I honestly can't remember them – but I'd have to start him on some medication, keep him under observation, send off blood tests, maybe get an X-ray . . . and then there was the paperwork.

At my peak, on a good day I could get all that done in an hour – hour and a half, tops. So at two in the morning, it meant I'd be getting back into bed at half past three.

After something like that, believe me, you don't just drop back off to sleep and pick up your dream where you left it. You're pretty wired. It's not a million miles away from the buzz you get after storming a gig. So, maybe it takes you an hour to fall back to sleep – that takes us up to four thirty. You have to be back on the ward at eight, which means getting up at . . . you get the idea. That's assuming you don't then get a call to casualty at five or something.

So that's your timetable if the patient lives.

If he dies – it's a quick scribble in the notes (*Time of death, etc.*) and back to bed. All done in fifteen minutes. Listen, I'm only human!

Was I a bad doctor?

I don't think so. Once I got there, faced with a dying man, the adrenaline would kick in and I'd do my best. I can honestly say that the thought of that warm bed never affected my judgement or the outcome of the various procedures and treatments that I was involved in.

But at that moment, as I was running across that car park and that thought flashed into my head, I did feel ashamed. Wishing death on someone? That's the opposite of what a doctor is supposed to do.[*] 'I just want to *help* people!' I'd said seven years earlier at my interview for medical school. How had it come to this?

Fundamentally, I wasn't cut out for life as a doctor – one of logic and reasoning. I'm a dreamer at heart. I live in my head and I'm always

---

[*] Years later, I talked to my friends about it, and they agreed they'd occasionally had the same feelings too.

looking for new excitements, but it took me a while to work that out, and in the meantime, I'm afraid my patients didn't always get a smooth ride.

The first time I had to break proper bad news to someone, I burst into tears. That's not what you want from a professional.

He was a man with a young family and his wife had died suddenly in our care. Cancer. There was nothing we could have done about it but he wasn't expecting it and frankly neither were we.

St George's, at that time, was one of the few medical schools that included some teaching about how to break bad news. Admittedly, it was only one forty-five-minute lecture, but it was better than nothing – just. If you've ever been in that situation yourself – of a doctor telling you something awful – you'll know how important it is for that doctor to get it right, as that moment will stay with you forever.

However, I was only a couple of weeks into the job.

We'd been told in the lecture that it was crucial to break the news *gradually*. So we should kick off with something like 'How ill do you think your wife was when she was admitted to hospital?' to assess how much of a shock the news was going to be. Then you gently lead them through the events leading up to their relative's death. 'Your wife was gravely ill . . .' Then something like 'I'm afraid we tried everything, but we were unable to save her life.'[*]

---

[*] It's a bit like the old joke about the man who left his cat with his brother whilst he was on holiday. When he gets back he asks his brother where his cat is. 'The cat's dead,' says his brother. 'Well, you could have broken the news to me a little more gently,' says the man.

'How?' says the brother.

'Well, you could have said the cat was playing on the roof and fell off and that you tried everything but eventually he died.'

'OK, I'm sorry,' says the brother, 'I'll remember that.'

'Anyway . . .' said the man. 'How's Mum?'

'Well . . .' says the brother. 'She was playing on the roof . . .'

The truth is, there's nothing really you can do to soften the blow, but you owe it to yourself and all concerned to at least have a go.

All these thoughts were in my head as I made my way to the relatives' room to give my patient's husband the news that would change his life forever. As I walked, I rehearsed my lines over and over in my head. 'How ill do you think your wife was . . .? She was gravely ill . . . We tried everything we could . . .'

As I opened the door and walked in, the man looked up at me.

'What's the news, Doc?' he said with a terrified look in his eyes.

'She's gone!' I said. All that training went flying out of the window in a single sentence.

It got worse.

'Where to?' said the husband.

'No. I mean, she's dead,' I replied.

Nice one, Dr Hall.

What followed still makes me shudder.

He burst into tears and seeing him so distraught, I burst into tears too. He didn't just cry, he started wailing and rocking back and forth in his chair. Then he started clawing at his face with his hands. Aged twenty-three and with just a couple of weeks under my belt as a qualified doctor, I felt completely helpless.

Looking back, I should never have been put in that position. It shouldn't have been me breaking that news, it should have been my registrar – but all too often they just weren't around. The general view at that time was 'We had to do it when we were at your stage, now it's your turn.'

I ducked out of the relatives' room and the ward sister looked at me and shook her head.

'Have you got any brandy?' I asked her, hurriedly drying my eyes.

It was something I'd seen in films – if you got given bad news, you qualified for a complimentary brandy.

'Er . . . will Scotch do?' she said.

Every ward at that time used to keep a bottle of booze on the drug trolley – you were allowed to prescribe it in moderation to help people sleep. So, I poured the new widower a large Scotch, which he proceeded to knock back in one go. So, I poured him another . . . and another . . . and then another. It then transpired that he was a bus driver, and in the panic of getting to the hospital, he had parked his double-decker bus right outside Casualty, blocking all access to the ambulances. Now, thanks to my medication, he was too pissed to move it.

It was still there the next day when I clocked on for work, a big red reminder of the awful cock-up I'd made the day before.

So, that first time I cried, and maybe a couple of other times, but after a few months, breaking bad news hardly bothered me at all. I got hardened, you see. I put my emotions on ice and froze them. You had to. You couldn't carry all that stuff around with you, or it would have been me on the Scotch.

It took me years after I gave up medicine to thaw them back out again. The good news is, I now cry at the drop of a hat – seeing a robin with a twig in its beak off to make a nest, watching *Long Lost Families* – actually just the sight of Davina McCall gives me a lump in my throat. I cry at my daughter's school plays – even though she's rarely in them – and I cry at the price of ice creams at West End theatres.*

With all that bad news flying about, hospitals do become huge repositories for dark humour. Not dark so much as pitch black.

Ready for a bit of dark?

Try this.

I had a patient die on me – no fault of mine, I tried everything – but when your number's up . . . Now, if a patient dies in hospital

---

* How can a scoop and a half of ice cream cost five pounds! Please. Someone tell me? HOW?

and the consultant looking after them isn't sure why, there's a post-mortem to try and establish the cause. As a junior doctor, if one of our patients was having an autopsy, we were encouraged to attend. On the whole no one bothered – largely because we barely had time to tend to the living, let alone the deceased, and besides, it wasn't very nice seeing someone you'd been chatting to only a couple of days earlier being opened up and having their brain weighed.

I arrived early to the morgue to see my patient's final indignity and was surprised to see the coroner. Now the coroner was only called if there were suspicious circumstances surrounding the death, if a crime had been committed, or if they'd died abroad.

The coroner was in the middle of a post-mortem on a young man who'd died whilst on holiday in Greece.

'These are usually a complete waste of time,' said the coroner, opening up the chest cavity and pulling out a black bin liner. 'He's already had a post-mortem in Greece, and they never put anything back where it belongs!'

I watched in horror as he then took off the top of the man's skull, reached into the hole where his brain should have been, and pulled out . . . a Union Jack tea towel.

'Their little joke!' he chortled.

Well, I made my excuses and left.

The main lesson I took home from my brief stint as a doctor was a simple one, one that everyone comes to realise eventually – but not usually until they are faced with death themselves. At the tender age of twenty-three, I realised that life is short.

Oh boy, is life short!

One case sticks in my mind. When I worked at Ashford Hospital, we used to take casualties from Heathrow. The West Middlesex Hospital took patients from Terminals 1 and 2, and we covered

Terminal 3 – and yes, our love of gallows humour meant there were a lot of 'terminal' jokes.*

A man was brought in – mid-sixties, probable heart attack. We tried to bring him back, but he wasn't having it. There was some confusion as to his identity, so I looked through his wallet. Sure enough I found his driving licence and name – but I also found a receipt for Knickerbox, the lingerie outlet. Someone tracked down his wife and we broke the news to her as best we could.

It turned out that they'd just come back from a holiday to celebrate his retirement. He'd clearly popped in to Knickerbox in the hope of livening things up. It was that detail that made it so heartbreaking for me.

Of course, I may have that wrong. Maybe he'd been knocking off his secretary all his working life and had bought her a couple of thongs as a parting gift.

'He'd been planning it for so long,' sobbed his wife. 'We were so looking forward to his retirement, to spend some proper time together.'

A light-bulb moment. Life's short, and there was no way I was going to end up like the dead guy with the lingerie receipt in Terminal 3.

To give up medicine, though, that was such a huge decision – and for what? To become a comedian? Come off it!

A couple of other things happened that made the decision a little easier.

In January 1989, my stepfather, Pop, died. He was fifty-four. It had been on the cards for a while, but that didn't make it any easier to deal with.

I was told by medical staffing that I could take the day off for the funeral – which was big of them. They then intimated that I would have been entitled to longer but 'he was only your stepfather . . .'

---

* 'The Terminal Three' was our nickname for the oncology team.

Sod that, I thought and took a week.

I didn't cry at the funeral – I tried really hard to, but I'd got so good at keeping a lid on my emotions that nothing came. Six months later, I was back at that same church for my old mate Patrick's memorial service. He'd died unexpectedly from a pulmonary embolism, aged just twenty-nine. Most of the old gang were there, and after it was over, we all piled down the pub opposite. As we went our separate ways, I thought I'd drop by Pop's grave. As I stood there, I started sobbing uncontrollably. It focused my mind on the 'life is short' thing, and as I left that graveyard, I was determined that things were going to have to change.

The ultimate tipping point was less dramatic. It came at the 1989 Ashford Hospital Christmas Lunch. Myself and a couple of other junior docs had decided to put on a bit of entertainment. Mark, the surgical registrar, brought his guitar and sang a song. A couple of others did bits. Then I got up and did a few gags. As I was standing there, looking out at those people laughing, I suddenly thought, *You're good at this, you find it easy. Instead of struggling every day at something you find hard and don't enjoy, try this instead!*

It hit me like a lightning bolt, and in that moment I made my mind up.

The job I had at Ashford was due to finish at the end of that July. It was a good one and was seen as a springboard for a future in hospital medicine. I was all set to get a good reference from my boss – who seemed to like me.

Three months before it was due to finish, he called me in for a careers chat.

'So . . .' he said, leaning back in his chair. 'What do you want to do next?'

'I'm not sure . . .' I said, fiddling nervously with my tie.

'Well . . .' he smiled. 'Are you going to go into cardiology or respiratory?'

'That's just it, sir . . .' I spluttered. 'I think I want to be a comedian!'

It was a bit like that Monty Python sketch when Michael Palin declares he's always wanted to be a lumberjack – except a curtain didn't open behind me to reveal a line of Canadian Mounties.

'Oh,' said my boss with a frown. 'You really don't know what you want to do, do you?'

He never raised the subject of my future again. If he'd sat me down and told me what a brilliant doctor I was and that I was just the sort of person the health service needed, I might well have changed my mind, but to his credit he didn't try to persuade me one way or the other.

I didn't apply for another permanent job – and when I finished my post in mid-July 1990, that was it.

I sat in my P-reg Toyota Corolla in the Ashford Hospital car park, pointed it at the exit, and put my foot down. I flicked on the radio as I came off the roundabout onto the mighty A308. The track that came on was 'We Gotta Get Out of This Place' by Eric Burdon and the Animals. It seemed that someone – specifically Eric Burdon – was trying to tell me something.

CHAPTER 9
OOPS!

'How ingenious is man? What other species would look at a fat man crouching in a corner in a tricorn hat and think, "What a brilliant idea for a jug?"'

Earlier in the year, seeing me as potential consultant material, my boss had encouraged me to take the exam to become a member of the Royal College of Physicians.

I knew that if I signed up for it, I was automatically allowed two weeks study leave – so I paid my fee and enrolled.

But I had other plans for that two weeks.

Instead of swatting up on rare disorders of the heart and lungs, I had decided to use the time to write a comedy play that I'd take to the Edinburgh Festival, which would then kick start my new career in show business.

The play would be so funny and so . . . incisive . . . Yes, that was the word! *Incisive* about the state of the health service that it would get rave reviews, a slew of awards and then would tour the country, finishing with a long run in the West End – by which time I wouldn't even be appearing in it – no, by then I'd be onto my third or fourth comedy play with a stack of commissions pending in my in-tray!

I even went out and bought an in-tray on the strength of it.

You'll be relieved to hear that at the end of that two weeks, I duly failed to gain membership to the Royal College of Physicians, but I did have my first and only draft of *Dog Murder One*.

I haven't reread it since Hayden Murphy gave us that stinging review and took my dreams, put them kicking and screaming into a sack, and drowned them.

I tried to for this book, but couldn't get past the first page. I'm afraid Hayden was right. It's a dud!

The gist of the plot was that a young city-type sets up a chain of nursing homes called Final Resting Places, where he euthanises the clients. Then at the end – in a plot twist you could see coming from a hundred miles away – he ends up in one of his own homes and the lights fade as he's about to get a taste of his own medicine. Move over, Harold Pinter, cancel all calls, Trevor Nunn – the new wave (me) is coming!

Why the title? Well, it was inspired by the story of a patient I had, who'd suffered a cardiac arrest at the top of a flight of stairs and fell down them landing on, and killing, her elderly Alsatian dog. Amazingly, we managed to get her back, but sadly not the dog. We were then faced with a dilemma. Should we tell her how her prize pooch had met its fate or quietly cover it up? In the end, I left it to the nurses.

With my new play fresh off the typewriter, I called Matt Bradstock-Smith and told him the good news. He didn't even ask to read it or want to know what it was about – as far as he was concerned if I'd written it, he was on board. Rob too didn't require much persuasion, nor his fellow graphic design student Suzi, who agreed without so much as an audition to play an elderly lady.

Theatre West End – the scene of our past triumph – couldn't fit us in. In fact, all the venues we were familiar with in Edinburgh were taken, which is how we found ourselves booked into a room in a leisure centre off the main approach road into the city – and a long way from where the action was.

The upside was that the canteen made the most fantastic French fries we'd ever tasted.

Once again, we'd be out all day glueing up posters and leafleting tourists – I spent so long trying to persuade some people to buy a ticket that I actually recognised them when they turned up in the audience.

Dog Murder One

The Cast
in order of appearance

Doctor Peter Lopez, Junior Hospital Doctor at Green Hills General, London SW.
.... Matthew Hall

Nigel Fenton, Hardworking estate agent and part-time entrepreneur, based in Knightsbridge, and living in South London.
.... Robert Mills

Miss Jolly, deaf, unwanted, octogenarian and mother of three.
Mr. Graveney, helpless widower and dog owner.
O.D., twenty-five year old depressive.
Jean Charlotsov, manageress of Eastbourne based nursing home.
Dr. Love, registrar orthopaedics, Sussex general Hospital.
.... Suzi Warren

Voice of Cardiac Arrest Bleep.
Charming diabetic man, with an interest in telecommunications
.... Matthew Bradstock-Smith

Thora Hird, warm-hearted OAP.
.... Herself

Written by Matthew Hall
Directed by Matthew Bradstock-Smith

Technicals Matthew Bradstock-Smith
Stage Managed by Richard Hall
Poster by Miss Warren
Additional groundwork by HB Nutters
Shirts by Jill's of Cranbrook
Mr. Hall's hair by Bad Luck Hair, Balham
Set Design by Eastbourne Council

What do you do when granny's living in 1941, granddad thinks he's the Post Office Tower and the boss is coming round for dinner? Thanks to disillusioned Doctor Peter Lopez and his entrepreneurial school chum, Nigel Fenton, the answer lies in 'Final Resting Places' - money making 'geriatricide' which takes care of Britain's unwanted elderly and solves the NHS Bed crisis at the same time. This new Black Comedy takes the P out of BUPA and puts the vet back into veteran.

**I look like a Lopez, don't I? Leaflet for my
punt for the Pulitzer: *Dog Murder One*.**

Then, boom! Hayden Murphy worked his magic and we couldn't give the tickets away!

Once or twice there were more people on stage (three) than in the audience (two).

Here's what I wrote in my diary shortly after that review came out:

I might rewrite the ending . . . I'm not going to send any postcards until I get some good news.

I never got round to the ending, and I'm not sure if anyone got a postcard from me that year.

On my last day, I went to a kilt shop and bought myself a pair of tartan trousers to cheer myself up. I only wore them once – well, I looked ridiculous in them! I only threw them out recently though, having clung to them for twenty-five years; they were a totem for my new life of freedom.

It was a big moment for me, that Edinburgh adventure – in two short weeks I'd learnt an enormous amount. It was also the last time that our dwindling group of merry men and women would go up there as a gang. After that, it was just me and Matt.

Given how it worked out, the final entry in my Edinburgh diary is surprisingly positive:

It would have been nicer had the show been a wild success, but it was certainly more fun than last year. In many ways Hayden Murphy did me a favour – he stopped me writing plays and made me concentrate on becoming a stand-up comic.

Harry Hill's first gig was on 23 September 1990 at the Aztec Comedy Club, a Mexican restaurant in South Norwood.

That's not strictly true. I was Harry Hall back then. Michael Caine has a good line about why he changed his name: 'There was already a famous actor called Maurice Micklewhite.' In my case, there was a cement business called Matthew Hall. No one buys a ticket to see a cement business.

I changed it because I thought Harry Hall was more showbiz, and I liked the way it contained 'Ha-Ha' too.

I also changed it because I didn't want any of my friends or family turning up to my gigs – and I certainly didn't want to see any of my old patients sitting in the front row.*

I'd got back from performing my big dud at the Edinburgh Festival and rather than a rucksack full of trophies, I was in the hole for five hundred quid and back living with my recently widowed mum.

---

* Later, when I tried to join the actor's union Equity, I was told there was already a lady actor called Hari Hall. So I needed to ask her permission to use the name (with my spelling). She turned me down, so if I wanted to join, I had to change it. I ummed and ahhed for a couple of weeks over alternatives – Harry Hole, Harry Hell and even Harry Carnegie were all front runners.

'Probably what you need to do is get a GP practice in a village with a really strong amateur dramatics group,' Jan said, vainly trying to look for a compromise.

Rather than tell her that I'd given up medicine for good, I'd eased her in by telling her I was taking a 'year off' instead.

She'd heard about people taking years off and although she was suspicious, she accepted it and probably appreciated the company. The way I'd rationalised it was that I'd spend a year going all out to get some gigs, and if at the end of that year I'd got nowhere further than The Hall Brothers had got, then I'd jack it in, apply for a GP training course and accept my lot.

For the next couple of weeks, I sat at the desk that I'd revised for my A-Levels at and attempted to write some jokes. Then I called the numbers in the back of *Time Out* to try and get some stage time.

There'd been a long enough gap between The Hall Brothers' last London gig for pretty much no one to associate me with them, so it felt very much like a new start.

Acts turn up and drop out of the circuit constantly – even acts that you'd think were good enough to make a living out of it. Sometimes they're not cut out for the lifestyle, other times they have responsibilities that mean they have to earn a regular living. I was lucky; I had no one relying on me and I had a way to pay the bills – by doing locum doctor work.

It was no easier getting gigs for Harry Hall than it had been for the double act – I still had to leave countless messages on answering machines. The difference this time was that instead of leaving it there, I followed it up with another message and then another, making a real nuisance of myself until it was easier for them to book me than have to field my calls.

If I didn't get a callback, I'd turn up at the club and ask to speak to the person running it – it was usually the same person who was tearing the tickets on the door. 'Oh, hi, I'm Harry Hall . . .'

At which point their faces would drop and they'd take out the bookings diary. I was dogged – I had to be. I had a lot to prove.

Believe me, it's not the funniest comics that get on, it's the pushiest.

I did pretty well to get an open spot within a couple of weeks of getting back from the Fringe, and nothing focuses your mind like a deadline.

I typed what I thought were my best gags onto a piece of A4 paper, and when I'd filled that, I attached another piece of A4 paper and filled that up. I ended up with a scroll of paper with my five-minute act on that was almost as tall as me.

I Blu Tacked it to the wardrobe door, next to the full-length mirror, and practised. You'll be pleased to hear that I still have that scroll of paper. There's a gag about a dolphin that's been scribbled out, and it appears that I started my set with 'I'm not a lonely person but I'm the only person I know . . . (BEAT) . . . I'm the only person I know.'

I timed it as somewhere between four and a half to five minutes; I knew that when you're the open spot, you really can't risk annoying the club owner by overrunning – no matter how funny you are.

I drove down from Kent and arrived in sunny South Norwood painfully early – at half past four in the afternoon. I was incredibly nervous, so I drove around the local streets for an hour, then parked up and went for a walk, running the lines endlessly in my head.

The comedy at the Aztec took place in a room above the main restaurant. There was a low stage in one corner, and the audience were seated at tables eating their fajitas and tacos and other shredded-meat-based dishes. The bloke running the gig was a sweet Liverpudlian comic called Rob Hitchmough. As I remember it, the first act on that night were The Crisis Twins – John Gordillo and Simon Clayton – who were a high-energy improv duo and always stormed it. I'd seen them on bills when I'd been shlepping around with Rob.

Then it was my turn.

There was a microphone, but I was too scared to take it off the stand, which meant I had to stand behind it stock still. I kicked off with my first line and it got a much bigger laugh than I'd expected and, to be honest, deserved – and it completely threw me! I'd been used to just the mirror for an audience, like some kind of bloated budgerigar, and I'd timed the act with me rattling through it.

The next line completely slipped my mind. Fortunately, the laugh gave me enough time to look at the back of my hand where I'd written my set list and I recovered enough to press on. More laughs. I started to enjoy it and straight away hit a slow patch. My five minutes flew by and before I knew it, it was 'My name's Harry Hall – goodnight!' And I was off to a healthy round of applause. Pretty good for five minutes of new stuff.

'I liked it!' said Mr Hitchmough, 'You've got some good lines. I can give you a paid half spot in May!'

I could not believe my ears, a paid booking from my first (sort of) solo open spot!

My next gig, a couple of months later, didn't go quite as well. I got a few laughs, but no booking and the third, at the Bearcat Club in Twickenham was my first proper death. I wasn't heckled; I got absolutely no reaction whatsoever. Complete silence. Even now I find a slow or unresponsive crowd difficult to deal with. These days I'd probably pick on someone in the front row just to get a reaction, but back then I didn't have the skills.* All I had was those five minutes rehearsed up – I couldn't jump ahead or cut a bit out. It was rigid. Once I'd started, it had to run to the end. I suppose I could have just walked off – but I had way too much pride for that!

---

* The best example I saw of someone trying get a reaction from a tired, quiet or disinterested crowd was San Francisco comic Ray Hanna. It was two in the morning and Ray was getting nothing – so he jumped off the stage onto one of the audience tables, then he took off his belt and started whipping the table with it. Then he stopped and saw me standing at the back of the room and said, 'Do you ever get that feeling when it's two in the morning and you're trying to get laughs out of your lousy belt?!'

As my tongue dried and stuck to the roof of my mouth and my lips glued themselves to my teeth, I started to speed up, another rookie error. I came off to a few polite claps.

There's no back door at the Bearcat; I was forced to walk through the crowd to get out. I put my coat on, pulled my hat down as far as it would go, and walked as fast as I could for the exit. I didn't stop to enquire what Graham, who ran the club, thought – there was no other possible interpretation of what had happened. I'd bombed and what's more, I had no idea why.

And that's how it went for the next six months or so – a few steps forward and a few steps back – but overall I got better at it and very slowly my diary started to fill with bookings.

Rob took my first publicity shots. Looking at it now, I'm not sure I'd want the sort of work this photo could get me.

I've played a lot of clubs over the years but like most comics I remember my first open spot at London's Comedy Store as if it were yesterday. By the time I played it, it wasn't in its original home in Soho, but as the notional birthplace of alternative comedy, it still cast a long shadow.

I was doing a locum at Southampton General Hospital at the time, but open spots at the Store were like gold dust. You'd have to wait a good six to eight months for one, so I wasn't going to miss it. I pulled a favour, got another doctor to cover for me, left early and set off up the M3. I was, naturally, incredibly nervous. I walked into the dressing room and sat down with the other open spots – my mouth too dry to even speak. The compère, a very funny Geordie comic called Mickey Hutton, came in and pointed at us each in turn and said, 'You'll die, you'll be shit and you'll be heckled off!'

I was in the middle, so I was going to be the shit one, apparently. He was mucking about, of course, showing off to the other pro's but we believed him. In the end, I got a few laughs and a lot of indifference, but in those days I was just glad to have got through it. Kim Kinney – the gatekeeper at the Store; the bloke who made the bookings; the one you had to impress – wasn't even there to see it. So, you could say it was a wasted journey – I didn't get booked and I had to phone up and wait eight months for another turn – but as the lights came on in the club and the bar staff started to clear up, Mickey took me to one side and said, 'You've got some good jokes, you'll be fine,' which meant a huge amount to me – it still does. I headed back down the M3, buzzing with excitement, stopping off at Fleet services on the way to have a full English. It didn't matter that the next day I was on call for emergencies, because Mickey Hutton, a man who made his living from comedy – the compère of the legendary Comedy Store, no less – had told me I was going to be fine.

From the start, I thought it was important to have a 'look'. I was never the jeans and T-shirt type. My view was that you got dressed up to go on stage, a throwback to the old days of variety – Tommy Trinder and Max Miller. To quote the old crooner Max Bygraves, 'You walk on, move around a bit and show 'em the suit.'

I wore a dark sixties suit – because they were the suits that were in the charity shops in the eighties. I'd had to wear a tie in my day job – so I liked the idea of casting it off as a small act of rebellion. But if you don't wear a tie, what do you do with your open shirt? To me it just looked a bit scruffy. So I pulled the collar up to make it look big. When people started commenting on the big collar, I had a couple made with genuinely big collars – they were very expensive and not the sort of thing I'd ever usually pay out for, but I saw it as an investment in the act and it paid off. I'd picked the glasses because I thought they made me look like Buddy Holly – I can see now that really they made me look like a 1950s accountant. Or worse, the local strangler.

I saw a pair of brothel creepers in the window of a shoe shop in Carnaby Street – again it was just the sort of thing I'd never have been allowed to get away with on the wards – so I went in and bought a pair.

I look back on those early months of freedom as being like the rebellious teenage years I never had. I picked up a sparkly waistcoat from another charity shop and added that to the ensemble for a while – until comic Ian MacPherson took me to one side after a gig at the Red Rose. He congratulated me on my act – which was a real thrill as I was such a fan of his – 'But I can see you dropping the waistcoat . . .' he said with a wry smile. I never wore it again!

(1)

Dolphins are supposed to be some of the most intelligent creatures
on this earth,second only to man if anyones can take over the
world it'll be the dolphins , except they can't get up
steps — fairly fundamental I would have thought

(2)

I'm not a lonely person but I'm the only
apter
I'm the person I know.Yes,I do have a limited social life,
people say I'm boring and I am actually registered with Lambeth
council as one of the socially disabled - I get a sticker for
my glasses and everything.I am eligable for certain benefits
I get two sessions a week with one of Lambeth's really
for instance interesting councillors - he plays in a band and everything
he gives me advice the other week he told me off for mentioning
over dinner how many times I get up at night to go to the toilet until I over dinner
do and I've noticed that my water is a different colour after a
really strong cup of cofee.
Apparently I'm entitled to positive discrimination on Dinner
party invitation lists.And I have been given special party
vouchers which allow me one conversation with someone at
the party who is operating the scheme.

In actuall fact I haven't talked to a girl for so long I've
almost forgotten how to fumble my words and appear incredibly
awkward.

I started late with girls (Comic pause: hopefully next year
sometime.

(3)

My voice didn't break until I was eighteen ,and even then it
broke into two higher voices.

My skin is smooth now but it wasn't always that way.They say
acne is made worse by certain foods like chocolate and fried
by
foods.Mine was made worse meat and two veg.My mother put me
on a diet of chocolate and fried foods for four years to
clear it up.It cleared up the acne,it was just the four year
migrains that I found rather ...
you can spend lying down in a darkenedroom as Lester Piggot
will tell you.

(2)

The other boys used to tease me about my glasses - they
came up with the ingenious name of four eyes you know
.....four.five six seven eight nine ten....

**The first twelve inches of my first set list. Not sure what
that stain is – could be red wine, could be blood.**

HOW TO BE A COMEDIAN: LESSON NO.2 – BAD GIGS

Probably the best bit of advice I ever got was from Ivor Dembina, the legendary promoter of the Red Rose Club in London's Finsbury Park: 'If it's going badly – get off!' he said. 'And if it's going well – get off!'

If you're having a bad gig, there's two things you mustn't do. One – speed up. And two – let the audience see you're rattled. I learnt the second from, of all people, Chris Evans.

I was over in Montreal doing the Just For Laughs comedy festival where Channel 4 were recording a couple of stand-up specials. Chris Evans, who was big on Channel 4 at the time with *Don't Forget Your Toothbrush,* was MC'ing one of them. Now Chris can be funny, but he's not a comedian – I mean, listen, I'm sure he could be if he put the hours in, but essentially what he does is presenting in a light and occasionally funny way.

He had already become a household name in the UK at the time, but no one had a clue who he was in Canada. No one knew who I was either, but I had a tight five minutes of gags that I'd honed the week before. To cut a long story short, he had a tough gig. Later, at the hotel where all the comics were staying, I was in the bar with The Agent and saw Chris sitting on a high stool on his own, with a faraway look in his eyes, nursing a drink, and I felt sorry for him.

'Hi, Chris,' I said. 'Why don't you come and join us?'

'Thanks,' he said and sat down at our table.

'How did you think it went?' said The Agent tactfully.

'Bit shit,' said Chris, 'but it doesn't really matter – I just did it straight down the bottle and didn't let on.'

I sat forward. He seemed to be suggesting there was a secret solution to a bad gig.

'What do you mean, Chris, down the bottle?' I said.

'Down the camera,' he said. 'I'm not doing the gig for those two hundred people in the room – they're not important. I'm doing it for the punters at home, the viewers. If I look like I'm having a good time, after they've dubbed a few laughs on it, it'll look like I am.'

And he was right!

The first time I really put Chris's advice into action was when I performed for the Queen at the 1997 Royal Variety Show. The best thing about doing that show is the day itself – it feels like proper old-fashioned showbiz.

On the bill that night were the Spice Girls, Celine Dion, Jim Davidson, Michael Ball, Cirque Du Soleil and the cast of Matthew Bourne's *Swan Lake*. I was sharing a dressing room with a Russian strongman called Vlad – who spoke virtually no English – and Dr Trevor James, whose act consisted of a giant puppet bird which, when he pulled a lever, defecated all over the stage – that was the gag and very funny it was too. The big surprise was to be an appearance from Ronnie Corbett and Ronnie Barker back together for the first time in ten years as The Two Ronnies. I'd met and worked with Ronnie Corbett a couple of times by then, and backstage, he introduced me to Barker. 'What are you going to do?' I asked. Barker explained that they were to come on dressed as the TV chefs The Two Fat Ladies on their trademark motorbike and sidecar – they'd then take their helmets off to reveal everyone's all-time favourite TV sketch double act.

'I mean, God knows how it will go down – it might be met by complete silence!' he said. He seemed genuinely nervous about how the audience would react.

In any event it got the biggest reaction of the night – bigger than the Spice Girls and Celine Dion put together. That's the thing about our great comedians – when we like them, we truly love them. They both came off beaming.

I, on the other hand, didn't fare so well.

Des O'Connor was sharing hosting duties with Jonathan Ross, and to be honest, I wished that I was being introduced by Johnnie – he'd always been a big supporter of mine, right from the early days.

'I won't do very long,' said Des as he went on to introduce me. 'I'll just settle them down.'

That sounded good to me – it had already been a very long night.*

Des proceeded to tell a very tortuous shaggy-dog story that had a number of false endings. Every time it felt like he was winding it up, I'd step a pace towards the stage, thinking he was about to bring me on – then the story would go off on another tangent.

Eventually, Des finished his gag and introduced me. Now, I liked Des – I had him on one of my shows and he was the funniest thing on it, but when he introduced me, it felt like he just put a little bit of distance between the two of us. It was a subtle thing, but it gave the audience a signal that he wasn't entirely convinced by my act – like he was covering himself in case I bombed.

'Well, this next guy should know what he's doing,' he said. 'He used to be a doctor and somehow [*Somehow? That's not a great sell, Des, is it?*] he's going to find your funny bone. Ladies and gentlemen, the madness [*Madness, notice – not comedy*] of Harry Hill!' Then he rolled his eyes. Thanks, Des.

---

* 'The longest night of my life,' said Mrs H.

It was like performing at the Dignitas reunion dinner, but I'm a fast learner and had Chris Evans's words echoing in my ears as I found the camera and played it all 'down the bottle'. As I came off I passed Jim Davidson in the wings – I don't know Jim, we're from different worlds, but at the end of the day, we're all comics.

'How'd it look?' I said to him anxiously.

'It *looked* fine,' he said with a smirk. I was booked for six minutes – when it went out they had cut it down to three!

When you watch it now, it looks like I'm having the time of my life.

I headed past Jim and kept on walking – out through the stage door, across the road and into the pub opposite, where I walked up to the bar and ordered three pints of lager.

I downed all three in close succession and felt the tension that had built up over the preceding weeks gradually evaporate.

'It wasn't as bad as you think,' said The Agent.

I hadn't eaten all day, and unfortunately I was now completely pissed and due to meet my sovereign at any moment in the time-honoured end-of-show line-up. I staggered back across the road, the pavement swimming in front of me, and into the theatre. Back at the dressing room, I started to get changed into my dinner suit and black tie – which was the protocol for anyone not in costume.

'How'd it go?' I said to the speciality act with the defecating bird, which he was busy rinsing under the tap. 'Smashed it!' he said with a broad grin. Meanwhile Vlad the Russian strongman was standing there in a necklace strung with fake tiger teeth and just his loin cloth.

'You can't wear that to meet the Queen!' I said with a surprisingly high level of indignation – well, it was cut very high over his thighs.

'Huh?' he grunted in a broad Slavic accent.

'We're meeting the Queen!' I said 'You'd better put something on!'

There was a real party atmosphere as we all lined up back-stage, waiting for Her Maj. Jonathan Ross was mucking about, wise-cracking with Scary Spice. Then as the Queen and Prince Philip appeared, everyone stiffened, standing to attention – like naughty school kids caught smoking behind the bike shed.

We'd been briefed that we shouldn't on any account talk to the Queen before she talked to us, and that we should address her as 'ma'am'. Legendary showbiz impresario Laurie Mansfield was doing the royal introductions.

I was sandwiched between an acrobat from Cirque Du Soleil and Michael Ball.

'And the comedian Harry Hill, ma'am . . .' said Laurie with a flourish of his outstretched hand.

The Queen stopped, looked me up and down and seemed to be momentarily at a loss for words. Maybe she could smell the booze.

'Well . . .' she said, after what seemed like a year. 'I suppose it will have raised an awful lot of money!'

To which I replied, 'Exactly, Your Majesty, I always say you can never have too much money!'

She gave me a look like she'd trod in something, then turned and greeted Michael Ball like an old friend. Des O'Connor rolled his eyes again and I could see Laurie Mansfield making a mental note never to invite me back.

I bumped into the Queen a few times after that, at various dos. What I love about her is the way she apparently has no idea who any of us are. At ITV's fiftieth birthday celebrations, I overheard her asking Ant and Dec where they 'fitted in', which was a great leveller.

The last time I saw her was at her ninety-second birthday bash at the Royal Albert Hall. The BBC had put together an eclectic bill consisting of Tom Jones, Sting, Shaggy and Kylie Minogue – all the Queen's favourites! I was there with Frank Skinner and Ed Balls as part of the George Formby Society, singing and playing 'When I'm Cleaning Windows'. There was a bizarre moment backstage where Frank and I were making our way to the stage and bumped into Sting, who then went into an impromptu version of 'Leaning On a Lamp Post' with us playing along.

We'd been told that at the end of this feast of entertainment, we should all file on, then the Queen and Prince Charles would join us to take the applause. As we assembled in the wings, I was right at the back of the line, I looked round, and there behind me, in a sparkly gold dress was the Queen.

'Oh, hello there!' I said, a little startled to see her.

'It's awfully dark, isn't it?' she said.

'Did you not bring a torch, Your Majesty?' I replied with a little chuckle.

'Hmm,' she said, once again completely thrown by my attempt at humour.

'Surely, you should have a torch bearer!' chipped in Frank.

Then the band started playing the National Anthem, and we were on.

POST CARD

26/2/97

1. Petting Zoo
2. ...ng
3. Bad Breath
4. 1st Class
5. London Bridge
6. Psychology of Sweets
7. Cats eyes

8. Bully - sticks + stones
   sunglasses
9. Deathrow
10. B.T smell.
11. Tramp beard
12. Chimps 20's
13. what's down there?
14. chased

*

CHAPTER 10
A TIGHT TWENTY

'Jesus walked on the water, healed the sick, fed the five thousand and raised the dead . . . classic Capricorn!'

Your first paid twenty-minute gig is a bit of a landmark for any comic, and mine was in early 1991 at The Tearooms des Artistes. It sounds fancy, but it was basically a wine bar at the arse end of Wandsworth Road in Clapham. Like most doing their first twenty-minute show, it was really fifteen padded out with stuff I knew didn't really work – but that's how you built your time. You always had to accept a ten when you only had five and a twenty when you had only test-driven fifteen.

You're at a disadvantage being new because you don't have any say in where you go in the running order – no one ever wants to go first, unless they're doubling up. So nine times out of ten you get put on first, which is a tough spot because the crowd aren't as warmed up – and by that I mean, pissed. Similarly, you don't necessarily want to go on last – particularly if it is a big bill or starts late, as the crowd might be a little fatigued or completely off their faces. Early on I realised that if I turned up a little bit late for the gig – just before or after it had started – they couldn't put me on first, and they certainly wouldn't risk putting me on last, so sometimes I could engineer myself into that coveted second spot. Devious, right? Like I said, I had a lot to prove!

I was on first at the gig in Clapham and it went pretty well – I came off relieved and happy that I'd done the time. It was a big milestone for me, and on top of that, I got twelve quid. On the bill with me that night, as well as a girl who played the guitar and sang funny songs* was a really funny and original impressionist called Alistair McGowan. Alistair had been making good money doing voice-overs and radio work, occasionally contributing his spot-on impressions to Radio 4's weekly satirical show *Weekending*.

We hit it off straightaway – and it turned out he lived just down the road from me in Balham. He was eighteen months ahead of me and had a good forty minutes of stuff and the audience loved him that night. Despite having only just met, I suggested we go to Edinburgh together that summer and do a two-hander. I was keen to go back up but couldn't see myself having enough for a whole solo show. I explained that I knew how to book the venue and do the promotion and accommodation and that basically he could just leave it to me.

Rob designed the poster and I got us booked into the Festival Club – a good, central, well-run venue – and secured us a two-bedroom flat just round the corner from it. I even drove Ally's luggage up for him as he preferred the train!

The show was called – predictably enough – *When Harry Met Ally*. We took it in turns to go first and it was a pretty sturdy hour of fun. Not groundbreaking – just two comics getting their acts together. We were supposed to be doing half an hour each, but more often than not I'd fall a bit short and Alistair would pick up the slack. I knew the form and was out leafleting all day and sticking up posters – Ally, less so, but I didn't mind, as I was very much the junior partner and was just glad to have the chance to be back up there. It was a good little bill and because he'd had a bit of exposure on Radio 4, we usually had a reasonable crowd. It was there that my mum first saw my act. She'd made the journey all the way up to Scotland and I'm sure breathed a big sigh of relief when she found herself laughing

---

* She gave it up after a couple of years – I was also there for one of her final gigs, where in the middle of it, she broke off and said, 'I'm *so bored* with my act!'

along at my gags. I have to give her credit – despite me turning my back on a career in medicine, she has never once made any serious effort to persuade me out of comedy.

...air, rage, oppression and impotence.

After last week's batch of Election comedy specials which mostly lost their deposits, it's a pleasure to welcome a new comedy act that is at least half-way funny. When Harry Met Ally (R4) are a pair of comedians, Harry Hill and Alistair McGowan, who made a name for themselves at last year's Edinburgh fringe.

They make an unconventional double act, since they don't divide into funny man and stooge. In fact, they're not easy to distinguish at all – though running jokes about Harry's baldness suggest that this may only be a problem on radio. It may also be intended: the pace and agility of their comedy demand that each can feed gags and each be fed. (In one of their most inventive sketches, they appeared as a pair of babies at their mothers' breasts, exchanging appreciative comments on topless barmaids.) McGowan is also a highly accomplished impressionist. This was a one-off show; they are worth a series.

Going Places . . . you know you're on your way when *The Oldie* like you . . .

Alistair had contacts – and when they turned up to see his act, they also caught mine. One of those contacts was a rookie radio producer by the name of Jon Magnusson – yes, the son of *Mastermind* Magnus. He was up in Edinburgh scouting for talent for a series of shows he was doing for Radio 2 called *The Pick Of The Fringe,* and he asked me to do four minutes on one of them. I don't remember much about it, but it was my first national exposure and seemed to go OK. Me, Alistair and Jon got on really well, and Jon said that he was about to take over the producer role at *Weekending* and that I should come along to the meeting, submit some ideas for sketches, and that he'd keep an eye out for me.

Weekending was a brilliant training ground for generations of comic writers, even though the show itself was never better than patchy. The beauty of it was that there was an open meeting for non-commissioned writers on Wednesday morning that anyone could attend – it was held in a room on the Light Entertainment corridor in Broadcasting House. You could literally just walk in off the street into Broadcasting House and say you were 'here for *Weekending*' and the commissionaire would let you in. There was nothing to stop you then marching through the building and strangling Tony Blackburn – but this was a world pre-9/11.

Although I had no real interest in current affairs, when I got back from Edinburgh, I bought four newspapers a day, read them from cover to cover, jotted down my ideas for funnies, and on the first Wednesday of September, pitched up at Broadcasting House. Those open meetings for *Weekending* were a bit of a bun fight. It was pretty much all men. All men and quite a lot of weird men. Some of them smelt like they weren't looking after themselves. Some of them looked like they'd been dressed by their mums. Usually all the big stories had been taken by the commissioned writers who had their meeting just before us non-coms. Jon Magnusson would walk in and say things like 'Has anyone got anything on the war in the Balkans?' At which point we'd pitch our various ideas and if he liked yours, he'd ask you to write it up.

The only sketch I can remember pitching was about a 'leaves on the line' story – where trains had been delayed basically due to the arrival of autumn. I suggested further delays due to a giant conker getting stuck in the mouth of the Channel Tunnel. Ah, satire!

The deadline for submissions was Thursday lunchtime, so I'd go and type up my offerings and fax them through to their office – you didn't ever know if your piece had got on the show until it went out and your name appeared in the impossibly long list of credits. What a thrill to hear my name for the first time as an actual comedy writer! Under Jon's patronage, I got quite a lot of my stuff on very quickly.

Within a month or so, it was enough to get a commission – it was this £120 a week that meant that, with the money I was getting from my club dates, I could stop doing locums altogether, so within eighteen months of giving up full-time work as a doctor I was finally self-sufficient.

Once you got commissioned, it meant that you could use the offices and typewriters on the Light Entertainment corridor to write your sketches. It was in one of those offices that I met Al Murray. He was not long out of Oxford University and was in a writing team with a couple of his old Oxford pals – which was nuts because they had to split the money three ways.

Also in the corridor at that time were Stewart Lee and Richard Herring, who had just started working on their own series.

It was great fun, a lot of camaraderie, and I loved the deadline and immediacy of writing a sketch on the Thursday that would go out the next day.

Jon's tenure as producer only ran for a couple of months – his replacement wasn't so keen on my whimsy and I started to get a lot of stuff rejected. I remember I had one sketch about Gorbachev and John Major* – I don't remember the gag exactly – but the producer told me she thought it wasn't quite right and that I should 'work on it some more'. I took it back to the writers' room and complained about it to one of the older writers, Michael Dines, who, as well as writing for *Weekending*, was one of the main contributors to *The News Huddlines*.

---

* I know, 'Yawn!' Right?

'Oh that's simple,' said Dinesy, scanning through the sketch. 'Just put him in the bath!'

'Eh?'

'Put Gorbachev in the bath. Don't change the dialogue or the gag, just add some sound effects of water, a few splashes and a bit of echo – that should do it.'

I took his advice, retyped it and it got on the show.

I get bored easily, and by Christmas I'd had enough of writing hack topical sketches and the thrill of hearing my name on the credits had worn off. I was also earning just about enough from my gigs by then to no longer need the money.

Where previously I'd read the newspapers every day, I was now leaving it all to the last minute. It came to a head one Wednesday morning when I was coming back from Birmingham on the train, having done a gig the night before with a carrier bag full of the week's unread newspapers, frantically going through them trying to catch up in the couple of hours it took for the train to pull into Euston station – so, I canned it.

The Edinburgh Festival was calling me again – and this time I was planning to go it alone.

**New Blood! When Harry Met Ally, Derek
Guyler and some other older white men.**

CHAPTER 11
FLIES OPEN

'My nan gets things mixed up. The other day she said to me, "Give me a hand with this jigsaw puzzle of a chicken, I can't find the picture of the chicken anywhere!"

'I said, "Nan, it's a box of cornflakes!"'

The Edinburgh Festival is a bizarre conceit. Essentially, hundreds of London-based comics travel four hundred miles, where they stay for a month at huge expense, to be seen by another hundred or so London-based agents and TV people. So why doesn't it take place in London?

Well, it's a bit like a holiday romance. Something changes with the geography. There's a pressure to it that can really bring out the best in you, and at the very least it serves as a deadline. You know that by late July, you've got to have a show.

In the nineties, you really only had to have three quarters of a show. Most of us went up with a sort of work in progress and tinkered with it in that first week. The whole thing was a lot less polished.

Having done a two-hander with Alistair McGowan, my sights were firmly set on a solo hour. Unfortunately, I only had about forty-five minutes of stuff to fill it. If comics ask me these days for advice about doing the Edinburgh Festival, I tell them not to worry about making sure that every joke is a new one – why beat yourself up? But the festival has changed enormously since the early nineties. For a start, back then it was really only two weeks long. Officially it was three, but the only people who did the third week were students or comics who couldn't get a venue in the first two. Now it's four weeks – it has to be for comics to stand any chance of covering their costs as it's become hugely expensive. In 1989, when I first went up it had a more amateur vibe – that's still the case to some extent, although the better venues and the prime-time slots have all been tied up by the big promoters.

The restraints now aren't artistic so much as financial. Comics these days, even if they do well, can be faced with bills for tens of thousands of pounds – the most I ever lost was five hundred.

That year I was also booked to do a twenty-minute set in a comedy showcase called *The Comedy Zone* alongside my friends Al Murray and Brenda Gilhooly and compèred by South East London's finest – Andre Vincent. The year before, the line-up had been Simon Munnery as Alan Parker Urban Warrior, Stewart Lee and one of my favourite double acts at the time, Chris and George – all held together by MC Mark Lamarr – so it had a good pedigree. Doing two shows also gave me a better chance of breaking even.

Brenda was doing her Gayle Tuesday 'Page 3 Stunna' act – a hilarious satire on the way glamour models were being manipulated by men.

A few words about my friend Brenda. I'd met her the year before in Edinburgh when she'd moved in with me and Alistair McGowan. She was his friend and was booked on the bill at Malcolm Hardee's gig, *Aaaaaaaagh, it's the Tunnel Club!** When Malcolm had booked her, he'd promised he would provide her with accommodation but that it was small – 'the size of a broom cupboard'.

---

* He called it that to make sure it was the first show you saw in the Fringe Guide. I remember once asking him how he knew that no one else was going to have a show with more 'A's' in it.

'Simple,' he said, 'I've got a bloke on the inside who phones me up if someone tries it on and I just tell him to add another 'A'.

When she got there, it was *actually* a broom cupboard. It was Malcolm's idea of a joke. So, she turned up on our doorstep in tears. I went from never having met her before to sharing a room with her, and I can honestly say I've never met anyone quite like Brenda. We'd lie in our twin beds, laughing our heads off into the early hours. She'd hit a bit of form with her act too; when she'd started, she did a version of herself. Then she hit on Gayle and things really took off – she toured with Paul O'Grady's monstrous alter ego, Lily Savage, as well as being a regular on his TV show.

That year, 1992, she was running Gayle out for the first time and loving every minute of it.

She'd finish on a song and if she was closing the show, me and Al would put on sailor hats and be her backing dancers.

This was also way before Al discovered his Pub Landlord character. At that time, he was doing a serial killer act. He would come on in a white tuxedo splattered with blood and would say, 'Good evening. I'm a murderer. I'd like to do some murders for you now.' Then he'd do the sound effects of guns and all kinds of stuff as he acted out various atrocities – including putting a dolphin in a microwave.

It sounds terrible on paper, but it was just one of the funniest things I've ever seen – and I must have seen it fifty times. I never once saw him have anything but a great gig. The crowd would be laughing and screaming in equal measure.

So how was I going to pad out forty-five minutes into the required hour? The short answer was: slides.

I interspersed my three quarters of an hour with slides of odd images I'd found that helped to give the show a sort of notional running theme. I had a whole bit about how great the robin was – cue a slide of a robin – and then I'd go into a rant about the red-backed shrike, about how it was 'a dirty bird that fouled its own nest'. There was another sequence about hair loss – photos from brochures I'd sent off for about hair weaves and wigs and cosmetic hair transplants, that fitted in around a few jokes I had about my own sad pate. Then I had a whole series of before-and-after photos from plastic surgery operations that I'd taken from a book I'd found in the medical school library and set to Frank Sinatra singing 'You Make Me Feel So Young'. Gradually the photos became more and more grotesque, ending up as photos of people mangled in car crashes.

I knew early on that I needed some music to help move it along. So I got straight on the blower to my old mate Matt Bradstock-Smith, who by then was working as a hospital doctor in Chichester. One of the things I loved about him was that literally all I'd have to say to him was 'Fancy going to the Edinburgh Festival?' and he'd be in the car and on his way over. He never once quizzed me about the show's content, so complete was his faith in me.

Well, that year he did have a request. He asked me if it was OK if at some point during the show he could sing a song about a girl he was soft on called Kath.

'What's the song called?' I asked.

' "Oh, Kath!" ' he replied.

Oh Christ! I thought, but what could I say?

'Of course, Matt,' I said. I was just glad to have him along. The only thing I had to work out was how to incorporate this very sweet heartfelt love song into my stream of absurd nonsense.

Well, there wasn't a way to incorporate it, which is why halfway through the show I would say, 'Oh I'm suddenly very tired! I think I might have a little sleep!'

Then I'd unfold a sun lounger, lie down and close my eyes. As I pretended to doze, Matt sang his song.

Oh Kath! I wanna call out your name!
I want you to feel the same way too
Coz I want to fall in love with you . . .*

When he'd finished, I'd 'wake up' and continue with the rest of the show like nothing had happened.

HARRY HILL "FLIES"
Harry Hill and his adopted son Alan
welcome you to an unusual caberet
experience. "Excellent" stage.
15 August - 29th August
8.30pm - 9.30pm
£4.00 (£3.00 Concessions)

Matt died in 2016 and what I wouldn't do to hear him sing it one more time.

By then I was Harry Hill. My solo show, called rather cryptically *Flies*, came down at nine thirty and *The Comedy Zone* kicked off at ten. That gave me plenty of time to walk across from the Festival

---

* I never did meet Kath, and Matt's crush remained unrequited.

Club to the Pleasance, have a chat with whichever comic was hanging around, and crucially have a pint.

Up until then I'd never really had a drink before I went on, but by the time I'd done my hour the pressure was off; the twenty minutes I had to do on *The Comedy Zone* felt like a breeze.

I'm not encouraging comics to drink before they go on, and these days I wouldn't have anything stronger than a Diet Coke, but that year, that pint, combined with the boost in confidence I got from doing my own show just loosened me up and let me experiment. It was that year at *The Comedy Zone* that I truly developed my comic voice.

Good jokes are all well and good, but what we remember about a comic is not so much what they say, but how they say it. Their voice, their persona or attitude. When you think of Tommy Cooper, you know what he's about before you can remember any of his lines. The same goes for Jo Brand or any of the greats.

It's the voice that you can't write, that you just have to discover by trial and error.

When I first started out, I wanted to be a deadpan comic, because those were my comic heroes at the time – Mr Jack Dee, Mr Arnold Brown, Mr Norman Lovett, Ms Jo Brand and Mr Stewart Lee. Stewart had lines like '*I went to a nice little place run by some Italians. It was Italy.*' That's what I liked, so that's what I wanted to be. I could write one-liners too. I'd come on and just do one after the other. There were a few of us starting out in the nineties – Milton Jones, Tim Vine, Matt Welcome, Anthony King . . . But one liners only get you so far; for your jokes to really sing you need to have an attitude. Take one of my favourite gags from Arnold Brown – the Glaswegian who chucked in his job as an accountant to become a comic. '*I was mugged for my trainers – but I had the last laugh. As the mugger ran off, I called after him, "They're not you!"*'

'They're not you.' That line contains so much information about Arnold, about his comic persona, his world view. Just brilliant.

Initially my comic persona was 'geek, unlucky in love' – the underdog, basically.

'My sex life is awful. I pulled back the duvet the other night and a moth flew out – (BEAT) – Didn't leave an address, no note, nothing! Never go out with a moth – never take a moth on a candlelit dinner.'

You get the idea, but most of the time I couldn't maintain that poker face – I wanted to laugh and horse around. I was trying too hard. My natural comic persona is more playful, more clownish, more silly, but I didn't have the confidence to break away from the mic and try something new. Until that Edinburgh.

I started to insert bits of songs, Bryan Adams's hit from *Robin Hood* had been in the charts for what seemed like months – you just couldn't get away from it. So in the middle of my act, I'd drop in the first line.

'Look into my eyes . . .'

Then I'd clunk straight into a one-liner.

'Not just jockeys, I think all small people should have to wear a number!'

A bit later, I'd do another line from the song. Critics always compared it to spinning plates – I'd have three or four running gags and a couple of bits of songs running all the way through until finally, at the end, I'd pay them all off by firing off the punchlines one after the other.

Or that was the idea.

I had a rough order and a few markers along the way but my act was never rigid. I never really knew what was coming next. I had a pool of gags that I could pick from and I'd sling them out as I gauged the mood of the crowd. If a line didn't go so well, I'd put in one I knew was a banker. If things were really flying, I might drop in a new line knowing that I had another banker up my sleeve to bring it back round if it bombed. I knew once I'd been belting them with zingers for a while that they needed a bit of a break – so I'd do a longer bit. I didn't want to be stuck with a script that I couldn't get out of. That's what actors do.

You have to be able to react to the situation in front of you, it takes practice and that only comes from stage time – it also meant that on occasion I had a bum gig. Some nights I'd tear the roof off, other times I'd struggle.

I remember one Edinburgh, I was sharing a flat with my good friend Sean Lock. Sean's probably my favourite comic and a lot of other comics will tell you the same. The so-called comedian's comedian. We love his fearlessness, his lovely long bizarre routines that only he could come up with and those killer one-liners . . .

'So tomorrow it's going to be muggy, then it's going to be Tueggy then Wednesggy then Thursggy . . .'[*]

It's just great writing – and he always surprises me. Don't forget I've seen a heck of a lot of comedians. Every bill I was ever on, I'd be standing at the back or in the wings, watching whoever was on before me. In the early days, I'd arrive at the start and leave at the end – and watch all the acts in between. Once you become a professional comic, it's very hard to just sit there and be open to laughing like you would if you just walked up off the street and bought a ticket.

Most of the time, I stand there knowing what the comic is going to say next. Not because I've heard it before but because there are just a lot of comic devices, tricks if you like, that we all employ to get the laugh. I'm basically just standing there ticking them off.

Sean is one of the few who always amazes me and who I can watch with fresh eyes, almost as if I'm a punter.

He's always given me good advice too. He has a razor-sharp mind, is incredibly well-read and sees things very clearly. So one

---

* Sean told me that after he'd come up with that beauty he took the rest of the day off.

night we were sitting in the flat at the kitchen table and I was complaining to him that I could never predict how my act was going to go over.

'It's concentration,' he said with a shrug, like it was the most obvious thing in the world.

'Huh?'

'Concentration,' he repeated. 'I've seen you before gigs, you're standing chatting to people – you need to concentrate on what you're doing next.'

He was right. I am a bit of a chatterbox. What he was saying to me in a roundabout way was 'It's time to get serious about it if you want it to work.' He didn't use the word 'professional', but that's sort of what he was saying. So I did, and he was right, and although I've had the odd bump in the road, after that pep talk I hit a sweet spot.

The Comedy Zone was a really exciting show to be in that year. It was standing room only with all four of us having a ball, and after it was done me, Matt, Al and Brenda hit the booze.*

The favoured late-night haunt of all the pro comics at that time was the bar of the Gilded Balloon on Cowgate, up a cobbled street below South Bridge. It would be stuffed to the rafters with comics, promoters, agents and the odd telly person.

It wasn't a particularly nice place to be unless you were plastered. There was a lot of anger in that bar; a lot of comics up against it with mixed reviews of their shows, poor audience numbers, money worries and, as if to compound it, everyone knew how everyone else was doing. This was in the days before newspapers and magazines dumbed down their reviews by putting stars on them. To find out what the reviewer thought you actually had to read the review – and we did. We'd pore over who got what and commiserate with those we

---

* Not sure where Andre went.

felt were unfairly treated and enjoy a little schadenfreude for those who we felt deserved it. It also hosted a late-night comedy show – *Late 'n' Live* – which could be a notorious bear pit.

I was there the night that another favourite of mine, Ian Cognito, lost his rag. He was doing his act and not getting much back, then the crowd turned. So he took them on. He slagged them off, then he slagged off the festival, then he grabbed a big carrier bag full of cassette tapes that he'd had made of his act to sell at his gigs and emptied it all over the front row. Then he walked off . . . and into the bar where he picked on another comic so relentlessly that the comic chinned him and left him sparked out on the beer-soaked floor. That's how volatile it could be.

After a while I stopped going there.

I'd have a pint, maybe two, and then I'd go back to the flat and take out a paint-by-numbers I'd bought in a local art shop and I'd quietly fill it in. By the end of the two weeks, I had a painting of two dinosaurs fighting which I titled *Edinburgh*.

I kicked off my first solo show by leaping out of a large trunk situated on the front of the tiny stage.

I'd get into the trunk just before Matt opened the doors and took the tickets. Once the audience were seated, he would start playing the Sinatra classic 'Come Fly With Me', which would be my cue to fling the lid open, stand up and start singing.

As we rarely sold more than about twenty tickets, I was only ever in the trunk for a couple of minutes.

A few days into the two-week run, I got a review in the *Guardian* that kicked off with: 'I have seen the future of new comedy and his name is Harry Hill . . .' And ended up with: 'he makes helpless happy laughter seem absolutely effortless.'

It was the sort of review you wouldn't even dare write yourself!

THE GUARDIAN
Wednesday August 19 1992

COMEDY

Harry Hill

I HAVE seen the future of New Comedy, and his name is Harry Hill. Harry is a 27-year-old ex-doctor who looks and acts a lot like an older Eric Morecambe. He's classless, ageless and completely peerless — and he sounds as if he's been cracking one-liners all his life. He could perform exactly the same act at an open air rock concert or in an old folks home, and as if to prove this point, he delivers his own intimate one-hour slide show — Flies — every evening, followed by a barnstorming 20-minute stand-up set in The Comedy Zone. Harry's warm material — which ranges from pipe-cleaner modelling to racism among wading birds — bears passing comparison with Vic Reeves, but Hill harks back to a time when comics addressed an entire culture, rather than estate agents on the one hand, and art students on the other. He makes helpless happy laughter feel absolutely effortless.
● *Festival Club (650 2395) and Pleasance (556 6550): Flies until August 29, 8.30pm. The Comedy Zone until September 5, 10.45pm.*

William Cook

That evening, I got into the trunk as usual. I could hear people filing in, and it sounded like a lot more than we were used to. Minutes went by and I was getting hotter and hotter in the trunk and running out of usable air. In essence, I was starting to suffocate. Finally, Matt struck up the opening tune. I flung open the lid of the trunk and jumped out. I'd been in the dark for so long that I was startled by the bright lights and dizzy from the lack of oxygen. Once I'd caught my breath and my eyes had stopped stinging, I peered out at the room – it was packed.

That's how it can happen. One rave review and suddenly you're a hit!

The show didn't go particularly well that night, partly because I was completely overwhelmed by the number of people who had turned up, but also because with praise like that, expectations were impossibly high!

But boy, was it exciting!

As a comic, when you're onstage, you have at least two voices in your head. There's the one that's doing the show, then there's the voice that's saying, *OK, slow down, stop here. Wait, now do the punchline* – the 'satnav' if you like that every comic has – that guides you through the gig. That night there were three voices: the usual two, plus an extra excited one that was telling me I was a success – running away with itself – telly spots! Radio shows! Big tours, the lot!

The next morning, I went to B&Q, bought a drill and made some holes in the trunk.

Me and Matt were only booked in to the Festival Club for two weeks – it was all I could afford – and on our last night, I came off from my stint at *The Comedy Zone* and my agent told me that he'd had a message from the Perrier Award judges that I should get along to the awards party because I might 'hear something to my advantage'.

The Perrier Award at that time was the big prize for stand-ups. To get a nomination – or better still win it – meant a big career boost. I can't speak for it now, but in the nineties it meant telly interest. If you won it, you'd almost certainly get a TV pilot and possibly a series. There was only one prize though – and I knew I hadn't been nominated – so why did they want me at the do? I didn't need to be told twice though – me and Matt hightailed it over there.

That year, the competition was particularly fierce. The nominations were Steve Coogan, Jo Brand, Mark Thomas, John Shuttleworth and Scottish comic Bruce Morton. What a line-up! I got there just as Steve Coogan was being presented with the award. He made a very funny speech, lifted the trophy, and headed for the bar. Then the judges announced a new award: Most Promising Newcomer – and the winner was . . . me!

It was doubly thrilling because I hadn't expected it. Matt wasn't mentioned, which seemed a little unfair – after all, he had sung 'Oh Kath!' every night for two weeks. Better still, we'd just performed our last show, which meant that no one was able to see it – which as a marketing ploy was dynamite! Just who was this mysterious newcomer?

We only did it once more. As part of the award, we were booked to play The Purcell Rooms at the Royal Festival Hall, where we royally died on our arses – but by then, it didn't matter.

There's nothing as exciting as someone on their way up. And at that moment, in that month of that year, it was me.

CHAPTER 12
TAP IT, UNWRAP IT

'Why do chimpanzees always go for that middle parting?'

That bit of Perrier buzz, plus Jon Magnusson championing me with the head of Radio Light Entertainment was enough to land me my own show on BBC Radio 4 – *Harry Hill's Fruit Corner*.

The loose idea for the show was that it was being presented by me and my family. So I had a brother called Alan – played by Al Murray. I had a nan, a mum and a dad* and, of course, a son – Little Alan Hill – played by Matt.

It was clear to me that I had to get Matt involved in the show after all his support over the years, but the problem was that, by his own admission, he was an extremely nervous performer and just couldn't deliver lines. So the conceit I developed was that he could only communicate by 'tapping'. At my command, he'd tap his foot on the floor – once for yes, twice for no – like a highly trained pony. It was, essentially, a visual gag and I could see that there was no way the BBC were going to pay him to make a tapping noise on the radio when pretty much anyone could have done it. I confided my dilemma to Jon, who knew how important Matt was to me.

'No one taps like Matt!' he declared, and put him on the same money as the actress playing my nan. I suspect he may well be the first silent actor to appear in a non-speaking role on the radio.

The show's finale, in time-honoured tradition, involved a celebrity

---

* My dad was played by Phil Nice, Arthur Smith's other half in the Hall Brothers' favourite double act, Fiasco Job-Job!

guest in a sketch doing something you wouldn't normally expect them to. It being radio, we could only pay a small fee, so we relied on older stars who weren't that busy any more. So, we had The Beverley Sisters – who turned up in gold jumpsuits and matching hats and finished off each other's sentences. And we also had *Carry On* star Bernard Bresslaw and my favourite Doctor Who, Jon Pertwee – the same one I'd written to aged seven for his autograph. Naturally we involved him in a Doctor Who sketch. At one point, he said 'Harry, could I have a word?' And took me to one side.

'I don't wish to interfere,' he said with the politeness of a bygone age, 'but you see where you've got the Daleks saying "Exterminate!"?'

'Yes, Jon?' I said.

'Well . . .' he continued, 'The Daleks always said it twice, you see? "Exterminate! Exterminate!"'

'Oops! Thank you, Jon, I'll change it,' I said. It's not every day you get Dalek advice from a genuine Doctor Who!

**The sign outside the BBC Paris studios advertising
my new radio venture 'Fruit Corner'.**

Although some of the guests were in the twilight of their careers, they were the only celebrities I'd met up until that point and many of them were icons of my childhood. We had Raymond Baxter off *Tomorrow's World* – I watched that every week before *Top of the Pops*; Stephen Lewis from sitcom *On The Buses* – everyone did a Blakey impression at school; and Richard O'Sullivan, the original *Man About The House* – how could one man be so witty!

We also had Richard Briers – the whole family used to laugh their heads off at his antics on *The Good Life*. In the break between rehearsals, I asked Richard if he had any advice for someone like me, starting out in show business. He didn't hesitate for a moment. 'Go for the fucking money every time, Harry!' he said with a twinkle in his eye.

Then, of course, there was Burt Kwouk. I'd met Burt at the Radio Light Entertainment Christmas party – which was the only works party that I've ever really enjoyed. At that time it was held in the Paris Studios off Regent Street – the same place that Spike Milligan and his gang had recorded *The Goons*. It consisted of cheap booze and trays of BBC sandwiches, but if you wrote for a show on BBC Radio, or had appeared in one, you got invited. Nicholas Parsons would be there, along with Ned Sherrin, Barry Cryer, June Whitfield, Paul Merton, Stephen Fry and Roy Hudd, so it was a no-brainer for all us hungry writers. It's easy to forget that back then, Burt was still a really big film star. His turn as Peter Sellers's manservant Kato in the Pink Panther films was a massive worldwide hit. Me, Jon and Al Murray made a beeline for him and chatted him up in the hope that he might be a guest on *Fruit Corner*. He agreed, and we got on well enough for him then to appear as a regular on series two. It was Jon's idea that I set him the task of catching a chicken – I think it was because he just liked that 'Hey Little Hen' song. I knew it was always good to finish a sketch on a song because it made the audience clap, and it was much easier than coming up with a punchline!

Years later, when me and Burt would go for a drink at Gerry's – the last of the great Soho watering holes – the pianist would start playing the theme from *The Pink Panther* as he walked down the stairs to the bar. Now that's star quality!

The jewel in the crown for me was when in series three Ronnie Corbett joined us as a guest.

Ronnie's faith in me was a big boost. A few years later in Edinburgh, I was backstage, waiting to go on when I got a message to say that he and his wife, Anne, were going to be in the audience. There are a few comics around who can tell you the same story – Ron had a house up on the Scottish coast, just outside Edinburgh, which, like his house in Croydon, also backed onto a golf course. Ron, his wife, Anne, and the family would head up there in the summer months for a holiday, and whilst there, would take in a few shows at the festival.

You'd have noticed Ronnie Corbett even if he hadn't been famous. His height made you do a double take, added to that was his amazingly dapper dress sense – he wasn't afraid to wear bright colours and tartans, and they suited him. When you saw him for the first time in the flesh, he looked, well, exotic. So him sitting in the audience in that tiny Fringe venue, trying to blend in was hilarious. Everyone had one eye on him during the show to see how he would react. Fortunately, thanks to the bright lights, I couldn't see further than the first couple of rows. I came on and did the first gag and that's when I heard it, that unmistakable laugh. 'Heh-heh-heh!' The audience heard it too, which made them laugh even harder.

He and Anne came to say hello afterwards and were very sweet to me. It was funny seeing him there with Matt, too, as they were both roughly the same height. He invited me and my new girlfriend (the future Mrs H) to join them at their holiday home for a barbecue.

This was immensely impressive to her – I think she thought that barbecues with comic greats were going to be the shape of things to come. We got on the train at Edinburgh, walked down the carriage, and I caught sight of another of my great comedy heroes. Sitting looking out of the window was Barry Cryer.

'Barry Cryer!' I blurted out. I just couldn't help myself. I remember going home from school for lunch as a kid and watching him on his gag-based panel show *Jokers Wild*.

Of course, he was going to Ron's too, and we sat with him. Ronnie and Anne had impeccable taste – the house was a beautiful white, low-built affair. It was a gorgeous day and Ronnie, whose dad had been a baker, was famously a great chef. Anne gave Mrs H a piece of advice that we still quote to this day. She was talking to Anne about being stuck at home every night when I was doing my show.

'How do you cope with the nights on your own, Anne?' Mrs H said.

'Get used to it, darling!' she said, rolling her eyes. We all think of Corbett and Barker as a great double act – but in their own way, so were Ronnie and Anne.

As we travelled back to the city later that day, I'm sure Mrs H and I were both thinking that maybe one day with a bit of luck, we might have that sort of life.

Mr. Harry Hill,
66a Warwick Gardens,
London, W14 8PP   3rd October, 1994

Dear Harry

Thank you for your note. It was a great pleasure to
do the show, and as I read the script I thought you
had caught me, and you and I together extremely well,
and I wasn't surprised that the reaction was quite as
full as laughs as it turned out to be, but it was a
great pleasure meeting you and working with you, and
indeed the whole cast.

Best of luck with the series and all you do in the
future.

Kind regards,

Ronnie Corbett

Letter from Ronnie Corbett. He'd always take the time to drop you a note. His manners were as impeccable as his dress sense.

HOW TO BE A COMEDIAN: LESSON NO.3 – WRITING MATERIAL

Turnover.

Turnover is what you need if you want to get anywhere.

All us stand-ups know comics who have a bulletproof twenty minutes that storms it wherever they go.

We all went through that stage – often it's your first twenty, the act you've had months, years even, to polish and hone.

Then they just stop adding new stuff. The act is preserved in amber and they wonder why they don't get picked up to go on panel shows or do slots on TV. They say things like, 'I don't understand it, I storm it everywhere but I can't get arrested on telly!'

It's turnover, dummy.

But you know, it's hard – it's really hard – to get good new jokes.

Here's how I work. At all times, I carry a small notebook with me. I say 'small', it's literally the size of a credit card – laughably small! In fact, it often gets a laugh in a meeting when I pull it out saying, 'I'll make a note of that.' The other people at the meeting see this tiny book – and laugh. It looks like I'm not taking their point seriously. Boom-boom.

In this silly little book, I write stuff that I need to remember – like something I need to do with a script, or a prop I need to get, or someone I need to phone – but I also write in it any stray ideas I get whilst I'm walking the dog, or on the Tube, or having a drink with a friend, or strangling a neighbour. I know that if I don't write these ideas down, I forget them, simple as that.

So sometimes they're ideas for gags, sometimes they're ideas for films or plays, or they could be TV formats, musicals – whatever. As I'm writing the idea down in the little book, I always firmly believe it is quite brilliant – revolutionary, even. The sad truth is most of them are complete and utter rubbish. It's just the way it is.

Very few good ideas ever just turn up on your doorstep fully formed, look up at you and say, 'Looking for a brilliant idea, guv?'

You think Einstein came up with $E=MC^2$ whilst operating a leaf blower? No, he got the idea in front of a blackboard. You've got to expend a lot of chalk to be a success.

So why bother writing these crappy ideas down?

Well, occasionally one is brilliant. Sorry, yes, it can happen, you just never know which one it's going to be.

Plus, when people see me on the Tube reaching for my tiny book and frantically scribbling something down, they think, *Ah! He's a writer!* Which I'm happy to take.

I have piles of these books, all numbered in a way only I understand. So picking one at random here's a page. It reads.

Think Twice
Washing machine – death stains
Lovely to look at, lovely to hold – Jesus
Mad to work here
Why so many white people on EastEnders?
Things: Mods or Rockers.

Here's another:

> HH Turns up in a town. Film it with Steve and Mark.
>   Other does the show right there in shop, etc.
> Accessing Gracenote Media database
> Caveman
> No Flash photography
> No sudden movements
> Contraceptive pills (hand out)
> Highly sexed cannibalistic tendencies
> On a tray, pills, body of Christ with drink

I have no idea what any of that means now but presumably did when I wrote it down.

On the whole I don't look at these micro-books unless I'm stuck – because I have another book.

The other book is bigger.

It's A5, in fact – it could be a fancy Moleskin like Hemingway used (must have had money to burn) or could be any plain A5 notebook. In this bigger book, I write gags from scratch as often as I can.

It all comes from gags for me. Whether I'm doing a TV show or a little film or a tour, the bedrock is gags. You might write a nice one-liner – great, that's going in the tour set. Or you might write a funny idea that works better as a sketch or a song or an item on a show. Also great!

When I was a club comic, when telling gags live on stage was my bread and butter, I'd make sure that for at least the first hour of every day I'd sit in front of this A5 book and try to write some. I still try to put aside some time to do this now.

I've never been stuck for something to write and have never

had a particular fear of getting stuck. Ideas I got. I think if you start worrying about getting stuck, you get stuck. If I stopped having ideas tomorrow, I've probably got enough written down already to see me through.

At the end of most of these morning sessions, I usually end up filling up a good few pages. Often, like the little books, it's rubbish and will never see the light of day. No, really, you think I'm being hard on myself? I'm not. Some of the stuff in those books, if I was forced to read it out loud, I'd blush. But, if I'm slow to think of something to write in the bigger book, I'll look in the smaller books for inspiration.

What I'm trying to illustrate with this tedious description of how I go about writing my jokes is that writing good, original gags is really hard! You have to go through a lot of dross to stand any chance of writing a bit of gold – but when it works, it's a fabulous feeling. You want to punch the air, or run out into the street and tell the joke to the first person you see.

For a while, if I'd come up with what I thought was a zinger, I'd run downstairs and tell it to Mrs H – but she's a tough crowd. She'd often just smile and say, 'Not sure . . .' and offer me a hot drink.

It's silly to even try testing a joke out on one person – unless they're a fellow comic. The acid test can only be the audience.

One option is a 'new material night.' These are shows where it's understood that all the comics will do five minutes or so of only new stuff.

The problem with them is that the dynamic is wrong for it to be a fair test of whether something is funny or not. The audience know you're trying new stuff, so they often laugh for the 'wrong reasons' – they laugh because you cocked it up; they laugh if the gag bombs because they're enjoying the moment rather than the material. It's a bit like those improv nights – the ones where the audience shout suggestions. They're laughing because they're enjoying the process, the game if you like – pretty much none of the stuff that ever comes out of that sort of improv would ever cut it outside of that conceit. Many times I've come away from a new material night thinking I've got a nice new five minutes, then watched as over the following weeks it gets chiselled down to maybe one or two gags if I'm lucky.*

You're better off trying out the gag by slipping it into your existing act – as awkward as that can be at times. You basically have to take a risk. You have to go from tried-and-tested, sure-fire laughs to unknown territory – and then back. It's much easier to stick with the stuff you know, but no pain, no gain.

I've had situations where I've written a gag and called a club to see if I could get on that night to try it out. Better still, you get two gigs – you double up – you try it out at the first gig and then fine-tune it for the second, based on the reaction to the first. If you had a weekend of gigs – two or sometimes three on the Friday, two on the Saturday – you could work up a good five minutes of new stuff.

I think that if it's a really, really, really good gag, you know before you've even tried it out, you just know. They're the most exciting ones, but every now and then, a less obvious gag surprises you.

Occasionally, it takes a while to get a joke to work. I used to have a long shaggy-dog story about my dad opening up

---

* They're good fun, though, those nights. A good social. I used to go to one every couple of weeks at The Meccano Club in Islington along with Lee Hurst, Jo Brand, Alan Davies, Dominic Holland, Nick Wilty – the whole gang. We'd all go to the local Pizza Express after and moan about why we weren't getting more TV work.

a bed shop. He calls the bed shop 'Beds! Beds! Beds!' – and then someone opens another bed shop directly opposite and calls his shop 'Beds! Beds! Beds! Beds!' The joke is then that my dad adds another two 'BEDS!' to the name of his shop and then the other guy does the same and it escalates and escalates until basically I'm standing on stage shouting 'BEDS!' repeatedly. Then I'd pause, and dismiss the whole preceding three or four minutes (because, yes, that's how long it sometimes ran to) by saying 'What a silly man!'

To be clear, that's not a punchline. The laugh, I think, was at how ridiculous I'd been in telling the story in the first place, the sheer audacity and stupidity of it.

The first time I told it, which was at a golf club in West Ruislip, it got nothing. And it's a long way to go for nothing. Imagine, there I am shouting, 'BEDS!' to general indifference and I know there's no real punchline at the end. The thing with a shaggy-dog story is you can't bale out – once you start on it, you're there for the duration. So I do the gag to nothing and have to turn the gig back round with some tried-and-tested stuff. That night I was on the bill with another of my favourites, Tim Vine.

'What did you think of the beds thing?' I asked him.

'Oh, that's great!' he said. 'Don't drop that, you just need to do it a few more times that's all.'

So I did and the third time I did it, it brought the house down. On tour I used to close with it.*

It was about confidence. Once I was confident in the gag, I could really sell it. That's a big part of what comedians are – we're salesmen.

---

* Dylan Moran turned up to the Comedy Store one night when I was on because he'd heard about my 'Beds! Beds! Beds!' joke and wanted to see it for himself.

There's nothing like knowing you've got a great new gag up your sleeve.

To comics, these 'A-list' gags are like chart-toppers to a musician. You have your singles – for a comic, it's those elusive openers and closers, the gags that set your audience up or leave them laughing. You also have your album tracks – your less direct stuff, your B-list gags. And just like a hit song, a good gag can earn you a fortune. Think about it, on a tour you go out every night and you tell those same gags night after night. Ker-ching!

So it's worth all the Sturm und Drang that went into coming up with them.

TV people don't really appreciate what a five-minute set is worth to a working comic. Whatever they offer you, you know that once you've done those gags on TV they're dead, you have to drop them from the act.

As I found out, to my cost.

It was 1994 and the Perrier Newcomer Award had prompted a bit of telly interest. That's what awards do really – they tell the TV industry and the media who to like for the next year until the next set of awards roll up.

I got booked on *Viva Cabaret*, a new variety show being made for Channel 4 by the same people who'd made Jack Dee's show.

It's easy to forget how exciting Channel 4 was when it first came out. These days it's mainly lifestyle and reality shows, but back then they were real risk takers. So at that time, if you were a left field comic like me, Channel 4 really was the place you stood your best chance of getting on.

For my TV debut, I had a suit made at the place where Jack Dee had his made – at Eddie Kerr's in Soho. Every comic who got a bit of telly at that time paid a visit to

Eddie. He made good suits, relatively cheaply, very quickly.*

The idea of the show, I think, was to try and recreate a sort of sexy underground cabaret club, reminiscent of Berlin in the thirties. There'd be a different comic hosting it every week – the only one I can remember is Mark Thomas – and they'd have a guest singer to finish – one night it was Tom Jones. They were making six in all, and they wanted me to do three. Three five-minute spots.

The aim of me going on the show was for the 'exposure', to increase my fan base, to get people coming along to my gigs and hopefully to drum up a bit more interest from TV. The problem was having done the best fifteen minutes from my act on TV, there wasn't much left for the live crowd to see that they hadn't seen already.

Cut to my first gig after appearing on *Viva Cabaret*. Expectations were high, there was a noticeable buzz when my name was mentioned at the start of the night, which was thrilling, but as I bounded down the stairs to the stage at the Banana Club in Balham, that buzz quickly turned to ashes in my ears.

It was an expectation I just couldn't match. Lines that usually killed were getting titters rather than big laughs. Then it happened.

'Heard it!' came a lone voice from the back, and the whole room seemed to nod in agreement.

---

* Eddie also famously made all the suits for the PG Tips Chimps. The story goes that Lee Evans's manager Addison Cresswell was in Eddie's picking up a suit, when he saw one hanging up. 'Is that one for the chimps?' he says.

'No, it's for Richard Morton,' says Eddie.

Richard is a particularly petite, skinny Geordie comic that Addison represented at the time. It's not funny if you don't know Richard, which is why it's just a footnote.

And you know what? That heckler was right, and there was absolutely nothing I could do about it. Well, what I did was some stuff that was so old it was new to them and I just about got away with it.

I was too scared to do any more gigs until I'd come up with some new stuff, and so I hit every new material night in town until I'd busted up a new solid twenty.

Turnover.

If you don't do them on telly, then you can do them forever – or for as long as you can sell them – because that's the other thing about jokes: the more you tell them the less funny they become.

Let's take a look at the life cycle of a joke.

Phase One

Congratulations, you've got a new joke! You don't know whether it's funny yet, and you can't gauge its full potential because you're not confident enough with it. You don't know where to put the pauses and the emphasis because you haven't fine-tuned it. So, you try it out a couple of times and if it bombs you try it again. Some comics say you should run a gag up the flagpole three times before you drop it, but I've had jokes I've been tinkering with for years.

Or maybe it gets you a big laugh on its first outing – exciting times – and you know you're on to something.

Phase Two

You've polished the joke over a couple of gigs, you're confident in its abilities, and you're excited about it! The audience senses that and they enjoy it as much as you do. This is the best the joke will ever go.

Phase Three

This is the plateau phase – the joke is working, you know you can rely on it; you know it's a good joke and it's paying its way night after night. It's no longer the new joke, it's taken its place with all the other jokes on the shop floor of your act, and when you're not working, those jokes all go on holiday together.

Phase Four

You're now too familiar with the joke and you've started to take it for granted – it's still funny, it still gets a good, reliable laugh, but not as big a laugh as it used to get and you're not sure why. Something's changed in the way you tell it. It could be that you're racing through it slightly, tossing it off, or maybe you've inadvertently changed a word here or there. Really, now's the time to drop it. You can sometimes breathe a little life into it by changing the order of your act because then you've got to be a little more 'on it', there's a little more adrenaline to focus your mind.

Some comics think that changing the order is the same as writing a new set.

We both know it's not.

Phase Five

If you don't drop the gag, eventually you don't even hear it as you're telling it – it's just automatic, it's not what it was. It needs to go.

The weird thing is, if you drop a gag and then throw it in maybe a year later, it can get a laugh that's almost as big as when it was in Phase Two.

Ah, it's endlessly fascinating, right?

Topical jokes are another matter.

Pity the comic whose entire act is topical.

That's a compulsory turnover problem right there. A topical joke is at its funniest – obviously – the closer it is to the thing it's referring to. So, if Theresa May does a funny dance at the Tory party conference – if you go on that evening and merely reference that dance – you'll get a big laugh. If you actually have a good joke about it, it'll raise the roof. Audiences love it! It's part of the live experience, the feeling that they're getting something one-off and special – and no doubt some of them will be tucking your joke away to tell at work the next day.

Remember when Madonna got yanked down the stairs by her cape at the Brit Awards? Yes, you do! She came on in a big black cape and had a dancer pull at it – it was supposed to come clean away but something went wrong and instead she got dragged down the stairs on her back. Kind of funny but then you thought, *Wait! She's sixty!*

I had a gig the night after it happened, and so yes, you guessed it, I went on with a black cape and got a stooge in the audience to yank it off – only I'd tied it so tight that the stooge ended up dragging me all over the stage. It was a really funny physical bit and was a great start to the show – but it was topical. A month later it would have gone for nothing.

The point is, I was probably first with that Madonna gag. What you don't want is to be the last – then it's the opposite of sharp. It looks lazy and sad.

The difficulty is that you get attached to jokes, you remember the good times when that gag delivered gales of laughter and you don't want to let go of it. We all know comics who had a gag about a film that was funny when the film came out – they got the laugh but held onto the joke long enough for the movie to come out on DVD. 'I see that *Jaws 4* came out on DVD . . .' as a way of giving them a reason to crowbar it into the set.

The weekend Margaret Thatcher was toppled, you never saw so many long faces at the Red Rose Club. All those left-wing comics were torn – they hated everything she stood for, but on the other hand they had forty minutes on her.

Careful what you wish for.

In the nineties, you didn't have to be left wing to work the circuit, but it helped. I guess you'd broadly call me a left-winger, one of the 'liberal elite', but that doesn't mean I necessarily want to talk about it in my act. All I really ever wanted to do was make the audience laugh, get paid and get rebooked.

Back then, I did feel under pressure to throw in a 'little bit of politics', as Ben Elton would have it. But that stuff only really works if you believe in it. The master of it at that time and probably still, is Mark Thomas – he could be absolutely mesmerising. He'd have the audience laughing their heads off one minute and gasping the next as he told them of some appalling abuse of human rights. By the end of his set, they'd be on their feet and ready to follow him in a torchlight procession from Finsbury Park to the Houses of Parliament, tarring and feathering every Tory MP they met along the way.

But I couldn't do that!

But, it was the nineties, and you had to.

So, you wanna hear how Harry Hill was setting out to shake the very foundations of our institutions?

OK, but don't get your hopes up.

So cast your mind back to 1990/91, the time of the Gulf War – the first one, the one we all watched on TV. So if you remember, it was all about Saddam Hussein invading Kuwait and George Bush senior riding in on his white Pershing missile. The left-wing comics on the whole talked about how the US were only after the oil, that they had a bad record on human rights themselves, that war should be a last resort. All good points worth making.

My gag was, 'Saddam Hussein, Hitler, Kaiser Wilhelm II – what is it about our arch-enemies that they always have a moustache?'

I rest my case, although I guarantee that I was the only act in London to have referenced Kaiser Bill since the days of the music halls.

Nurse Tiffids
Barbara Cartland
Dad Fire Brigade
Mum – No-one und.
    ↖ Valium

SHoplifting
Pancakes
  Pope sex
_____
Birds of feather
Bank Robbery
Hide + seek

Travel suitcases

Lottery Wardrobes
Shopping for others.

CHAPTER 13
LAYING ONE

'Don't take your baby into the bed because there's a chance you might roll over in your sleep, roll on top of the baby and . . . put your back out.'

My follow-up to 1992's Edinburgh smash *Flies* was called *Eggs* and was sold out for the entire run before I even got there. Sadly, it met with universal disdain from the critics. It actually prompted an outraged letter to the local paper when we previewed it in a wine bar in Chichester.

Little to laugh at

Sir, – Chichester Festivities. Presentation of "EGGS" July 7, 1993, Bishops Kitchen.

Having read the previous write-up, I had anticipated a presentation of good old humour-cum-comedy act on attending the duo of former doctor Harry Hill and Chichester GP Dr Matt Bradstock, at the Bishop's Kitchen 6.30pm sitting.

Alas – no.

Much of the material was offensive to the extreme (IRA theme – "all these car/lorry bombs – too much choke" . . .); the derogatory jokes of certain physical characteristics of some elderly ladies was objectionable, and the "film" on the beginnings of Harry Hill's love life and the subsequent sexual birth contortions of his lady love degrading indeed.

While Dr Bradstock only played a "stooge role" in the main, I note his comments that "it's great fun getting up in front of a bunch of people" – maybe it is not great fun for them, particularly if he is ever confronted by one of his elderly female patients who seeks his professional services.

We expected real comedy – we need real humour, and the £7 a head seat and a show lasting 68 minutes failed to provide. Festival organisers – if you need the support of the public at future events then just ensure that you provide dignified presentations.

What a flop!

Harry Hill
Bishop's Palace
July 11

Rising star Harry Hill sadly proved to be the surprise flop of the Festivities.

The comedian, whose following is growing since his appearances on Channel 4's Viva Cabaret, must have left the stage with relief.

Perhaps the £7 entrance price deterred the kind of people who are more likely to appreciate his quirky sense of humour.

His fast-moving act flicks from subject to subject, with a steady flow of non-sequiturs and running jokes.

But the show, especially a sketch about Nintendo, left many members of the audience baffled and bored.

Some were not even stirred to politely applaud at the end, which is revolutionary for a Festivities audience.

Harry's act relies too heavily on being manic and not enough on being funny. Jokes which inspired laughter were appreciated more for their rare appearances than anything else.

Admittedly that night was a bit of a mess – I was busking it to a large extent – and the crowd were mainly over sixty and very conservative. I had an ill-judged gag about the IRA bombing campaign – 'All these cars exploding – too much choke! Just ease the choke button in a bit . . .'

That night it got a gasp.

The show wasn't in any better shape by the time we got it up to Edinburgh.

It was a very ambitious production. I can't remember much of the detail, but I know I'd made two sort of pods from cardboard boxes that me and Matt appeared through at the start. I had this running gag about how Matt was trying to escape by tunnelling out. So every now and then he'd empty some earth from the bottom of his trousers like on *The Great Escape*. The gag ended with Matt appearing from his pod with a wheelbarrow full of earth, which he then upturned onto the stage. I bought a couple of big bags of potting compost but it was very dry, and Matt would get very sweaty. The first time we tried it, I looked at his face – it was covered in potting compost – and I just burst out laughing.

The other problem I had was one of expectation again. Because I'd been touted as the 'future of new comedy', the audience expected me to be side-splittingly funny from the moment I came on. I suppose I should have been!

Al Murray made a brief appearance in the show as some sort of official. That year he was appearing in the Jewish rock band Guns 'n' Moses and the three of us were sharing a flat with Brenda.

Matt had his keyboard with him, and Al had his drum kit set up in the front room. Anyone who knows me will tell you that I love to sing, so in our down time we routined some songs. It was such good fun that we booked ourselves a late-night slot at the Fringe Club as Pub Band. I was notionally Tony O'Pub, Matt was Matty Beer and Al was Ale Murray. I have a cassette tape of that night. We kicked off with 'Amarillo', segued quickly into 'Delilah' and finished with

```
"EGGS" PROPS   Date: 29 May 1993

MATT

Trunk
DAT player
Cine screen
Suit
Specs x3
Alan's beard
Ice cream tray
Distributor cap
Tinned salmon
Marrow
Spanish money
Watch
Car keys
Saucer
Frying pan
Lighter fuel
Nest
White coat
Goggles
Snorkel
Petri dishes
Tweezers
Microscope slides
Deck chair
Hamper
Thermos
Books
Newspapers
Blueprint
Earth  ·
Growbag & Mechanism
RAF kit
Flying helmet
Adapted trousers  .
Wheelbarrow —
Shovel
Broom
Black hat
Black roll-neck
Nap sack
Black make-up
Blow-up woman
Cans lager
```

Looks like the shopping list of a serial killer.

'Avenues and Alleyways', then after shouts of 'More!', did a pub-style version of 'Bohemian Rhapsody'.

I ad-libbed a line about 'Imagine a world where all the pubs join together as one – when will there be a Harvester for the world?'

It was a rowdy crowd of pissed drama students, but it went down a storm. On that tape you can hear me laughing so much I can hardly get the words out. Al's tight drumming and splashy cymbal work are hilarious.

We knew we were onto something, so when we got back to London we did a run in the upstairs room at the Camden Head in Islington. The idea was that Al would compère, I'd do my act then we'd all come together for Pub Band to finish the night off.

We met up at the flat Al shared with Stewart Lee and Richard Herring in Tooting and ran some ideas. The best bit, in my view, was a mash-up of Madonna's 'Material Girl' with a selection of old-time music-hall songs. It's hard to explain it on paper but it killed every time.

Al had decided he wanted to ditch his serial killer act and had come up with a character – Billy-Jack Ritchie – based on an American Catskill comic. It was inspired in part by the Billy Crystal character in the movie *Mr Saturday Night,* which we watched on repeat because we liked it so much.

So on the first night at the Camden Head, he came on wearing an oxygen mask and wheezed out his new material. I don't remember any of the gags – which, maybe, isn't such a great sign.

It didn't go so well and Al, who was used to big laughs with his regular act, lost confidence in it, and on a whim the next night, decided to go on pretending to be the landlord of the pub downstairs. It went down a storm and inadvertently gave him a whole new direction.

So Al would do five minutes, then I'd do my twenty or so, then Pub Band came on and killed – it was a really exciting week.

We decided to take it to Edinburgh, calling it *Pub Internationale* after the 'gentlemen's' magazine of our youth, *Club International.*

We kicked it off with an act we called 'The Two Simon and Garfunkel', which was me and Matt dressed as the famous pop duo doing an eccentric dance to a Herb Alpert track. The dance finished with the trick I'd learnt in the Cubs panto all those years earlier – I jumped into Matt's arms and he carried me off.

Al had built his five minutes into ten. I did thirty, then we played a short super 8mm film of us horsing around in the streets of Tooting to the theme from *The Professionals* TV series to cover the costume change.

I wore a pale blue drape coat that I'd picked up from a thrift store in Miami, and a rubber quiff I'd bought from a joke shop. By then we'd added some new bits; we'd complain that we'd all been done for drink driving then sing The Cars' hit 'Who's Going to Drive Me Home . . .'.

A particular highlight was me singing 'Yesterday'. I'd sing the verse straight but when it got to the chorus – 'Why she had to go . . .' – Al and Matt would play this demonic version of it and I'd scream it at the top of my voice and smash up a chair – and then finally I'd break a beer bottle over my head. It wasn't a real beer bottle – it was a sugar-glass one – and it was my job the next day to patch up the chair and soak a label off a bottle of Bud and stick it onto the fake one.

After each song, I'd shout, 'Please take your glasses back . . . to . . . the . . . bar!'

We'd finish on 'Bohemian Rhapsody' then the encore was a double-time version of 'Tie A Yellow Ribbon'.

So it was a pretty packed hour.

We were all on flying form and having the time of our lives.

There was a real buzz about the show and it was heaving every night. Vic Reeves came one night, Chris Evans on another. We were duly nominated for the Perrier Award up against Alan Davies, Jeff Green, Owen O'Neill, the American comic Robert Schimmel and the Australian double act Lano and Woodley.

I think we were the hot favourite – that's what The Agent reckoned, but in any event, it went to the Aussies.

Part of our reward for being nominated was a night at the Lyric Theatre in Shaftesbury Avenue.

Up until that point, the biggest audience we'd played to was maybe a hundred and fifty people. The Lyric held nearly a thousand.

It sold so well they stuck in another three nights. Vic and Bob came again on the same night as Ronnie and Anne Corbett.

It really did feel like we were the toast of the town!

That first night though, that was somethin' else!

Those old Victorian theatres are just perfect for comedy. Even though it was packed, you felt right on top of the crowd. It was a Sunday night – the one night of the week when the regular show *Five Guys Named Mo* didn't play. Princess Diana was all over the papers at the time – she'd just split with Prince Charles – and my sister Michelle was a dead ringer for her, so we put her in a Lady Di wig and gown, pimped her up with some sparkly jewellery and stuck her in the royal box.

'I couldn't believe Lady Di was there,' said my friend Steve Bowditch over a pint in the bar after. 'Someone said they thought it was a double, but I knew it was her cos of the way her diamonds twinkled.'

There was such a huge reaction when I came on that I felt physically winded – I could hardly catch my breath. The front of the stage had a set of wide steps down into the front row. I know because when I hit myself over the head with the bottle, I rolled down them.

After that we toured the arse off it. We played every little arts centre and two-bit theatre in the country. Attendance was varied – we didn't have the profile in the rest of the country that we had in London – but it nearly always went down well. When we played the Hazlitt in Maidstone, the audience got a double treat as I introduced Vic Reeves, who came on in a blonde fright wig and sang 'Goldfinger'. During the first half, whilst I was on, he'd sat at the side of the stage at a small table drinking our rider. Forty minutes into the show there was an almighty crash as the table went over. He explained later that it only had three legs.

'I only live nearby,' he said. 'Why don't you come over and stay the night!' So we all piled in the car and followed him and his driver. Well, let me tell you, he didn't live nearby. It was about an hour away down tiny country lanes in the pitch black – we nearly lost him twice.

When we got there, we carried on drinking and Matt connected up his keyboard, Al set up his drums and Vic plugged in his electric guitar. I've got a Hi8 video somewhere of forty minutes of prog rock noodling at chez Vic. What a night! Eh? Come on! Living the dream!

CHAPTER 14
START SPREADING THE NEWS

'Never get anyone trained in tai chi to back you into a parking space – you'll be there all day.'

In May 1995, there was a huge buzz going around the stand-up circuit because David Letterman was bringing his show to London for a week and was looking for a British comic to do five minutes.

Now, although his show was never broadcast on regular TV over here, to my generation of comedians, David Letterman is a complete legend, a true original, the first really funny modern chat show host. So many have tried to copy what he did, but few have ever got close.

The rumour I heard was that Lee Evans was the front runner as he had a movie out – *Funny Bones* with Jerry Lewis – and so had a bit of profile with the American audience – plus he was quintessentially British and always reliably funny. If not Lee, then Eddie Izzard, who was probably the other big British comic at that time.

It never crossed my mind that I'd be in the running.

Then The Agent called to say that they were 'interested in talking to me' and that I should go to his office at a predetermined time and await a transatlantic phone call from the producer. Seems terribly old-fashioned, doesn't it? I'm not sure why he didn't just give them my number.

Anyway, I turned up and sat staring at the phone, waiting for it to ring.

Sure enough, it rang, and I answered it.

'Hi, Harry!' said a very enthusiastic American man.

'Hello!' I said in my poshest English accent – I don't know why, but whenever I talk to Americans, I go all lah-di-dah, like I was in the Bullingdon Club with Boris and Dave.

'What is it you would like me to do?' I asked.

'Well . . .' said the producer. 'I'd like you to do the five minutes you'd do on the show!'

Fortunately, I was gigging every night and was match fit – I did five minutes of gags down the phone. Remember, this wasn't a Zoom call or FaceTime – he couldn't see me. All he could hear was my voice, but he was really laughing on the other end of the line. I mean *really* laughing.

'That's just great, Harry, I'll be in touch!' he said as he hung up.

'How'd it go?' asked The Agent.

I told him how the guy had been really laughing and that he said he'd be in touch.

'Yeah,' said The Agent with a scowl. 'They always say that.'

Which to be honest took the shine off it a bit.

A week later he called me to tell me that they wanted me to do the show, that I was the chosen one! I'd be on *The Late Show with David Letterman* and I would meet David Letterman and we would become friends and we'd go on holiday together!

Well, maybe not that last bit.

I can't tell you how exciting that was and how much kudos it gave me with all the other comics!

On the day of the recording, I was told that if the show overran, there was a chance I wouldn't get on.

In any event, I never even got in the car to the studio. There I was, all done up in the big collar and suit, waiting in my flat when I got a call telling me to stand down.

I was gutted.

I can't tell you, I'd been so pumped up and ready and then, whack! It was all over.

There was a silver lining, though. They told me they'd fly me over to New York to do the show there instead.

'Yeah, they always say that,' growled The Agent.

A couple of months later, I found myself on a plane flying business class to New York with The Agent sitting next to me.

'Dave is a little bored with some of the current bunch of comics,' said the booker for the show. He was incredibly relaxed about what he wanted me to do. The show's attitude was very much: 'We trust you to do your best bits, that's why we booked you.'

I had a few spots in comedy clubs in New York to try the stuff out.

That's when I got my reality check.

I found the New York crowds incredibly tough.

It seemed to me I had a couple of problems – one was just the way I looked. All the other comics were dressed casually, T-shirt and jeans, and they had a similarly laid-back style to match.

They would amble on and do all that 'Hi, where you from?' stuff – a very gentle upslope to their material – which on the whole, to me anyway, was pretty run-of-the-mill, the sort of stuff that wouldn't have cut the mustard at the Red Rose or the Bearcat. Virtually every line would start with 'Hey! Have you noticed . . .?'

So, when I came on in my suit and big collar, all guns blazing, singing, 'Chicken, liver, carrots, onions, everybody's talking 'bout, casseroles!' they didn't know what to make of me.

The look, the accent, the material were all just incredibly foreign to them.

They would literally spend the first few minutes discussing me. I could hear them saying 'Where's he from?' and 'My God! What's he wearing?!'

It was weird and, worse, incredibly distracting.

I had a routine where I asked a member of the audience to say 'Quack!' – then I'd throw bread at them saying 'See how you like it! I've seen you down the duck pond!' It got a good laugh, but I got taken to one side by the club owner who instructed me curtly, 'Not to throw bread at the diners.'

That week before the *Late Show* taping, everywhere I went, I struggled. I adjusted my references – they call biscuits 'cookies', they call mobile phones 'cell phones', they call shire horses 'Clydesdales' – small things that were easy to tweak, and the act started to go a little better.

By the time it came to Friday, I was so nervous I spent the whole day pacing up and down in my hotel room.

At around half past four in the afternoon, they sent a huge stretch limo to pick me up and take me the two blocks to the Ed Sullivan Theater on Broadway. The traffic was so bad it took forty minutes. There was a big crowd of autograph hunters at the stage door as I arrived and when the doorman opened the car door, they surged forward – then they saw it was me and put their books away. No one had any idea who I was!

I got shown to my dressing room and was told that Dave would be making his way down from his office to the stage shortly and that on no account was I to leave my dressing room until he'd passed through, because he didn't like to see his guests before the show started.

So, I sat and watched the wall-mounted monitor as they ran the title sequence.

'Tonight on the *Late Show* – Terri Hatcher! Jon Stewart! Harry Hill! Paul Shaffer and The CBS Orchestra . . .'

I sat and watched as the show played out. Then I sat and watched as they re-recorded the titles, missing my name off.

Then there was a knock at the door. It was the booker.

'They've run out of time, I'm afraid!' he said.

I couldn't believe it – bumped again! All that way, all that preparation, all that adrenaline, wasted. As I walked back to the lift, the doors opened and out walked the man himself, David Letterman.

I froze, thinking, *Is it OK if he sees me after the show or am I supposed to stay in my dressing room till he's* left *the building?*

'Hi!' he said. He looked different – smaller, more wiry – than he does on TV and his face was plastered with thick, thick, tan make-up.

'Hello!' I replied nervously.

'Are you the kid from England?'

'Yes.'

'Sorry about that, we'll bring you back,' he said and kept walking.

So back home I went. Three months later, I flew to New York again. Only for a couple of days this time – because I had my five-minute set worked out.

Friday came around, the limo turned up, took me to the show. I sat in my dressing room, I watched the show and watched them re-record the opening titles without my name. I got bumped again! This was ridiculous. They were taking the piss, surely?

'We'll bring you back!' said the producer.

By the third time, I was sitting in that dressing room as cool as a cucumber, expecting not to get called as they announced, '. . . Walter Cronkite and Harry Hill!'

Then, after thirty-five minutes or so – there was a knock on the door.

'You're on!' said a girl with a clip board.

Doh! I thought, *It's actually happening!*

Suddenly, I was in the lift, then I was walking backstage at the Ed Sullivan Theater. The Ed Sullivan Theater! Where Elvis made his TV debut, where the Beatles began the British invasion. I was standing in the wings, getting mic'd up and talking to Biff, Dave's famous floor manager.

I looked across, and there was Dave – maybe only twenty feet away. I remember it was really cold. I'd heard that Dave liked the temperature chilly to make the audience more alert and so more likely to laugh. Some of the band still had their coats on.

'When you're done, stay where you are and Dave will come over and shake your hand,' said Biff. 'Then we'll go to an ad break. If he really likes you, he'll ask you to join him on the couch, but that doesn't happen very often, so don't expect it.'

I'd been asked what play-on music I'd wanted when I first got booked – and because of the Beatles/Ed Sullivan thing, I'd asked for the opening chords of their first number-one hit 'Please Please Me.'

'Our next guest is a very funny man who visits us all the way from the UK,' said Mr Letterman, shuffling a cue card in his hand. 'Please welcome, the very funny – Harry Hill!'

And off I went.

I still got a little bit of the weird reaction I'd experienced in the clubs, but because Dave had endorsed me, they got into it pretty quickly. That room wasn't so different to playing a regular Victorian theatre back home – the audience were right there in front of me. I knew the five minutes back to front by then, and once I'd got a few laughs under my belt, I started to relax and have fun. What gave me that confidence was that I could hear Dave laughing, off to the left and slightly behind me. So it felt like it was going well.

'Thanks, Harry! Take a bow!' It was Dave. He took my hand in his cold hand and the cameras cut for the ad break. Then he said the magic words.

'Why don't you come and join me?' He gestured to the couch. I'd made it! I sat down next to him as they repositioned the cameras and got ready for the last little segment where he tells the audience who's going to be on the show on Monday and then signs off.

'So, you work mainly over here or . . .?' he asked.

I explained that I'd only worked in the UK and we chatted idly about nothing in particular. Then one of the production team came and sat down beside me and tapped me on the shoulder. I turned to face her.

'Oh, hi!' she said 'I've been sent here to distract you because Dave needs to concentrate on the next item!'

I think maybe he had a button under his desk that he pressed if someone was being boring.

Six months later, they asked me back. This time I was waiting in the wings to go on and when Dave saw me, he gave me a big wave. 'Hi Harry!' he said smiling. He looked genuinely pleased to see me.

Although Dave seemed to love my act, even to the extent that occasionally he'd lapse into an impression of me,* the only work I ever got offered from those appearances stateside was the part of an English butler in the movie *Garfield 2: A Tail of Two Kitties.*

It started with an audition in a basement in Covent Garden.

'You're acting with a CGI cat,' said the casting agent from behind the camcorder she was taping me on. 'Go as broad as you want!'

So, off I went, mugging and generally horsing around, which is my preferred style of acting – well, let's face it, it's my *only* style of acting.

'Maybe rein it in!' she said, pulling a face.

As I left, I didn't hold out much hope of getting the part. In fact, by the time I got home, I didn't even want it.

'I never found *Garfield* funny, anyway!' I said to Mrs H. 'And it's not even the first movie!'

Then The Agent called and told me I'd got the job. It was for a huge amount of money too. It would have meant filming for a month in the UK and a week or two in Los Angeles. Yes, suddenly I was going to be an actor in a Hollywood movie! Then I got the dates through and it coincided with my stand-up tour, Hooves.

I was so upset! I was moping around the house, gutted that I wouldn't be sharing the screen with what had now become my favourite cartoon cat.

---

* 'You like the lining! You like the lining!' he'd say, opening his jacket and flashing the lining.

The director then came back and said, 'Don't worry, we'll get Harry to do the voice of one of the other CGI animals in post-production.' So that cheered me up a little.

'Yeah, they always say that,' said The Agent.

Cut to eighteen months later and I'm in a voiceover studio in Soho doing the voice of Claudius the Rat.

Cut to six months later and I open a copy of the *Mail On Sunday** to see a big splashy interview with Joe Pasquale who is about to appear in the new movie *Garfield 2* as the voice of Claudius the Rat.

I was furious! I dashed the colour supplement to the ground with all the venom I could muster and turned the air blue with the filthiest words I could think of.

'What's up with Dad?' asked our nine-year-old daughter.

'Your father's upset that he didn't get the part of the voice of a rat in *Garfield 2*,' said Mrs H witheringly. She then insisted on taking the kids to see the flaming movie.

'How was the rat?' I said grumpily to the nine-year-old when they all got back.

'Very believable!' she replied.

---

* I swear it's Mrs H who buys it!

CHAPTER 15
LUV 'N' STUFF

'The first time I met her she was wearing an off-the-shoulder outfit – off the shoulder, down to the ground with a zip running from the top right down to the bottom. It was a sleeping bag.'

If you're in show business and thinking of attempting to spend the rest of your life with someone, for God's sake, don't marry a fan. Show business can be a very rough ride at times. For every peak, there's a precipitous drop just round the corner. You need a strong person to help you navigate through those difficult times.

Find someone who is at least your equal. Someone who you're not just attracted to but who the very thought of upsetting makes you as unhappy as it would them.

I met my someone at a party in South London in 1986.

Rob was at the Chelsea School of Art and had taken me along as his plus-one. I liked those art school parties – the people there looked much more exotic than those at the med school dos. The party was at a Victorian terraced house, the sort that are two a penny in London. It was a sunny day and clutching the beers we'd brought, Rob and I ventured through the patio doors into the garden, and there she was – bleach-blonde hair and red lipstick, with a ring of other students round her, holding court. She looked fabulous and was funny too, with a dry line in sarcastic put-downs. I knew immediately that she was something special. Here was a girl who could hold her own. Rob introduced us. Her name was Magda Archer, and she was one half of an illustration duo with a fellow called Peter Quinnell called, naturally enough, Archer/Quinnell, a double act but in the Gilbert & George mould.

She was a little bit haughty at that first meeting, and in my sixties suit and glasses, I was immediately conscious of being the square medical student. Despite that, Rob and I proceeded to show off relentlessly and eventually, whilst not exactly falling for my charms, she did seem vaguely intrigued.

It took me ten years to wear her down – talk about the long game.

Over that ten years, I only saw her very rarely – normally when I was Rob's plus-one if he was stuck for a date. Then in 1996, my chance came. Archer/Quinnell were having an exhibition in a little gallery in Waterloo, and Rob took me along to the private viewing. I'd just had a bit of TV success and was feeling flush, so I bought one of their pictures. When the exhibition came down, she generously offered to deliver it round to my one-bedroom basement flat near Earl's Court. She claims that when she came round that first time, she walked past the bedroom and glanced in and saw a pile of cash on the bed. She's probably right – we were all paid in cash for gigs in those days, and I'd occasionally while away the hours Fagin-like counting it.

I made her a cup of tea and chatted with her for about an hour but essentially she just dropped off the painting and that was that. As soon as she'd left, I called Rob, who tipped me off that she was single again. 'You should call her!' he said.

Her number was on the back of the picture, so I did just that. She'd mentioned in passing that she'd just bought a new washing machine, so that was my opening gambit.

'I need a washing machine and was wondering whether you had any advice on what make and model to buy?' I asked, wondering if anyone had ever used a more obscure chat-up line. The conversation flowed freely for about forty minutes, and it felt like we were getting on really well. Having established that Bosch were pretty reliable and that on no account should I get a 'combined washer-dryer', I seized my moment. 'Maybe we should go out for a drink or something?'

'Oh no,' she said, 'I couldn't do that.'

Are there any more at home like you? With my brother and sisters (that's me on the right).

Hello girls! Me aged about nine, I think, at Holimarine Holiday Camp, Weston-super-Mare. Looks like I could do with a couple more of those economy burgers.

Matt and me, boozed up in Edinburgh.

Trying to be as cool as Stewart Lee, and not quite pulling it off.

Me and my long-suffering real-life Nan, Alice Botting. I'm the one on the right.

I think I got the big collar off her too. Me with Jan.

Nice to see him. Is there anything more satisfying than making your hero laugh? Bruce Forsythe and me in Steve Brown's studio.

Not now Burt! Me with the legendary Burt Kwouk.

Show time! Looking worried outside the Ed Sullivan Theatre.

There were three of us in this marriage. Me, Magda and Hattie the Fox Terrier.

Selfie with her majesty and her son Charles, just before she kicked all those balloons into the audience.

Unholy alliance! Me with Simon at the opening of *I Can't Sing!*

I taught him everything he knows! Paul Hollywood on
the set of Tea Time.

Cannon and Ball? Look again! It's Lord Robert Winston and me.

Out to catch the big one. With Grandpa Theo, Herne Bay.

It seemed I'd read the situation all wrong, so we said our goodbyes and I hung up.

A couple of minutes later, the phone rang. It was her. 'Sorry, yes, I'm up for going for a drink,' she said.

I was so excited at the prospect of our first date that I immediately phoned my girlfriend and told her it was over! Yes, sorry, when I said I 'waited' for ten years there were, well, 'dalliances'.

A week later, I took her out for dinner in Islington and we've been together ever since.

If by 1996 Magda was slightly easier to win over, her fox terrier, Hattie, was a tougher nut to crack. The two of them were inseparable – wherever Magda went, Hattie went too. One of our early dates, a picnic by the river, was particularly trying. As we sat on our picnic rug, munching our Scotch eggs, Hattie chose to dive into the river and then run at me like some kind of lunatic canine dive-bomber, shaking her wet fur all over me. She'd then run back into the river and do it all over again, back and forth, back and forth until I smelt like a big, bald, damp dog. I was furious. Magda found the whole thing hilarious, which didn't help. Another time Magda nipped out, leaving me alone in my flat with the dog. No sooner had the front door closed behind her than I looked up to see Hattie taking a dump on my new beige carpet. She was testing me. I was pretty uptight back then. Up until Magda turned up, I'd pretty much done what I'd liked when I liked. I indulged myself and, on the whole, people indulged me because I was a semi-famous comedian.

What Hattie was trying to tell me, I think, was, 'This is not just about you now – you need to accept that your life is going to change if you think you stand any chance of hanging on to her.'

So change I did.

We had a few arguments in those early days as Magda retrained me to be less inward-looking. I was generally pretty grumpy and monosyllabic over breakfast and had used the excuse that I wasn't a 'morning person'. Other people had just accepted it like it was some irreversible character trait.

'What do you mean, you're not a morning person?' she said dismissively. 'Make an effort!'

So I did, and, hey presto, I became a morning person.

We were married within a year of our first date and had the first of our three girls a year after that.

It's not easy living with a comedian – let's face it, it's not easy living with anyone. She's had a lot to put up with. We're all pretty insecure at heart and need a lot of attention. I routinely come home after every TV recording saying how badly it went and how 'I need to get out of this business'. I'm rarely completely happy with the results, and when I watch the shows back, I give her and the kids a running commentary on why this bit didn't work, or why a particular prop is wrong. If I'm on tour or gigging, I'm home late and buzzing so much from the adrenaline that I can't get to sleep. Then the next morning, I'll be pitching some mad idea to her for a show or trying out a gag.

I used to be a worrier. I'd worry about work, I'd worry about money, I'd worry about whether a gag worked. Magda is most certainly not a worrier. Nothing phases her. On the rare occasion that I've had the press on my doorstep looking for a story, it's her who's sent them away with a flea in their ear.

I need someone like that.

It's not easy being the 'plus-one' either – where people ignore your other half or shove them aside to get to you. We don't really do the showbiz thing. If we wanted to, we could probably be out every night of the week at some launch or premier. We tried it a couple of times in the early days, and both agreed it wasn't worth the hassle. If it's an industry do that I can't get out of, I'll go alone, show my face and scarper at the first opportunity.

She gave up the illustration when the kids came along, and once they were old enough to go to school, she bounced back as a fine artist. The fashion house Marc Jacobs recently licensed some of her work for a clothing range. There was much excitement in our house when Harry Styles and Dua Lipa were pictured wearing her designs. At the launch at Harvey Nichols, I was proud to be her plus-one.

Early days – me and Mrs H.

I'm not sure what kind of parents we've been.

When my daughters hit their teens, they naturally started doing some of that teen stuff – wearing short skirts, plastering their faces with make-up and drinking in the park. This awoke a bizarre conservatism in me that I never knew I had. I took to shouting things at them that I'd only ever heard in those kitchen-sink dramas from the sixties. Stuff like 'Get that muck off your face!' and 'You're not going out dressed like that!' and 'No daughter of mine drinks Thunderbird out of a bottle on a park bench – you'll use a glass like your mother!'

But for some reason, it just seemed to make the situation worse.

So I talked to a friend of mine who recommended I read a self-help book called something like *Talking To Your Teen So Your Teen Can Talk To You*. So I tracked it down on Amazon. I was sitting on the stairs reading it when one of the girls arrived home from school.

'What's the book, Dad?' she said.

'It's called *Talking To Your Teen So Your Teen Can Talk To You*,' I said earnestly, ' and I'm hoping it will help us communicate better.'

To which she replied . . .

'Loser!'

I never finished the book, but I learnt something from that short exchange. I stopped my heavy-handed interventions and gradually they grew out of most of what was winding me up.

I think the kids have turned out as funny, confident, talented young women as much in spite of my parenting skills as because of them.

CHAPTER 16
ROAD KILL

'The Bible is a good book, but if you drop a Bible from a height, you could kill a small mammal – so it's not all good!'

It's very easy to forget when you're playing to packed houses at the Edinburgh Fringe Festival and in tiny cellar bars and function rooms on the London club scene that pretty much no one in the rest of the country knows who you are which was only too apparent when I found myself booked to play a forty-five date national tour, Savlon 2000, in some of the largest venues in the country.

The rationale was that it was better to under sell a thousand-seater than sell out a three-hundred seater – because you might have sold three hundred and one tickets in the big venue and made more money. Technically, I suppose that's true, but it was me who was having to do the shows staring out over rows and rows of empty seats.*

Give that option to any comic and they'll always go for the smaller sold-out venue and take the financial hit. A sell-out – even if it's sixty seats in a room above a pub – is just exciting! If, as an audience member, you file in to a room that's only a third full, you sit waiting for the curtain to go up thinking, *Hmm not many in. Can't be any good, I'm backing a loser. I wonder if it's too late to get my money back?*

The show reeks of failure from the start.

---

* Actually, in that situation, (and we've all been there), they'll often put a sort of curtain up or drape the seats in black fabric so you can't see them – almost like the seats themselves are in mourning.

That's not to say you can't still have a good show in that situation, but the dynamics change.

Me and Al Murray were once booked in to play Dundee Rep, which on a good day seats 450. We'd sold so few tickets that the house manager moved us to the foyer. It went off fine – we got paid, we got drunk, we went home.

My Savlon 2000 show kicked off with me singing 'I Know Him So Well', dressed as both Elaine Paige *and* Barbara Dixon. I then went on to describe donuts as a way to smuggle jam – or 'Trojan Buns' – and then detailed the best way to transport an owl. ('Roll him in newspaper and cut two holes for the eyes – so that he might see the vista.')

A few good gags and a helluva lot of whimsy, interspersed with lines from 'Return Of the Mack'. My big finish was getting someone up out of the audience who I deemed was scared of cats to 'desensitise them to cats' by bringing my rubber cat, Stouffer, ever closer until finally it was right in their face and I was making agitated cat noises.

You had to be there – except a lot of people weren't!

That night I picked on a man in the front row who was very reluctant to join me on stage – it's always a tricky moment that, because if you let that one person off and try to get someone else up, the audience then know that it's not compulsory – that all they have to do really is say no. Then the whole thing takes forever and nine times out of ten, you end up onstage with someone who *wanted* to be picked – an attention seeker who won't shut up and let you do your frigging cat desensitisation routine so you can go and have your pint of lager and a lie down!

So, usually, I find it's best to insist – which is what I did with this reluctant man. Although I noticed it wasn't just him who was reluctant – all the people around him were waving their arms about and shaking their heads. Eventually, he gave in and got up onto the stage, along with his white stick.

Yes, he was blind.

I don't know whether you've ever tried a principally visual gag on a blind person, have you . . .? Well, the news is, it's still funny – but not in the way I'd intended it to be. Fortunately, he loved every minute of it, as the tables were turned and it was my turn to squirm. It was one of those lovely moments you can only really get in a live show – where the audience were aware I'd cocked it up and really enjoyed seeing me try to fight my way out of it. If you're wondering (and I know you are), I got round it by shouting what I was doing, '*The cat is now six feet away from your face! The cat is now two inches from your face and has got its mouth open!*'

I'm not sure it was ever as funny as on that night.

For my first couple of tours, I only did an hour or so and had a support act – my good friend Steve Bowditch. I'd met Steve when I was first starting out at the Comedy Pit in Streatham. I'd gone along to support Alistair McGowan, and Steve was on the bill. In those days, his act was a sort of stream-of-consciousness prop act. He'd hold up a shark's fin and move it about singing the theme song from *Flipper*, then he'd hold up a magic wand. 'The power of the wand,' he'd say. His best bit at that time was several pieces of brightly painted wood that were connected by hinges. He'd move it around and sing the Channel 4 ident music and the pieces of wood would align into the familiar multicoloured C4 logo.

I'd never met anyone like him – he was a decade older than me, was from South East London and kicked around with Malcolm Hardee – in fact, he was one third of Malcolm's occasional comedy troupe The Greatest Show on Legs, who famously performed a naked dance with only balloons to cover their modesty.* Steve's whole attitude is that life should be fun.

---

* By modesty here, I mean, of course, genitals.

He had a great put-down line if he was ever heckled. He'd stop what he was doing and look at the heckler with a wry smile. 'Hmm, I bet you were at work today, weren't you?' he'd say. 'Me? I was in the park!'

That's Steve's outlook right there – why be at work when you could be in the park?

Another time someone shouted 'Wanker!' at him in the middle of his act. Steve stopped what he was doing and looked at the heckler long and hard. 'Hmm . . .' he said. 'What is your point exactly?'

By the time we went on the road together, he'd ditched most of the visual stuff and was doing one-liners.

'Winston Churchill once said we shall fight them on the beaches – nice bloke, but I wouldn't wanna go on holiday with him.'

Or he'd put on a Blakey moustache and just make Blakey noises for two minutes.

Anyway, I loved his act, and he was great fun to travel around with. He has an ingenious mind and, above all, a childlike playfulness. Well, I soon knocked that out of him!

It's a tough gig being the support. Rather than seeing you as an added extra, a lot of the time the audience consider it as something they have to endure to get to the main act. Picking a support act is a fine art too. You don't want someone who's too funny and is going to tear it up. You don't want someone who's doing anything similar to what you're doing either and, of course, you don't want someone who's going to bomb every night.

Whilst I was on the road I had an enquiry about appearing as a regular on ITV's reboot of the eighties hit show *Saturday Live* – the series that had launched acts like Ben Elton, French and Saunders and Harry Enfield. It was a must-see for my generation of comedy fans, made stars of its line-ups, established so-called alternative comedy beyond the clubs and made the telly people realise that there might be something better than *Summertime Special*.

So, as the wheel turns, ten years later, ITV were bringing it back. Lee Hurst was booked as the host, Alexander Armstrong and Ben Miller were on board, doing various regular characters and Simon Munnery was doing every other show as Alan Parker Urban Warrior. All good people, and thinking back, I can't work out why I was so reluctant to do it!

Maybe I was just worried about blowing all my material again. Maybe it was because it genuinely was live. It may even have been the money – who knows! All I do know is that they kept asking me and I kept saying no.

What you should know about TV people is when they want you to do something, the more you say you're not interested, the more they want you to do it! ITV wanted me to do it, The Agent wanted me to do it – but I was holding out. That is until the Savlon 2000 tour hit Grimsby.

Now I've got nothing against Grimsby, but how I came to be booked into the 1200-seat Grimsby Auditorium is beyond me. Even The Agent would admit that was wishful thinking.

'How many have we sold?' I asked, preparing for the worst as me and Steve were being shown to the dressing rooms.

'Eighty-five,' came the answer.

At least round it up to a hundred! I thought.

There wasn't enough black cloth in all of Grimsby to cover the unsold seats.

It's very difficult to get yourself in an upbeat, 'Let's slay this crowd!' mood when your show has sold so badly. I did my best. I went on, I did Paige and Dixon – but about ten minutes in, I heard seats flipping up and footsteps followed by fire doors opening and closing. It turned out that twenty of the eighty-five were people who worked at the Grimsby Auditorium, and after ten minutes they'd seen enough.

The next day, I called The Agent. 'Tell *Saturday Live* I'll do it!' I said. I couldn't face another night like that.

I knew Lee Hurst well from the circuit,* and I knew him to be a great compère, a brilliant improviser and someone who always had an original take on topical gags. In those days, he also had a man-of-the-people vibe, broad without being naff – so he looked like the perfect choice to host the show, but live? To me that seemed unnecessarily risky – what if I went on and died? At least when I'd died on the Royal Variety, they'd been able to save it in the edit. I could be dying on my wind piece every week for two months!

That summer of '96 was an exciting time. It was the year the England team got to the semi-finals of the European Championships – against our old adversaries Germany; the year everybody was singing Frank Skinner's 'Three Lions' song – even at funerals. Britpop was in its pomp – Oasis and Blur were at each other's throats – a sort of Poundland Summer of Love.

I'd go out three nights of the week and run my five minutes in the clubs and hone it up so that by the time I got to Saturday, I knew what I was doing. After the first couple of weeks, I noticed that the audience were much more pleased to see me and that I didn't have to work so hard to win them over in the opening few moments. It was working for me, I was getting through. Ratings weren't great for the show and something about it didn't quite work. To this day, I'm not sure what it was. The mix of acts? The music? I mean, Tears For Fears weren't exactly hot that summer. Perhaps our biggest hurdle was the enormous amount of nostalgia that existed for the original series. We had no equivalent of 'Loadsamoney' or Stavros The Greek in our version, and inevitably the zeitgeist eluded us.

---

* It was Lee who organised a minibus full of comics including me and Alan Davies, to go down to the Isle of Dogs and leaflet against the rise of the right-wing BNP.

SATURDAY
LIVE
c r e w
2 5 MAY 1996
valid above date only

Mind you, it worked wonders for my ticket sales! I did all eight shows and being the first act on after Lee, I grabbed everyone before they turned off and went to bed. I needn't have worried about it being live either – it suited me really well. It meant I could feel the crowd like a regular gig and give them what I wanted and not have it mucked about with in the edit. I remember that first night having Chris Evans's words ringing in my ears and just making sure my eyes were glued to the camera. They were never as good as proper live gigs, but they came across really well on TV, and my style of short bits matched the viewers' late-night attention span.

By the time the show had finished its run, I was due in Edinburgh for the festival and was greeted like a conquering hero! The run was sold out in advance and tickets for the autumn tour were flying off the shelves! I'd called the show '96 Comeback Special' – and that's very much how it felt.

HOW TO BE A COMEDIAN: LESSON NO. 4 – BUILDING YOUR ACT

'How long did I do?' is probably the most common question a comic asks after he or she comes off stage.

Most stand-ups, particularly when they start out, are completely obsessed with duration.

I remember clear as a bell, coming off after the late show at the Comedy Store one night. As I walked past the compère – Lee Hurst – he said with a little outrage in his voice. 'But you've only done eighteen!' It sounds petty, right? It's not! I was booked for twenty. I was short by two minutes – that's ten per cent!

It sounds obsessive but we comics know the difference between doing eighteen minutes and twenty-two.

That four minutes might be ten jokes – sixty if you're Tim Vine. Two minutes is five jokes. If you did twenty minutes instead of twenty-two, then maybe you can drop five jokes that you're bored of.

Turnover.

We're not just obsessed with how long *we* did either – we're obsessed with how long the other comics on the bill did too. I can remember one comic literally running in to the Meccano Club at one of our new material nights and proclaiming that across town, Boothby Graffoe had just done 'A whole hour – all new stuff!' The rest of us were all left shaking our heads, looking at our set lists and muttering, 'A whole hour? . . . And . . . all *new*!'

I maintain that if you can write a reasonable five-minute set, you can probably write twenty.

The big jump up is to forty, because then pace comes into

it. Over forty minutes, pretty much every comic knows there'll be a lull somewhere, at maybe twenty-five minutes. So, you have to recognise the lull and either try to fix it – usually by doing something high energy like a physical bit, or if you're Bill Bailey, a song – or you've got to be sure you've got something coming round the corner that will bring them back.

Once you've done forty, then really there's no limit. You stop worrying about time. You can do an hour, two hours, whatever, but in my opinion, for what it's worth, you don't really want to see any stand-up comic for more than an hour. I don't care who they are – Billy Connolly, Al Murray, Richard Pryor, Victoria Wood, Stew Lee, Jo Brand (OK, we get the idea!) and that even includes me!

When I'm in the audience, I always clap loudly and ask for more, of course, but I don't actually *want* any more. What I should really do is clap and shout, 'Enough!' But well, that looks chippy.

Of course, we all do ninety minutes to two hours – we wear the length of our sets as a badge of honour. That's partly because we're all egomaniacs, and partly it's to justify the ticket price! Plus, if you do a full show, you don't have to pay a support act – and more importantly you don't have to travel around with the support act and face them every morning over breakfast.

Actually, acts like Bill Bailey – where it's more than just a bloke in a suit with a microphone – can easily sustain for longer. I can honestly say Bill's is the only show I've ever been to and genuinely wanted more.

It's partly why I introduced a band and puppets and big physical set pieces into my act – because I could feel the audience's interest dropping off after about an hour and ten.

The Yanks have got it about right – no one there seems to do more than sixty minutes. When I saw Seinfeld live at the O2 back in 2011, he had a terrible cornball support act who did maybe half an hour (seemed longer! Ouch!). Interval, then Seinfeld. Tight hour. Didn't even break a sweat. No encore. Did anyone complain? NO! We were all back home in time for *Newsnight* – what's not to like?

Seinfeld's maybe a special case. There were a few of us comics there that night to worship at the altar of Jerry – Ricky Gervais (who knows Jerry well), Lee Mack, Chris Evans, a few others. Was Jimmy Carr there? Feels like he should have been. I forget. Anyway, we got invited backstage for the 'aftershow', and we all stood round agreeing how tight the show had been. There was just no air in it – no audience interaction, no settling down, only great material. He hardly even acknowledged the crowd, he didn't need to – every line was a zinger, no filler and we marvelled that there was no one like him over here in the UK – then it hit me. 'It's because none of us can be bothered to get it that tight!' I said, and we all nodded in agreement.

1. Animals win
2. Chris helpful
3. Scab
4. Nib
5. Poodle - noodle - stroodle
6. Fish paste
7. What nut ?
8. Rough Ball Park
9. Person, purpose.
10. Cobblers + keys
11. Life support machine.
12. Think of a s. ienie inknown bottles
13. Toby Jug.
14. Certain smells — coronation 6

CHAPTER 17
BOING!

'Never say never . . . Whoops – said it twice.'

Having previously been told by the BBC and Channel 4 that my idea for a Harry Hill TV show – a version of my radio show *Fruit Corner* – could in no way work on TV, suddenly, after the *Saturday Live* career bounce, they were both falling over themselves to commission it.

The Agent was cock-a-hoop.

'I've never had this before!' he said, working out how best he could screw them into the ground financially.

I must admit it was exciting.

Having written countless treatments and draft scripts and had them all turned down, in the end, all they wanted off me was a couple of lines outlining what the show would be.

I wasted no time in getting the old gang back together – Matt, Al, Brenda, Burt, Steve Bowditch and Stewart Lee as the script editor.

We needed a director and the obvious move would have been a young hot shot with something to prove – we went for the opposite. Robin Nash was in his seventies when I started working with him. With a booming voice, a Zapata moustache and impeccably dressed in a bow tie, he had absolutely nothing to prove – he'd been Head of Comedy at the BBC in the eighties, had produced *The Two Ronnies* and *Generation Game* and directed *Top of the Pops* for years.

Robin was directing *TOTP* when 'Bohemian Rhapsody' hit the number one slot.

'How did you cope with having a seven-minute song in the top slot?' asked Stewart.

'Simple!' replied Robin. 'We played the first half one week and the second half the week after!'

He was a lot of fun, and because he was that bit older and hugely experienced, it meant that me and Stewart behaved ourselves. The content of the show was pretty odd, so we didn't need any fancy camera tricks or chicanery. I wanted it to look like one of those old studio shows from the seventies. He shot it just as he would have shot *The Two Ronnies*. It's like that old saying about needing to know the rules before you can break them – but really his rules were pretty good rules.

We did have a disagreement early on, though.

It was about rehearsing my stand-up. I said that I didn't need to rehearse it – that I'd do what I'd done on *Saturday Live* – hone it up in the clubs and deliver it down the bottle on the night. He explained that there was more than one camera and that I needed to learn to play all of them. So, yes, if I was doing a punchline, I'd deliver it on the mid shot, but if I was doing an action – like for instance, when I did my parody of a goal kick – he'd be cutting wide, so I needed to turn and face that camera, otherwise it would look odd, like when a newsreader is facing the wrong way. In other words, you either play all the cameras or none of them.

The real reason I didn't want to rehearse the stand-up was that I knew I wouldn't get any laughs in the rehearsal room and camera runs and was worried it would kill my confidence and timing, but he was deadly serious. He took me to one side and said, 'Listen, Harry, if you don't rehearse your stand-up for the cameras, you'll end up like . . .' And he leant in and whispered the name of a very famous comedian in my ear. A name which I have sworn solemnly to never reveal.

OK, it was Freddie Starr.

Yeah, right? This was before Freddie went off the rails – at that time he was still riding high, and I thought if I could be as funny and successful as him, I'd be well chuffed . . . But anyway, I feigned shock and seeing how strongly he felt about it, rolled over.

I mean, who was I to argue with the man who'd directed the cameras for Legs & Co. when they'd performed to ELO's 'Don't Bring Me Down'?!

The *Harry Hill* show was a sort of ragbag of characters and sketches loosely held together with my stand-up and the conceit that every week there'd be a badger parade, which inevitably would end up being cancelled.

'Parade's off!' Al Murray would say, which meant I had to visit the badgers in their grooming bay, which then led in a cranky way to a big *Crackerjack*-style song finale with the rest of the cast and two dancers dressed as badgers.

I know, on paper, you can understand why I struggled for so long to get it on TV!

I'd got the idea for the badger parade on the Savlon 2000 tour. We were in Liverpool and I was bored with the show. We drove past a charity shop with a number of toy badgers in the window.

'Stop the car!' I yelled. Steve, the tour manager, pulled over.

'I've got an idea!' I said and popped into the shop.

'How much are the badgers in the window?' I said.

'Sorry, chuck, not for sale – they're for display purposes only,' answered the woman at the till.

'Oh, come on!' I said, 'Everyone has their price, surely?'

She ummed and ahhed for a bit.

'OK, fifty pence?' she said. So that was it, I bought them, tied them to a bit of fishing wire, and that night, before the show, I made an announcement: 'During the badger parade this evening, please no sudden movements or flash photography as it may startle the badgers!' Then at the end, as the audience were filing out, I dragged them across the front of the stage on some string to German oompah music. At the stage door, all I heard from people was questions about the badger parade – so I felt like I was on to something. After that, whichever town we went to, we kept an eye out for toy badgers and just added them onto the end of the piece of string.

The pilot went really well. In many ways, the pilot was as good as it got.

Writing what is essentially a sketch show is one of the toughest things to get right – particularly if there's no theme or structure to it. The worst brief I can get as a writer is to 'write anything you like' – that's when you can end up staring at a blank page.

Monty Python are probably the best example of that sort of sketch show comedy – they hardly ever repeated any characters. One of the things that's exciting about their show was that you literally had no idea what was coming next.

It's much easier if someone says, 'Write ten sketches about conkers,' or something specific.

One solution is to have a roster of characters in slightly different situations that you can come back to every week. The most extreme examples of that are *The Fast Show* and *Little Britain*.

So, for a series of eight shows, I'd write eight badger set-ups and eight badger grooming bay sketches that led to eight songs, eight Burt Kwouk Chicken gags, eight Harry and Burt at Home sketches, eight Big Brother Alan bits – well, you get the idea. After a while, it felt a bit like I was writing the same show every week. Although Stewart was the script editor, I don't really remember him ever giving me anything much in the way of rewrites beyond the first couple of shows.

Really, I should have asked for some help, a couple of co-writers, maybe let Al write some bits, but my ego wouldn't allow it. I was adamant I wanted to write it all myself. Actually, I think the fact that it all came out of my head is what made it distinctive, but a lot of it was really just stuff that appealed to me. For instance, a long sequence about minced beef featuring a one-off character 'Matty Mince', which was Matt Bradstock-Smith dressed up in a mince costume. I really only put it in because I liked the idea of seeing Matt dressed up in mince.*

There were only a few things that survived from the Radio 4 show – mainly, guests doing things you didn't expect, so we had Chas and Dave singing Oasis, Huffty (off *The Word*) singing Jimmy Nail, Ian Lavender singing Madonna, Billy Bragg singing 'Agadoo' and Peter Davison singing Pulp.

CHAS & DAVE

P.O. Box 73, Aston, Stevenage, Herts. SG2 7JT
Fax: 01438 880151

Dear Harry,
    Thanks for your note.
Your show is excellent!
We enjoyed our chat too.
I thought of a silly idea today.
If you like it we could do
more of the same.
    Give me a ring or fax me.
            Chas.

x

Well, Chas liked it!

---

* I remember Matt being in a really bad mood that day because he'd been told he couldn't smoke because the mince had been stuck on using a highly flammable glue.

As I remember it, I'd write a draft and then we had a week's rehearsal in a room behind a church in West London. I'd fix the script up a bit, and then we'd all head down to Teddington Studios to shoot it. There was absolutely no waste – the only sketch I can ever remember cutting was one that was Stewart's idea, with me in the bath in some obscure reference to a scene from *Spartacus* that Stew thought would get people talking. I'd never make a show like that these days. I always like to over-record so that I have the option to cut five or ten minutes of stuff that doesn't work – or if I'm spoilt for choice, bounce it into another show.

No, those shows needed to be twenty-three minutes long, so that's how much I wrote.

Teddington was a real thrill as I knew that's where Benny Hill and Tommy Cooper had recorded their shows.[*] It had a separate block that housed a 'hospitality suite' – a bar and a canteen – which every day offered a different roast. So we'd pile down there at lunchtime, have a big roast lunch and hot pudding and all the cameramen would get pints of beer at the bar – it's a wonder we got anything done in the afternoon at all! It was a novelty for all of us – trying on costumes, wigs and make-up. It was me and my friends mucking about and getting very well paid for it.

At around 7 p.m., they'd let the audience in and because we'd rehearsed it, all we had to do was hit our marks and do the lines. The more complicated stuff that involved costume changes, we recorded earlier in the day and played in. I'd rebelled against that idea when it was first put to me, knowing that we wouldn't get anything like the laugh we'd get doing it live, but as Robin explained, 'If we do that, we'll be here all bloody night!'

For one series I had the idea that we'd do fly versions of popular shows. This involved having tiny fly-sized sets made

---

[*] The studios are luxury flats now.

under a Perspex box into which we released a load of flies. You can't just catch flies, so we had a 'fly wrangler' who provided them. One of the funniest things I've seen was watching Robin Nash shouting at the cameraman to 'Put the camera on the fly's face!' as we were filming our fly version of Jane McDonald's *The Cruise*.

Another test for poor Robin was a sketch called 'Interspecies Quiz'. The idea was to have two panels – one of dogs and the other of birds – competing in a quiz to see which was 'best'. I was seated in the middle and would ask the representatives of their species various questions about *EastEnders* and they would 'buzz in' with their answers.

I don't know whether you've ever tried filming a panel show where dogs compete with birds, but let me tell you, it's not the sort of thing you can knock off in ten minutes.

For a start, the dogs don't necessarily like each other and try to attack their teammates, or alternatively, try to mate with them.

It turns out they don't like birds either, particularly chickens. It also transpires that birds do not necessarily obey simple hygiene rules when faced with a rival panel of growling dogs.

I didn't want the birds to look anxious or the dogs to look aggressive; I wanted them to look pensive, deep in thought, as though they were enjoying the quiz.

An hour into the shoot, with the set covered in bird shit, someone had the bright idea to lock off the camera, shoot each animal individually and then reassemble the scene in post-production.

In many ways, I was still writing for radio; I hadn't quite cottoned on to how long things took to shoot or what was achievable. That sketch on the radio would have involved a couple of dog barks, a few clucks and a few buzzes.

It was a rookie error, but sometimes the naivety and blind

enthusiasm you have when you're new to something leads to some nice surprises. It's important to try to hang on to at least a little bit of that as you travel forward.

I cast Brenda as Bridie McGinty – Paddy McGinty's sister. This is a good example of what I was saying about my references being obscure and rather partial. The song 'Paddy McGinty's Goat' was a big hit for Val Doonican in 1964, which told the story of a goat that was blamed for various incidents in the fictional village of Killaloo in Ireland. I'm not sure it was the sort of cultural reference that Channel 4 – the home of *The Word* and *Big Brother* – were looking for. Anyway, Brenda would come on to the tune of 'Paddy McGinty's Goat' with Eileen the stuffed goat under her arm. Each week she'd detail what had 'got her goat' – which would be some minor bugbear, like slip-on shoes – and would then sing a version of 'Paddy McGinty's Goat'. She'd finish up by saying 'Come On, Eileen!' And leave to the strains of 'Come on, Eileen' by Dexys Midnight Runners. Ratings gold, right?

One viewer-favourite was Stouffer the cat.

Stouffer was based on a rubber cat puppet I'd picked up on holiday with Mrs H in a shop in Nashville called 'Hot Dogs and Cool Cats' that only sold cat and dog themed items. The original was black and only had one paw but when I got the C4 show, I had him remade in blue with two hands and named him after the hotel we were staying in.* Stouffer sat in a chair that I was holding with an obviously false arm. The joke was that I was obviously doing Stouffer's voice and operating him – a piss-take of Rod Hull and Emu and Bob Carolgees' Spit the dog. On his first outing, one of the Channel 4 commissioners expressed concern that you could see my lips moving as Stouffer spoke. Don't get me started on commissioners.

---

* He had a cousin, Radisson, which was the name of the hotel up the road.

I'm not sure what the general reaction to the show was – I was kept away from the dirty business of ratings. I know that Charlie Catchpole in the *News Of The World* ran a review with the strap line 'Video Killed the Radio Star', attacking it for not being as good as its Radio 4 iteration, *Fruit Corner*, but by the end of the run, he was asking for tickets for him and his kids to come to the recordings.

In my experience, it's often the case that after the first show of a new thing, people are a bit non-committal. Usually it's week three when they start telling you you're a genius. It just takes them that long to get into it.

The fact is, you always put your best show out first, then your second best and you bury any show that was a bit weak round about show seven – so you can finish on a good one – if you've got one left.

I remember Burt coming in for the rehearsal about three shows in saying, 'I think something must be working. I used to get people saying to me "Not now, Kato!" on the Tube, but this morning someone said, "Have you caught that chicken yet?"'

The only notes I got back from the channel were that 'he moves around too much', which was a fair point – even the smallest movements on camera seem huge on TV.

Each episode used about five or six minutes of my stand-up – and it had to be the best bits, the one-liners and the running gags – and the schedule of one series a year meant I had to turn over at least an hour of new stand-up, which meant a tour every year.

So for three years, it was a national tour and then write and record a series. Added to that schedule was the fact that me and Mrs H had two of our three daughters in '97 and '98, so you don't really need me to tell you that I was absolutely knackered for most of those years at Channel 4.

Looking at them now, at best they're patchy and the third series is actually pretty ropey. It's never been repeated, you can't buy it on a DVD, and I think that's probably for the best!

Years later, after I gave up *Burp*, Channel 4 got in touch and asked me whether I'd put together a 'best of' show of highlights to celebrate Channel 4's thirty years of programming. I called it *Whatever Happened to Harry Hill?* because just three months after giving up *Burp*, I'd seen a byline in *Heat* magazine asking that very question. Three months out and according to them I was washed up!

I framed the show as a documentary, looking back at the shows through interviews with the principal players: me, Al – with a grey wig – and Burt. The idea was that it was all leading to a special reunion show, then at the end – yes, you guessed it – the badgers refused to go on.

'Parade's off!' said Al, some fifteen years after he'd first said it. We recreated the grooming bay, I got the original badger puppets down from the loft and we finished off singing 'Price Tag' with me as Jessie J, Al as Tom Jones and Burt, improbably, as Will.i.am.

Really, it was a chance to get the old gang back together. Robin had died some years earlier, so I directed it. Burt was pretty frail by then and Matt had recently been diagnosed with cancer, but being the trooper he was, that didn't stop him dragging up in full slap and a mini skirt as a Raga dancer.

Much like the original show, this special went largely unnoticed, but I'm so glad we did it when we did.

Matt died about eighteen months later, and Burt not long after that.

Me and Burt had kept in touch over the years. He had a wonderfully dry sense of humour.

My mum had bought a house with a Chinese name and knowing I knew Burt, asked me to ask him what it meant. So I called him up and explained the situation.

'Let me get this straight,' he said in that raspy voice of his. 'Your mother bought a house off some Chinese people and wants to know what the name of the house means in English?'

'Yes!' I said brightly.

'So why the fuck didn't she ask them?!' he said.

On the subject of Peter Sellers – which is all anyone would ask him about – he remained tight-lipped. Virtually everyone who ever worked with Sellers wrote a book spilling the beans. Not Burt, who had worked more closely with him than anyone and on his biggest hits. Then one day we were chatting, and he turned to me and said, 'What you have to remember about Peter Sellers is . . .' I sat forward – at last he was going to offer me his insights into one of the greatest character comics who ever lived – '. . . he was completely fucking *mad*!'

Yes, I thought, *that probably covers it!*

When Burt died, his wife asked me and Barry Cryer to handle the funeral. Although I'd known him all those years, he didn't talk much about his background, so I had to do a bit of digging. It turned out that he was from a wealthy family in Beijing and had been sent over to America to be educated. When Chairman Mao took over, his father sent Burt a letter that read simply: *If you come back, they'll kill you.* So he never went back. He came to London and, like a lot of young Chinese men at that time, got a job in a restaurant in Chinatown. A lot of the waiters were moonlighting over at Pinewood as extras for the film *The Inn Of The Sixth Happiness* – starring Ingrid Bergman. One day, one of the waiters was ill and Burt took his place – capitalising on the idea that to Western eyes 'we all looked the same'. He got picked out by the director for a speaking role and that was it – he was an actor.

When Burt died, he was a great age – amazing really when you consider the amount of booze and fags he'd consumed. A long life well lived and although it was a sad day, it was also something of a celebration.

When a young person goes, it's different – there's very little in the way of positives.

Matt dying was a tough one. We were great friends and although we hadn't seen a hell of a lot of each other in later years, he was always one of the first people I'd phone up if I had a bit of news or to try out an idea I thought might be funny. He was very good at giving me an honest opinion about a show or a gag and because we went back so far, I was happy to take it from him.

When he was near the end, me and Al went to see him at the hospice – naturally, it was upsetting and we sat at the end of his bed, not knowing what to say or how to react. After a bit he opened his eyes and said, 'For Christ's sake, one of you say something!'

The only good thing that came out of it was the lesson he taught me about dealing with death. He accepted it. Not immediately, it had taken him a while, but once that happened, he made it much easier for those close to him to accept it too.

'I'm not scared of it,' he said. 'It'll just be like before I was born – and that was OK.'

I learnt that the last thing you want to do is to be dragged, kicking and screaming, to the grave.

There was a massive turn out to his funeral – almost too many to fit in the crematorium. Me and Al both talked about our friend. His wife, Jane, reminded me that when she first 'went back to his place', there was a line of tiny shoes by the front door. *Oh good, he's got kids!* she thought. They were his shoes.

The coffin went out to ELO's 'Mr Blue Sky'.

A little later, Al and I organised a fundraiser for the hospice that had helped care for him at the Lyric Theatre in Shaftesbury Avenue – which was in many ways, where it had all started for us. Al, me and some of Matt's comedy friends – Sean Lock, Tim Vine, Brenda and, of course, Stouffer the cat. I cut together a little video from some of my vast home movie collection of us all horsing around in our twenties. We then reprised our old Pub Band set with Steve Brown taking Matt's place on the keys.

He would, as they say, have loved it.*

The C4 show wasn't recommissioned after that third series. I had a hunch it wouldn't be. I remember going to the Channel 4 Christmas party and spotting the controller over the other side of the room. I thought I'd go over and say hello.

As soon as he saw me, he took a detour – behind a sofa, edging along the wall to the nearest door to escape. That signalled to me that maybe all was not well!†

When a show doesn't come back, it's always reported in the press as 'cancelled' or 'axed' – but it's not usually as dramatic as that. They just say they don't want any more and usually ask you if you've got any other ideas for shows. It wasn't like that with the C4 show, though. The message I got from The Agent was, 'No more shows and no more anything.'

At that point, things looked pretty bleak for me career-wise.

A couple of weeks after I got the news of the show's fate, I did a gig in a little fringe theatre above a pub in Battersea. It didn't go particularly well and as I was walking home around midnight with my little suitcase full of props, a cabbie spotted me and slowed down. He leant out of the window of his taxi and said, 'When are we gonna see you back on telly again, H?'

'Not for a long time!' I said, then added melodramatically. 'I'm washed up!'

---

* But he couldn't, because he was dead.

† Which is why the last episode featured a scene where I was shot by the controller of Channel 4 – played by my ventriloquist dummy, Gary.

I hardly slept a wink over that period, tossing and turning, haunted by visions of returning to the sound of seats flipping in an empty Grimsby Auditorium. I knew that I couldn't ever go back to civilian life – I'd been out of medicine so long there was no way back – and here I was with a mortgage and a young family to support. It was starting to look very much like I was one of those one-hit wonders.[*]

* It wasn't even a proper hit – so more of a half-hit wonder.

CHAPTER 18
LIFE LESSON

'I remember my dad sending me to sit on the naughty step – so-called because of the erotic carvings he'd done on it. Naughty, but nice!'

At the last recording of *Harry Hill*, I was joined on stage by a man carrying a big, red book under his arm. No, it wasn't my accountant – it was Michael Aspel.

I took one look at him and said, 'I thought you were dead!'

I wasn't lying, I honestly did.

'Harry Hill . . .' he said in that slightly disinterested way of his. '. . . This is your life!'

That was a pretty surreal moment – for a start, I was only thirty-six years old.

I was immediately taken through to a sort of holding bay whilst they set up for the TV recording. I'd been a big fan of the show growing up – it was must-see TV. I remember seeing Lewis Collins from *The Professionals* on it and wondering why Martin Shaw hadn't made it to the studio!* Was there some beef we didn't know about? Shaw had recorded a video, which was played into the studio, but he was only in Devon, which was a mere two and half hours on the train.

As I sat there, waiting to be called, I wondered who on earth they were going to bring on for mine. I didn't know any celebrities – the most famous person I knew was Burt Kwouk, and I'd seen him just twenty minutes earlier.

---

* I never liked the ones where it wasn't celebrities, but people of high standing like Douglas Bader or a sporting icon.

Then Mrs H turned up and boy, was I glad to see her – it turned out it had been a very stressful couple of months. Initially she'd been in two minds whether to agree to it, but claims she remembered me saying early on in our relationship that 'If *This Is Your Life* call, make sure you say yes.'

I don't remember saying that – but it does sound like just the sort of cocky thing I might have said back then. Having said yes, she'd also had to struggle to keep the thing a secret from me – she reminded me that at one point I'd become so suspicious of the various phone calls she'd been making that I'd asked her if she was having an affair.

After an hour or so, I took my place next to her on the familiar set of *TIYL* and Aspel started to work his monotone magic.

First through the doors was my old school friend and co-founder of Staplehurst Chemical Industries Adam Starkey. Then one by one they all trooped through – Matt, Rob from The Hall Brothers, my mum and dad and other family members – even my old biology teacher. One by one they each stepped up to deliver their pithy anecdotes.

The weird thing was that whilst I recognised the stories, there was something odd about the way they told them. They didn't sound like themselves at all. Mrs H explained later that a researcher had interviewed each of the guests on the phone and then written up their version of the anecdote, which they delivered back to them in script form for them to learn. That way the production knew what they were getting. Hence the android effect. Celebrity-wise Keith Harris was there with Orvile who'd both been guests on the show – it turned out that when Matt had sat down, he'd noticed a high cushion and because of his short stature he sat on it so he could get a better view of the proceedings, until a runner from the production moved him on explaining that the cushion was 'for Orvile'.

Wendy Craig made an appearance by video link – a bit of a stretch as I'd never met Wendy, but my sister and I had a long-running joke about her which involved us sticking photos of Wendy Craig in various odd places in each other's room for a reason that now escapes me. The then BBC royal correspondent Jennie Bond turned up – a lovely lady, but I'd never met her either – I'd merely made a few jokes about how I fancied her because she was 'more attractive than Virginia Wade and more accessible than Valerie Singleton'.

Burt was there, of course, and Stew who had been told they were cutting his anecdote the day before via an answering machine message.

The big surprise at the end was Ronnie Corbett – which, whilst it was nice to see him, only really served to remind the audience at home of what a proper star looked like and how far *This Is Your Life* had gone downhill.

I had a real laugh during the taping; I was on good form, wise-cracking and gently undermining the whole thing and enjoying watching my friends squirm in front of the cameras. When it was aired, all my stuff was cut out and it looked like I hardly said a word. My friends sounded like robots and I looked like a stuffed dummy.

There was a big buffet afterwards – which was probably the best bit of the night. The producer told Mrs H that she'd done 'quite well' because 'Harry looked at you three times and held your hand once.'

I thanked Michael Aspel, and he told me that on the night he'd sprung it on Bernie Winters, Schnorbitz – the fourteen stone St Bernard bitch he replaced his brother Mike with – had broken free of her lead and got to the buffet first, bolting down two thirds of it before any of the VIPs could get near and coating the remaining third with dog saliva.*

---

* If you're on that show, you do get to keep that big red book – not immediately – because it's full of photos and screen grabs from the night itself. I used to think it contained a detailed history of the person being 'done' but there's no text whatsoever, just the screen grabs. So you had to wait a while for them to print them off. In my case, I didn't get the book until over a year later and only after several requests from The Agent to the production company asking where it was.

HARRY THRILL

TO say comic **Harry Hill** was shocked when *This Is Your Life* host **Michael Aspel** pounced on him is putting it mildly. Harry actually blurted out: "I thought you were dead!" The red-book-carrying smoothie assumed Harry was joking, but he was serious. "It was hilarious," reports my spy.

GOT ANY GOSSIP? CALL ME, POLLY GRAHAM OR J
0171 293 3950 OR E-MAIL US AT: matthew.wrigh

Red-book carrying smoothie.

CHAPTER 19
ALL NEW

'Black sky at night . . . night! Black sky in the morning, Oh! I've woken up at night again.'

When a show doesn't get picked up, it's always a bit disappointing, (unless it's my version of *Stars In Their Eyes!*) but so far I can honestly say, it's always been for the best. Nine times out of ten it makes you embrace fresh opportunities and come up with something new.

Your real problem starts if they keep wanting more. That way you run the risk of getting stuck creatively. Don't get me wrong – some people are perfectly happy to be in that position, but to me the certainty of knowing exactly how every year is going to unfold would drive me crackers. It sounds too much like work.

The problem at the heart of success is that it's boring. If that makes me sound a trifle ungrateful, let me explain. If you have a hit show, what do the channels, your agent, the public, want you to do? More of the hit show, of course. Everyone's getting fat on the hit show! Everyone's dipping their beaks into the hit-show trough. If you're a creative person having nailed one idea, you want to move on to the next. No one is interested in taking a risk on something new when they have something that they know delivers ratings and inevitably money.

The irony is that when you've got the hit show, that's the time when you're getting all the offers to host other shows. You're offered book deals, board game spin-offs, voice-overs, adverts – but you've got no time to do them because you're too busy working on the hit show.

No, it's much better to have a flop!

I'm kidding, the money's better on a hit, and like I said to Her Maj that time, 'You can never have too much money!'

Who was it that said, 'Art for art's sake and money for God's sake.'

Listen, it's complicated. There's a delicate balance to be struck between art and commerce and when I've worked out what it is, I'll let you know.

In the meantime, my approach is to treat all of it – success and failure – like a big game. In the end, it doesn't really matter whether the show's a hit or a flop so long as I enjoy the process – otherwise I might as well be back on the wards. Of course, I want everyone else to like what I'm up to, but if I don't like it, you probably won't either. There's no point in me trying to second-guess what I think you might like either, as that way mediocrity lies.

I used to covet other people's success but not any more. I look at it like this: if another comedian is doing better than me with a hit show, it means that the channel is making money out of it, the commissioners are making careers out of it, and so they're more likely to commission comedians to make shows – so that's good for everyone.

Landing a TV show is a bit like finding love; all the time you're desperate for it, it eludes you – no one finds 'desperate' attractive. Just be funny! Be confident in your charms and eventually they'll come knocking on your door.

Besides, most hits end up as flops, because if you carry on churning out the hit, the standard drops. There's nothing as angry as an audience who feel that their favourite hit show is not as good as it used to be.

When the C4 show wasn't picked up, I went back to my roots. I hit the clubs, worked on the act and went back out on tour.

Then I got the call from ITV. It turned out that the then controller David Liddiment was a fan of the C4 show and had the idea that maybe I was the missing link between the alternative world and the mainstream. So, it was arranged that I'd meet him for lunch. I liked David because he liked me – but he was very difficult to read that day.

He welcomed me with the weakest handshake I've ever had.* We sat down and ordered our food. In those days, knowing someone else was picking up the tab, I would order as much food as I could cram on my plate. I've since found out that the problem with that is that if your host only orders a salad he has to then sit there and watch as you wrangle your knickerbocker glory.

Virtually straight off the bat, Dave said, 'So, Harry, what do you think of the shows we have on ITV?'

Ouch!

What I wanted to say was 'I never watch ITV! My mother always told me it was common!'.

It's true. We were never allowed to watch *Magpie* – the much cooler ITV version of *Blue Peter* hosted by the lovely Susan Stranks, Jenny Hanley and Marc Bolan lookalike Mick Robertson. They were so much more happenin' than Valerie Singleton, Peter Purves and John Noakes.

The Agent, who was also at the lunch, shifted uneasily in his chair.

'David!' I exclaimed. 'Surely you don't need to hear my opinion of your output!'

Luckily, at that point the waitress arrived, and I gave her my order – all three courses of it.

'And can we have some extra chips as well?' I heard myself saying.

All David ordered was a bowl of buttered asparagus – it was going to be a long lunch for him!

---

* For completeness, the firmest handshake I've ever had was from Gordon Ramsay one year at The BAFTAs – it was like getting your hand caught in a car door.

I've found the best way to handle these sorts of meetings is to ask the controller or commissioner about 'what they're excited about'. That normally gets them talking whilst you plough into your coq au vin.

For David, at that time it was *Who Wants To Be A Millionaire?* – which had only just launched and was massive. It was pretty much the only TV show anyone was talking about. He described it as a 'once in a lifetime' show as he pushed the fronds of asparagus around his plate.*

We chatted about comedians that we admired and the whole thing passed off perfectly happily.

I had no idea whether he was going to commission a show from me, though.

A nerve-wracking couple of months later, I heard that he wanted two series of a more mainstream version of the Channel 4 show.

In my view, when it comes to comedy, there's probably very little point in commissioning less than two series – it always takes at least one series to get it right, and commissioners should take the long view rather than having an itchy finger on the trigger – because if they stay with a show, truly develop it and get it right, that show can run for years and is a brilliant return on their investment as opposed to one series and goodbye, which isn't. Listen, if I wasn't as busy as I am, I'd offer to run half these channels for them – but like I say my workload won't allow it!

In no time at all, the story hit the newspapers, who reported it as a 'three million-pound deal on ITV', which apparently made me Britain's 'highest paid telly comic'. This came as news to me – from what I could make out from the deal, I was on less money than when I had been at Channel 4.

---

* He only ate about four. 'You leaving that?' I wanted to say, grabbing the plate and scraping it onto my own, but I held back.

Harry Hill
& Guest

DAVID LIDDIMENT

Head of Entertainment Group, Network Television

requests the pleasure of your company

at a Christmas Party

on Sunday, 11th December, 1994, at 8.00pm

in Studio 8, Television Centre

Buffet Supper

R.S.V.P. Charlotte Ross
Room 4152
BBC Television Centre
Wood Lane
London W12 7RJ

Black Tie

Tel: 081 576 1964

Friends in high places – even back in 1994,
years before he signed me up.

Some agents love those sorts of headlines because it makes them look good and I guess attracts other acts to their stable. I always found it incredibly embarrassing. Maybe it's that middle-class thing where you 'never discuss money' – I don't know, it just seemed to me crass and also asking for trouble.

It just wasn't true either!

When the tabloids shouted, 'Three million!' that's what ITV were paying to the production company to make the show – then out of that came all the salaries – not just mine – so, it was rather misleading. The other problem was that whenever Mrs H read a headline like that, she'd go out and buy a new coat and the window cleaner would add a nought to his bill.

As a nod to the idea that I'd sold out by going to ITV I wanted to call the show *Harry Hill Lite* as if it was a low-calorie version of the Channel 4 show, heading off the critics by getting in first.

They didn't like that, so we settled on *The All New Harry Hill Show*.

Of all the shows I've made, it's the one that the least number of people remember; it doesn't even have its own slot on Wikipedia – it's been amalgamated into the Channel 4 show.

It opened with a title sequence of me riding a firework-style rocket over London and bashing into the ITV Tower on the Southbank – knocking the 'V' off in the process. I thought it was a great idea until someone pointed out the similarity between it and the events of 9/11, just eighteen months earlier, but it was too late to change it.

We then cut to the studio to see some elderly dancers – billed as The Sevenoaks Cardiac Rehabilitation Centre – doing a dance routine, then I'd emerge dancing and singing from a giant revolving collar. I'd then do the requisite five minutes of stand-up and introduce 'Sir Steve Redgrave' played by five-foot-two septuagenarian Ronné Coyles in a Steve Redgrave Lycra one-piece.

I'd been introduced to Ronné by none other than Keith Harris – of Orville fame – a lovely bloke who had been a semi-regular on the Channel 4 show as the proprietor of the puppet-only bar, Orville's.

After the C4 show finished, I got a VHS tape through the post with a note from him saying, *If you ever get another TV series and are looking for a stooge, here's your man.* On the tape was an excerpt of Ronné on the Michael Barrymore show *My Kind Of People*. In it, he ran down a series of impressions of Bette Davis and Peter Lorre, finishing on a frantic tap dance. At last, an all-rounder! I invited him in and he was full of stories from the good old days of variety.

He'd started life as a boy soprano – appearing in one of the Crazy Gang films – then he became an ice juggler. 'The first thing we did when we arrived in a town was to visit the undertakers – because at that time, they were the only people who had any ice,' he said.

Then he became a trapeze artist – until he forgot to tie on his safety harness and fell into the orchestra pit at the Chiswick Empire. He landed in the grand piano and woke up a week later in hospital.

By the time I met him, he was making his living playing the dame in pantomimes up and down the country.

I'd asked Matt to be a part of the ITV show, but by then he'd decided he'd better get himself a proper career and had settled down as a GP in Bognor Regis. So Ronné was perfect – he acted as a sort of assistant – a nod to the Anthea Redferns and Isla St Clairs of TV days gone by – and better still, he could deliver lines!

I'd do a bit of business with Ronné, then it was time to set up 'The Hamilton Challenge', where I'd set disgraced Tory MP, Neil Hamilton, and his wife, Christine, a task. On the first show, it was interspecies tennis – where the two of them had to play mixed doubles with a horse and a donkey.

Then it was time for the 'Celebrity Hobby That You Didn't Know About But Will In A Minute'.

One of the big attractions of doing the show on ITV was that with the extra exposure and budget, we'd be able to attract a better class of celebrity than Huffty.* So let's look at the six celebs we got over that first series of *The All New . . .*

Nigel Havers kicked us off – with his hobby, radish carving – then Gail Porter and Dan Hipgrave (Gail's other half and the guitarist from Toploader, silly!). Show three saw Dora Bryan taking me paintballing. Show four Rick Parfitt,† show five Les Dennis, finishing on Patrick Mower on show six. All of them lovely, talented people but it's not the sort of line-up that was necessarily going to find people circling the show with a marker pen in the *Radio Times*.

---

* Nothing against Huffty! I love her!

† I really liked Rick and we kept in touch. He invited me and Mrs H to a press junket on the Orient Express, which took us from Paddington to Southampton, where we got on a coach which took us to the aircraft carrier the *Ark Royal* where Status Quo did an open air gig on the flight deck. I can safely say it was one of the longest days of my entire life!

I learnt then that to build a show around getting a particular celebrity was making a rod for my own back – you never got the one you wanted and in reality you started at the top of a very long list and worked your way down.*

Looking at the few bits and pieces of it that are available on YouTube, it's actually much funnier than I remember – and more consistent than the Channel 4 iteration – but was it more mainstream? Nah! It doesn't seem at all like an ITV show – if anything it looks like a piss-take of one!

Again, it was a lot of fun to make but was I upset that it didn't ever come back for its second run?

Not really! I wasn't short of ideas and the ITV deal had also included provision to make a pilot of a show that poked fun at the week's TV . . .

---

* My abiding memory of that show is of Ronné grooving with Rick Parfitt on the dance floor at the wrap party.

CHAPTER 20
SECOND COMING

*'Barbara Windsor, Barbara Castle – what is it about the name
Barbara that makes you want to visit Windsor Castle?'*

Really if you want a career as a TV comic you need to find a format
that allows you to be funny in the same way that you are in your live
shows, but that doesn't eat up all your stand-up. For Brucie, it was
the *Generation Game*, for Romesh Ranganathan it's his *Ranganation*,*
for Lee Mack it's probably *Would I Lie To You?*

In that sense, *TV Burp* was the perfect vehicle for me.

I got the idea for a weekly comedy show about the week's TV from
Garry Bushell. Yes, that Garry Bushell, the TV critic for the *Sun*. I
know, right?

From the moment I started doing spots on TV, Garry had always
been a vocal supporter – which was strange in a way. You'd probably
think of Garry preferring older-style comics like Jim Davidson and
Nigel Farage† but there was something about my act that tickled
him. When he went on holiday, he asked me to cover his TV column.
I must have been having a slack week, or the money was good. Either
way, I said yes.

Unlike the TV critics in the broadsheets who cover maybe one or
two shows a day, the tabloid critics only have a weekly column, so try
to cover as much as they can, especially the big shows, the shows that

---

* Is there a show that's a combination of the two? *The Rangation Game*? If you're
reading this, Romesh, call me.
† Satire's not dead!

people are actually talking about like *EastEnders* or *Corrie*. Garry would make the main piece about some bugbear of his,* and then there'd be shorter pieces, sometimes just a few lines – it was all very gag-oriented.

TV critics tend to work a week in advance, so I sat down to watch a bunch of preview copies with a pen and paper – jotting down ideas for gags as I went.

My main byline was 'What does Saucy Siss think he's playing at?' which was about Peter Sissons sitting on the edge of his desk. I accused him of 'sexing up the *Nine O'clock News*'.

There was a piece about Dot Cotton's singing voice – suggesting tracks that she might sing at a funeral, and another complaining that *Live Aid* got 60 million viewers back in the eighties but still 'didn't get a series'.

It came easily to me – I enjoyed it – and I was feeling pretty smug as I faxed my copy through to the editor David Yelland.

Within an hour or so I got a gushing fax back from him – it seemed he liked it as well.

Subsequently, whenever Garry took time off, he'd get me to stand in for him, and the more I did it, the better I got at it.

In fact, I started to look forward to Garry going on holiday almost as much as he did. Then at some point I thought, *Maybe this could be a TV show?*

So The Agent said he'd make a few enquiries.

The good news was that ITV agreed to fund a broadcast pilot. We got a producer and a director and some writers – Paul Hawksbee was one of them. Paul had written a lot for Frank Skinner's topical *Fantasy Football,* which was big at the time. We got some preview tapes of TV shows and did a dummy run in a pub out in Canary Wharf.

---

* Often about Jo Brand being a man-hating feminist. She's not, but she could have Mr Bushell for breakfast any day of the week.

It was just me at a desk with a TV on a stand, playing clips and then making gags off the back of them.

Even after that basic run-through, it was clear to all of us that we were onto something. It seemed like such a simple idea I kept asking people whether anyone had done something like it before.[*]

I remember the long car journey through the rain back from Canary Wharf to Clapham and the cab driver asking me what I'd been up to. I explained I was trying out an idea for a 'TV show about TV shows'.

'Good luck with that!' he said, pulling a face at me in his rear-view mirror.

Little did he know that *TV Burp* would become the most popular and influential TV show in the history of light entertainment.

OK, maybe not – just trying to build the tension.

We tried various writers on *TV Burp* before we settled on my personal dream team of Paul Hawksbee, Daniel Maier, Brenda Gilhooly and David Quantick. We tried Richard Herring, Dave Gorman, Chris Addison – all great comics – but none of them had the staying power – or frankly the time – to trawl through the hours of crap TV that was necessary for the job. Most of these guys were working every night on their acts.

No, it takes a special type of lunatic to sit for eight to ten hours a day watching everything from *Life On Earth* to *Ice Road Truckers* and *Emmerdale*.

The first series had fewer clips and was pretty sketch-heavy, which was a mistake because the sketches weren't what we were best at.

---

[*] Well, there was a sort of forerunner to it – comic Bob Mill's *In Bed with Medinner*. If you haven't seen it, then search it out on YouTube. Basically it was Bob crouched next to a VCR wired to a TV. He'd load up a VHS of one of the shows he'd seen – like Granada's *The Estate* – and press play and take the piss out of it. It was cripplingly funny.

They were long and drawn-out and *TV Burp* worked best when it was fast and furious.

I remember the director, Peter Orton, saying to me roundabout series three that we needed to 'slow it down – it's just too fast for people to keep up with'.

My reply was, 'They've got to keep up!' My whole attitude was foot-to-the-floor from the moment the titles finished.

Gag, gag, gag . . .

I was trying to make a show with a laugh count as high as you got when watching a great stand-up in a comedy club. Why would anyone settle for less?

I didn't want smiles or titters either, I wanted belly laughs. Now that's a laudable ambition, and I reckon a lot of the time we managed it – but Christ alive on his wee donkey, did it create a rod for our backs!

The main reason for the surfeit of sketches was that although most of the broadcasters – Channel 4, ITV and Sky – gave us advance copies of their shows, the BBC refused to give us permission to use clips from any of theirs.

That was a big hole to fill. We had decided very early on that whilst it would be a lot easier for us to make a show using clips from some of the low-rent satellite channels, it felt a bit like shooting fish in a barrel. It was important to us to keep it broad, to try and cover the sort of shows that everyone was talking about – which meant big shows like *EastEnders* and *Strictly*. We had to find a way round the BBC ban.

It turned out we could use a loophole called 'fair dealing'. Fair dealing is where you use a clip, without getting permission from the rights holder, on the grounds that it's for 'the purposes of comment or review'. It was set up to help make serious documentaries where an interview or video clip might not show the owner of the clip in a particularly flattering light and so they'd have every reason to want to hide it from view.

Fortunately 'comment or review' is a fairly woolly phrase, so we decided to roll the dice and see if we could get away with it.

If you watch those early shows, you'll notice that some of the intros I do to the clips are needlessly long-winded. I'd say things like 'I was pleased to see that in contrast to other soaps, *EastEnders* ...'. This was to cover our backs under the fair-dealing clause – should the Beeb decide to come after us. By series eleven, of course, I didn't bother with any of that, because it was clear by then that no one had the appetite for, well, a fight!

We contacted friendly journalists, who agreed to lend us their advance copies of BBC shows after they'd watched them. We had a machine that could copy their tapes onto multiple VHS's at the same time. For any live shows, we'd simply tape them as they went out. We basically set up a pirate video factory, but for TV shows that no one wanted to buy!

The first time we tried it, we got an angry phone call from the executive producer of *EastEnders*.

'How dare you!' he shouted down the phone at my producer. 'I've got actors here in tears from what you've done!'

Really? I thought. *In tears?*

I guess, any actor appearing on *EastEnders* for more than a couple of episodes might end up pretty close to tears. I often feel like crying after watching the Christmas special.

His anger seemed comical to me. I think he thought he was producing high art rather than a silly soap about a fictional square in the East End, which was paid for by licence payers like me.

Don't get me wrong, I love *EastEnders,* but Dickens it ain't.

So, I'm afraid it just made me want to include even more *EastEnders* clips.

The BBC didn't bother to pursue us because in those early days nobody was watching the show.

By the time *Burp* got popular, it was too late, they'd set a precedent – and that prickly *EastEnders* executive producer had moved on.

The downside for the *EastEnders* actors was that because we were 'fair dealing' their clips, they didn't get paid. All the actors on *Corrie* and *Emmerdale* were remunerated, but the *EastEnders* actors weren't – maybe that's why they were crying.

It's what led to me being heckled by Martin Fowler actor James Alexandrou at the Soap Awards. 'Where's our money?' he shouted.

'I write the show, not the cheques!' I replied.*

When *TV Burp* first started, ITV really didn't know what to do with us.

They put us out at half past four on a Saturday afternoon. Then they put us out at ten past eleven on a Thursday night.

You can tell a lot about how successful a show is by the quality of the stuff being advertised around it. The most popular shows attract a very high tariff for those ad slots – so you'll get the blue-chip companies – the cars, the banks, John Lewis and M&S. During that first series of *TV Burp* I remember seeing an advert for Saniflo, the macerator toilet flush system, in our ad break – that's when I knew we might be in trouble.

Before each of the first three series, The Agent would call me into his glass-sided office and tell me 'ITV are planning to cancel the show', which, of course, did wonders for my state of mind going into an eight-week run.

But in many ways, the underdog position suits me best, and I'd always come out fighting.

The message that kept coming back from ITV was that the reason nobody was watching *TV Burp* was that 'no one knows who he is!'

---

* Pleased with that.

Which is why they wanted me to do *An Audience With . . .*

They reasoned that it was a popular vehicle for established comics going out at prime time and would drive people to the show.

My reasoning for not wanting to do it was that yes, *An Audience With . . .* had been a big show in the eighties and nineties with household names like Billy Connolly, Victoria Wood, Kenneth Williams and Ken Dodd in the driving seat*, but back then those sorts of shows – where actual celebrities, the top brass of British light entertainment, like Barbara Windsor, Michael Parkinson, and movie stars like Michael Caine turned up – were a complete novelty. We'd never seen them all together in one place, off duty, having a great time like they were all members of one big club. Half the fun of those shows was spotting who was in the audience. 'Look! There's Saint and Greavsie!'

Add to that the comic host gently taking the piss out of them – I can't tell you, when those shows started up they were absolute dynamite. Everybody would be talking about them the day after they were broadcast.

By the time they got round to asking me, the novelty of seeing celebs off duty had dimmed somewhat for both the viewers and the celebrities. Add to that the fact that I didn't have any celebrity friends – as witnessed by the turn out on my *This Is Your Life* – and you can see why I wasn't jumping at the chance to do it.

'Who would come?' I said to The Agent.

He looked at me and with a straight face replied, 'David Bowie?'

David Bowie! David effing Bowie! I mean, it was ridiculous! Did he really think the Thin White Duke, who was living in New York at the time, would hop on a plane and make his way over to

---

* Although the funniest of all was probably Freddie Starr. I love the way he baits the celebrity crowd – a true anarchist. It's difficult to associate that charismatic man with the character he became in later life.

the ITV studios to see a comic he'd probably never even heard of?*

'OK!' I said 'I'll do it!'

Cut to the night in question. I'm pacing up and down behind the curtains, feeling more and more anxious. I peek through the curtains and there is Kriss Akabusi sitting next to Richard Stilgoe and Hank Marvin. For younger readers – ask your grandma!

Moments later, the producer pops his head round my dressing room door. 'Steve Wright's just called, he's got a snuffle and can't make it – break a leg!'

If you ask my wife what the worst night of her life was, she'll reply without hesitation, 'The evening of the recording of *An Audience With Harry Hill.*'

It's pretty high up on my list too.

I had gone through all my previous set lists, selected all my best jokes and routines and assembled them into what I hoped was an hour of blisteringly funny comedy.

It was tough from the start. In my heart, I didn't really want to be there and instead of having fun with it, I saw it as something I had to get through.

As I walked out onto the stage, there was a rather muted round of applause, considering they were all supposed to be there to see me.

After the first ten minutes or so, I thought to myself, *OK, this isn't going to be great, but I'm just about going to get away with it.*

Twenty minutes in and I actually thought I was going to be the

---

* That's a little unfair. I'd been chosen by DB as the token comic when he hosted Meltdown on the Southbank – featuring all his favourite bands. I came out dressed as the clown in the 'Ashes To Ashes' video with Ken Dodd-style false teeth and proceeded to murder the song.

first person to do *An Audience With . . .* and be booed off by the celebrity audience.

They were lit up like a Christmas tree and there, plumb in the centre, was Chris Tarrant. I don't know if they gave him a cushion to sit on, a slightly higher chair or his own spotlight, but he seemed to tower above the rest of the audience, and you know what? He didn't laugh once. How do I know? Because he was such a big star, the director had a camera trained on him for the entire performance! Yes, he had his own camera! In the edit, afterwards, I remember fast-forwarding through his reel – nothing. He sat there like the Buddha, with a look on his face of 'How much more of this have I got to sit through?'

I mean listen, I understand, it was a tough night but throw me a bone, Chris! What we should have done is recorded the audience during the warm-up man's act,* who, if I'm honest, went over better than I did.

When I came off, I headed straight to the dressing room and felt like bursting into tears.

When I told this to Paul O'Grady some years later, he said he'd felt exactly the same after doing his. He told me that when he'd told that to Ken Dodd, Ken had replied. 'That's nothing – I *did* burst into tears!'

It's weird when you die at an event like that – where the expectation is that you'll storm it.

'It was better than you think,' said The Agent.

'That was great. I'd never heard of you before!' said Hank Marvin generously.

'Bit tough . . .' said Dave Gorman ruefully.

The Agent was right though. It was better than I thought, and

* Comedy magician Miles Crawford.

after it had been dubbed with canned laughter, it looks like I'm doing fine. Well, to the casual viewer it does. When *I* watch it, all I can see is me going through the motions with a look of cold fear in my eyes.

Needless to say, it wasn't the miraculous turn around in the *TV Burp* viewing figures that ITV had hoped for.

No, that happened when they accidentally broadcast an episode of *TV Burp* at half past five on a Saturday.

I'm not sure if it was a clerical error, or if ITV had run out of stuff, but when *Burp* went out for the first time in a reasonable slot, it got unexpectedly great ratings. Suddenly, everyone got very excited and we were promoted to Saturday teatime.

I was never happy with the title *TV Burp*, even though it was my idea. How long had we spent trying to come up with a better one? It had felt like days.

'Sideways TV', 'Shout At The Telly' and, oddly, 'Gogglebox' were all run up the flagpole.

'Who's gonna watch a show called "Gogglebox"?'

It turned out that one of the newer execs at ITV didn't like the name either and had requested a meeting with me to discuss it.

'What's this meeting about?' I said to The Agent as we stepped into the lift on the ground floor of the ITV building and the steel doors clanged shut.

'He doesn't like the name of the show,' said The Agent.

'Well neither do!' I said.

'Me neither,' said The Agent.

'What's he want to call it instead?'

'I dunno.'

'But we're on series three!' I said, shaking my head. 'Who changes the name of a show halfway through making it? We'd just lose all the people that have started watching it, wouldn't we?'

'Maybe,' said The Agent.

'So what are we going to tell him?'

'Ah, well . . .' he said, looking incredibly pleased with himself. 'I've got a plan for that. If he insists we change it, I'm going to suggest we change it to *Harry Hill's TV Burp*.'

'That's what it's called already!' I said, as the doors squealed open onto the twenty-first floor.

The exec cut to the chase pretty quickly.

'I don't like the name, so I want you to change it!' he snapped.

'What do you want to change it to?' I asked innocently.

'I dunno,' he said, 'but not that – it's affecting the ratings!'

'Where has this come from?' I enquired. 'Have you done some market research or something?'

'No, but I asked my secretary if she watched your show and she said no, she didn't because she didn't like the name.'

In other words, he wanted to change the name for no other reason than a bit of casual office banter.

I stole a look with The Agent. Was this really why we'd been dragged halfway across London?

I pointed out the possible folly of changing the title of a show halfway through its run.

'Look,' he said, his head going up and down like one of those nodding dogs on the back shelf of a Ford Cortina. 'I tell you what I'll do. I'll get some research done, some focus groups, and if it comes back that people don't have a problem with the name, well, that's fine, we'll leave it alone, but if they do – you're changing it!'

In a wonky way, that seemed fair.

The next time I saw the exec was at the British Comedy Awards where I was picking up the award for Best Entertainment Show and Best Entertainment Performance for *TV Burp*. I was sat next to him – which I hadn't asked for, so the cynic in me thought that maybe he was keen to bask in a little bit of reflected glory. Of course not! He was there to show his support! As I sat down clutching my trophies – two playing cards encased in five quids' worth of plastic – I turned to him.

'Did you do the research on the name?' I said.

'Yes,' said the exec, knocking back a glass of warm retsina. 'Turns out people do hate the name.'

'So?'

'But they love the show, so we're not touching it.'

That was the same night that the TV Naturalist Nigel Marven brought that huge python along and it nearly escaped off the stage. Some might say it wasn't the only snake in the room that night . . . not by a long chalk.

How To Make An Episode Of *TV Burp*

If you fancy making an episode of *TV Burp*, just follow these simple steps.

Monday

Watch TV from maybe eight thirty in the morning till ten o'clock at night. Well, OK, not all the way through – I'd take a half-hour break for elevenses and then another half-hour for lunch. Usually I'd drop off to sleep at about four thirty – often in front of the *Emmerdale* omnibus. I'd then have maybe an hour and a half or so for dinner, then I'd be back at it – swapping out the videotapes, pumping the VCR until it glowed red hot. I had a rule that I'd never work past ten at night – but if we were really up against it I'd often not stop till eleven.

I wasn't the only one – all the writers were doing exactly the same thing. We'd watch the shows on a VCR that was rigged up to another VCR that contained a blank tape. So, if we saw something we thought might be funny – a rockery that looked like a face, or a pig that appeared to be talking – we would rewind the master tape, press record on the blank one and dub off the short section that contained the joke.

Simple, right? Usually! Occasionally you'd forget to press pause and dub off an entire show, or you'd inadvertently cut the top off the clip or sometimes you'd just get a bit of static if the SCART lead was loose. The most common problem, though, was that when you actually looked at the clip again, it just wasn't funny.

11.30 – bedtime.

More often than not, during the night you'd be woken by a series of clunks as the motorcycle courier posted another twenty tapes through the letterbox. Clunk! There goes *Coach Trip*! Clunk! *Freaky Eaters*! Clunk! *Eddie Stobart Trucks and Trailers*! Clunk! *The Apprentice*! Clunk! *Ibiza Uncovered*! Clunk! *Snog, Marry, Avoid*! Clunk! Clunk! Clunk! Clunk! . . . Well, you get the idea with that!

So that's Monday.

Tuesday

We'd have a writers' meeting, where we'd all share what we'd recorded on Monday and the live stuff that had gone out over the weekend.

We all had different areas of expertise.

Paul Hawksbee had a brilliant eye for a routine – so he'd find a selection of clips that built from one to the other – that back-and-forth style where it looks like I'm talking to the clip. So, for instance, Paul spotted the way Delia Smith pronounced 'hummus' – as 'who-mousse'. So I'd play the clip of her saying, 'Who mousse,' and I'd say, 'Who mousse?' back at her. Then we'd play another clip of her saying it, and I'd say, 'You mousse?' Then we'd play another one, and I'd say, 'Me mousse?' And so it went on.

Daniel Maier was particularly good at spotting patterns in shows. I'll never forget the excitement in the room when he spotted two extras on *Holby* – one that only did 'lengths' of the corridors and one that only did 'widths'.

Brenda had a comic's eye for a visual gag – it was Brenda that suggested I get chased round the desk by the bust of the Queen Vic (I added the riff from 'Riverside (Let's Go!)').

David Quantick just has a bizarre way of thinking. So, for instance, Dave brought in a clip from *Emmerdale,* which really was just a shot of Zac Dingle in the foreground, but in the background, through a window, you could see a goat. 'Window goat on *Emmerdale!*' he said in his West Country twang, and for some reason, it got a laugh.

After the meeting I'd have a chat with the producer, a hairy north Londoner by the name of Spencer Millman.[*]

When Spencer joined the show, he took it to a whole new level. First, because he was really tough on me – if he didn't like a gag or had the vaguest suspicion of a bit of 'filler', he'd tell me to cut it, in big capital letters. *CUT IT!* I used to dread his emails.

One of the main reasons the show improved under his command was the number of clips he let me run in the show. The previous producer had told me that I could only include a hundred clips in my scripts because 'the machine only takes a hundred'.

So, I'd always have to be a bit more selective in what I included, mindful of that limit.

The first week he took over, Spencer asked me why I hadn't included a couple of clips that he thought were strong.

'Because the machine only takes a hundred clips!' I said.

'Who told you *that*?' said Spencer, almost spitting out his Monster Munch (Spencer was definitely a candidate for *Freaky Eaters*).

Maybe the previous producer thought it made me focus more on

---

[*] That surname may ring a bell. It's the same as Andy Millman's – Ricky Gervais' character on *Extras*. Spencer and Ricky worked together on *The 11 O'Clock Show*.

what was really funny, or maybe he was sparing the production team extra work – every one of those clips had to be sourced, permission sought, and if possible a master tape got hold of.

My argument for including more was that nobody ever really knows what is going to be funny and what's going to bomb, and so the more material we played into the audience, the more stuff we had to choose from.

After that, I think the most I ever got up to was 160 clips. For a twenty-two minute show!

Fundamentally, Spencer trusted me, so if I felt strongly about a particular idea, he'd let me try it. One that sticks in my mind is the wobbling jelly thing we used to do.

I wrote in the script:

CUT TO: A jelly on a plate, wobbling.
SFX: 'Wipe Out' by The Surfaris

In his notes to that script he wrote: *REALLY?*

I told him I just had a hunch about it.

It turned out it was inexplicably really funny, and we played it into virtually every show for a whole series.

Those returning items were like gold dust to me.

To my mind, they were like regular characters. Stuff like the jelly, chasing the bust of the Queen Vic, spotting a bald man with glasses in a clip, Heather from *EastEnders*.*

So I'd have my chat with Spencer, I'd talk to any members of the

---

* Steve Benham – the guy who played Heather was an extra really, not an actor. He's a big bloke – so big, in fact, that his other job was as a bed tester. 'Bed tester? What's that?' I asked. 'Well when they bring out a new bed, they get me or someone like me to lie on it – to check it doesn't break,' he explained. Nice work if you can get it.

team, look at clips and talk to the art department about props. Another important conversation was with the costume designer, Leah Archer, mainly about the end-of-part-one fights.

As the show progressed, the fights got ever more extreme.

We had Heather Mills versus Hitler ('Come on, Hitler!'), 'Bowl-headed girl' versus 'Cushion-headed boy', John Wayne's hat versus Agatha Christie's handbag, a king prawn fighting a baby – I mean anyone who tells you that 'surreal humour doesn't work on mainstream TV' can take a running jump.

All these costumes had to be sourced or made, and it all had to be turned around in three days.

So, I'd get home from the meeting – a forty-minute drive on a good day – I'd have a cup of tea and sit down and watch TV. But not like most people – I couldn't just slump in front of something I enjoyed. No! I had to slot in another VHS and watch something that nine times out of ten I hated watching!

Don't get me wrong, there were some shows that I did like. *Pineapple Studios* was one. It was a little-known documentary series about the day-to-day running of a dance studio in Covent Garden, tucked away on Sky One. I think it's safe to say no one would have looked twice at it if we hadn't featured it every week for a whole series.

I remember distinctly when the first one of those came in. I knew we were onto something – Louie Spence, Debbie Moore – and, oh God, the 'triple threat' of Andrew Stone! Add to that Michael Buerk's deadpan narration – and a sizeable chunk went in every week for about six weeks.

There were a few shows like that, ones that we promoted by championing them. *Hole in The Wall* was a particular favourite of mine – Dale Winton shouting 'Bring On The Wall!' It was so dumb, it was brilliant. What could be funnier than Vanessa Feltz in a tight-fitting silver Lycra body suit and a red crash helmet being knocked into eighteen inches of water by a large piece of polystyrene?

Word came through that they were planning to can it after the first series, but because their ratings had shot up after we'd featured it, and everyone was going around shouting 'Bring On The Wall!', they commissioned a second series.

Unfortunately, they decided to give Dale's job to Anton Du Beke (a bit of a cheek as he'd been one of the team captains under Dale!), so we made a team decision not to feature it. Nothing against Anton – you couldn't meet a nicer guy – it was just that we preferred Dale! It never made it to series three.

What *Burp* giveth, it could also taketh away.

Freaky Eaters was another one we saved from TV landfill. That was great for us – even if by the end of their second series, I was pretty much only getting laughs by turning to the side camera and repeating what they were saying in a silly voice. 'Hoops!' or 'Chippy Chips!'

By the time series three of *Freaky Eaters* came along it was clear they'd run out of food for people to be scared of – I mean brown sauce? Really? Chips again? Come off it. So we stopped covering it and it was retired. Still, it was fun while it lasted, a lot of fun.

Wednesday
Watch TV all day and night (see Monday).

Thursday
Record the show.

This was the fun day. I'd get into the studio at about ten, check the props and costumes, we'd record any sketches – all those bits where I appeared to join in with the action in a clip, which the art department and the director Peter were brilliant at recreating, then we'd break for lunch. After lunch, we'd record the end song and sign-off, then we'd rehearse the show. I usually had an hour before they let in the audience, during which I'd make any last-minute changes to the script, have a cup of strong tea, a banana and a Mars bar, and then off we'd go.

It usually took about forty minutes to run the show and another forty minutes to record any pickups. We'd record maybe thirty-five minutes of material, which would cut down pretty easily to twenty-two.

Afterwards, I'd go for a beer in the green room and say hello to any guests and get home roundabout eleven and have my dinner.

Friday

In the morning we'd have another writers' meeting at 10 a.m., where we'd share the clips we'd sourced on Wednesday and Thursday, then after lunch I'd go to the edit of the recording from the night before and sign it off.

In the evening, I'd go through my notes from the week's two writers' meetings and make a rough plan for the following week's show.

Saturday

I'd start writing the following week's show at 9.30 a.m. and have it written by 6 p.m. at the latest, then I'd email it to Spencer. At 7.30, I'd sit down with the family and watch the *TV Burp* I'd recorded on Thursday, then watch *X Factor* – which was live and make notes on that.

Sunday

I'd have the morning off but probably drift back to watching stuff in the afternoon and evening.

So that's how you make a show about the week's TV – simple, right?

Let me know how you get on.

Plea for help. This photo was taken by TV Burp writer Daniel
Maier after a particularly arduous weekend's viewing.

HOW TO BE A COMEDIAN: LESSON NO. 5
- A FEW WORDS ON AWARDS

'Awards are for people with big egos and low self-esteem!' declared Mrs H – as I was leaving the house to go to the BAFTAs for the first time.

Timing's everything.

She's right, of course. You shouldn't really need an award to tell you if your work's any good – and honestly I don't.

But I did then!

Let me be clear, I love awards ceremonies – to watch, on the sofa with a box of Celebrations and a gin and tonic, and it's very flattering to get nominated for one. But going to the actual awards ceremony? Not so keen.

To be honest, I always felt a little bit lonely at them. Mrs H never wanted to come and as I keep saying, I don't have any proper showbiz friends – well, none that are up for awards anyway!

On the rare occasion I did meet someone I knew, I tended to get dragged away from them by The Agent to meet this person or that person. It's called 'networking' but it felt like being paraded around like a prize cow.

And they're long, long, long nights.

The maddest one is the National TV Awards. They don't even have judges! They're voted for by the general public – I mean, I ask you! I did go once, though. That year it was being held at the Royal Albert Hall. I was up for, well, *TV Burp*, what else?

I didn't want to go, but if I didn't go, it spoilt the night a bit for the production team. Production teams up and down the country *love* awards ceremonies – largely because they're young, they can get trashed on free booze and they can rub shoulders with Kevin McCloud from *Grand Designs* or Brian Belo from *Big Brother* and no one knows who the hell they are, so they're not screaming their name as they walk up the red carpet or trying to take their photo as they stagger to their cab at two in the morning three sheets to the wind.

The producers of awards ceremonies naturally really want you to arrive via the red carpet because it forms a couple of minutes of valuable content in their show. It's one of my favourite bits as a viewer, seeing the celebs turning up, looking uncomfortable and not sure of themselves in their new shoes, but for me, walking down that red carpet on my own with strangers screaming at me and photographers firing off their flashguns just made me feel silly and out of my depth.

I worked out I could avoid the melee by getting the car to drop me round the back of the venue. That way I could sneak in unnoticed. Mean of me, isn't it? To deprive the viewing public of that shot of me looking anxious in my grandad's 1970s mohair dinner suit. I'm sorry, but it was just my way of staying sane.

The year I went to the National TV Awards – can we just call them the NAFTAs? They wouldn't let me in through the stage door – I needed some sort of pass – and as I walked up the great red runway, I bumped into June Brown – Dot Cotton off *EastEnders*. I'd never met June before, but was a fan. 'Walking my way?' I said, glad to see a friendly face and we started walking up together.

About halfway up, she said she needed to have a fag and walked back down again. I carried on into that beautiful edifice, the Royal Albert Hall – that perfect distillation of neoclassical values. The Royal Albert Hall! Where Wagner himself had conducted the orchestra (that's Wagner the German composer and polemicist, not the Brazilian-born singer who was a runner-up in series seven of *The X Factor**). The Royal Albert Hall! Where Sergei Rachmaninoff once performed his legendary Piano Concerto No. 3. The Royal Albert Hall! Where in 1933 Albert Einstein, no less, addressed a meeting of his peers.

'Oh look!' I said as I met up with the rest of the *TV Burp* team. 'There's Lacey Turner off *Easties*!'

It was hosted that night by the veteran newsreader Sir Trevor McDonald, the unflappable anchor of the *News at Ten*. Sir Trev's a great journalist but boy, could he kill a gag stone dead. Me and the *Burp* writers had wanted to put together a montage of all the jokes he'd murdered at the NAFTAs like it was a stand-up video. A new release for Christmas – *Sir Trevor McDonald: Live From The Albert Hall!* – but ITV quite rightly said, 'No!'

Apparently the architects of the Albert Hall were heavily influenced by the design of ancient amphitheatres, and it certainly felt gladiatorial that night. All the celebs were seated on the flat bit in the middle and the members of the public encircled us from above in the balconies and boxes, waiting to give us a thumbs up or a thumbs down.

The other difficulty with awards ceremonies was that on the whole it means I am in a room full of people who I've taken the piss out of – some of them on a regular basis and who, in the case of the cast of *EastEnders* hadn't even got paid for it. I remember that night standing in the aisle at the Albert Hall and spotting Steve McFadden, your own Phil Mitchell, heading towards me, and he didn't look happy. I remembered

* And father of Wagbo!

someone telling me that they cast soaps by choosing people who are like their characters, so I started to get worried. My mind raced back to the various episodes of *Easties* I'd watched where Phil had laid someone out with a well-aimed punch.

Why didn't I turn and run?

Two reasons. First, I was in fight-or-flight mode – actually there's a third 'F' in that list – Freaked out. I was literally rooted to the spot – I couldn't fight or flight. The second reason was, hey, I'm a fan, remember? Who doesn't wanna meet Phil Mitchell?! It would be worth a black eye! By this time, Phil was 'upon me' literally – right up close.

'All right, Harry?' he whispered in his Phillest of Phil voices.

'Yes, Phil,' I said. 'I mean Steve McFadden!'

Like I say, I was nervous.

'Yeah,' he went on. '. . . It's funny, I like it.'

Then he kept walking – because standing behind me was Barbara Windsor.

I'm afraid to say that one of the most notoriously low rent of all the awards ceremonies was the British Comedy Awards.

It was held in a TV studio for a start. The whole room was lit up with harsh white studio lights, so it was baking hot. There was no food, just bottles of cheap wine – the type you'd buy from a French supermarket when you were interrailing – and bowls of weird snacks that you'd never heard of, as if the producers had bought them from a stall in Wembley Market.

The executive producer of the BritComs at that time was the legendary Michael Hurll. Michael had been in TV light entertainment for so long that he had once shared a room with John Logie Baird. Not quite, but he'd worked alongside Robin Nash on *TOTP* and *The Two Ronnies*.

He told me that one year he'd wanted to give Mel Brooks a lifetime achievement award. Somehow he got hold of his phone number and called him up.

'Yes?' said Mel Brooks.

'Oh, good evening, Mr Brooks. My name is Michael Hurll. I'm the executive producer of the British Comedy Awards . . .'

'What do you want?' asked Mel.

'We'd like to present you with our lifetime achievement award—'

'Fuck off!' snarled Mel, and hung up.

Michael was a lot of fun, full of stories of the good old days in show business.

He once produced a panto in the seventies at the London Palladium starring Cilla Black. Cilla's rider was 'a fridge full of champagne'.

'As soon as she'd signed the contract, I sent a runner out to buy the smallest fridge he could find!' he laughed. Of course, Cilla couldn't drink the whole fridge's worth, but what she didn't drink, apparently – she took home . . . every night . . . for eight weeks. That's a lot of bubbly! Well, you would, wouldn't you? Good for Cilla!

There's lots of talk around awards ceremonies about 'goodie bags'. My kids became obsessed with them. They'd heard about the ones at the Oscars – where apparently there's a room that the nominees file into that's like a small branch of Harrods.

They do it slightly differently over here – there's a bag, sure, but I'm not sure I'd use the word 'goodie' for it. Typically, it would contain a bottle of water, a scented candle, a voucher for a discount spa treatment, a tiny promotional box of some weird chocolate truffles that had four days left on the use-by, a shampoo (thanks, guys!), a dog shaving kit, an odd liqueur that was flavoured with a herb you'd never heard of, and some lip salve that was only half a centimetre long when you wound it to its maximum. There was also a leaflet with a code written on it that if you phoned a certain number and told them who you were and quoted the code you'd get a free pair of odd-looking shoes – but really, who could be bothered?

It was a load of old tat, basically.

Still, my brother seemed happy with the liqueur he got for Christmas, my mum loved the truffles, and I still wear those shoes!

It makes a difference, of course, if you win. Award ceremonies really start to do in your melon when you lose – which is most of the time, unless you're Ant and Dec.

You arrive as a potential winner – but go home a bona fide loser – and no matter what anyone tells you about 'not wanting to win' and how pleased they are for 'the boys', take it from me, they're not. They're seething with jealous rage – it's why at the dinner after the BAFTAs all the cutlery is plastic.

No, schadenfreude is the fuel that show business runs on – for a lot of show people it's the only thing that gets them out of bed in the morning!

In 2008 when I was awarded a couple of BAFTAs* I was genuinely gobsmacked – never, in fact, had my gob been smacked quite so hard. The ceremony was held at that high temple of light entertainment – the London Palladium. *TV Burp* was up against some heavy hitters that year; *Have I Got News For You*, *Strictly Come Dancing* and *I'm a Celebrity . . . Get Me Out Of Here!* (which incidentally is my nickname for the BAFTAs).

---

* What do you mean 'it must have been a slow year!'?

The favourites to win that year was *I'm a Celeb* and Ant 'n' Dec had seats on the front row – a dead giveaway if ever there was one that they'd be triumphant. I don't know 'the boys' as they're called in the business (not sure why, they're both in their mid-forties), but I've met them a couple of times and liked them, particularly Dec – well we've all got a favourite Ant and Dec, haven't we? So there they were in the front row and there I was – maybe eight rows back – sandwiched between Piers Morgan and The Agent. Behind me was James Corden, who was also about to get his first gong for *Gavin and Stacey*, and he was quite, well, how shall I put it? 'Hyper'. He kept swinging on the back of my seat like a kid in a car who needs the loo. I felt like doing what my dad used to do to us if we were playing up – sticking my hand round the back of my seat and smacking his legs!

Anyway, when Keeley Hawes and Nicholas Hoult announced that I'd won, I sprung to my feet and headed towards the stage. As I passed Dec, as a gag, I lent down and whispered in his ear, 'It's over for you two!' He laughed. A nice showbiz moment there for you. Of course, it hasn't quite panned out that way! These days, they win everything and I don't even get invited!

I didn't have a speech in mind, so drawing on my *Freaky Eaters* 'Chippy Chips' catchphrase, I said something like, 'Baffy waffy wif waff wafta!' Or words to that effect. As speeches go, it wasn't exactly the Gettysburg Address, but it was good enough for the *Daily Mirror* to print it in full the next day.

Once you've been handed the award you get taken off to be processed, so me and my new best friends Keeley and Nicholas got taken round the back to have our photographs taken. I'm not sure Keeley was a particular fan of mine, as I remember turning a corner backstage and stumbling upon her saying to Nicholas '. . . and I've never found anything he's said remotely funny!'

Maybe she was talking about the host Graham Norton, but they both looked at me like they'd been caught with their hands in the slagging jar.

I got my revenge. As we stepped in front of the press, I whispered to Keeley, 'I always do cross-eyed for photos!' She giggled and for the next three or four photos, she went cross-eyed.

I didn't.

It's a nice photo – I look strangely normal for once.

Me with Keeley Hawes picking up a
BAFTA . . . Nice photo, Keeley!

It was a great night for the *Burp* team. The producer Spencer, the director Peter, Brenda, Dan, David, Paul, all the team and yes – The Agent – all enjoyed themselves.

Stop being a curmudgeon, Harry – yes, OK, I enjoyed it too.

People were all over me like gnats on a Maidstone girl's legs.

The following year, we got another one.

Three BAFTAs – have you any idea how intimidating that is? Sitting down at a blank screen to write a show and looking across and there's three BAFTAs that seem to be saying to you, 'Come on then, Mr Big Shot – Mr Baffy Waffy Wafta – let's see what you come up with now!'

I mean, I suppose they could have been saying something else – they could have been saying, 'Don't worry, Harry, you've won three of us, so you must be good. No need to worry – you'll have this done in no time!'

For all I know they might have been discussing global warming: 'We really do need China to sign up to the Paris Treaty for it to have any chance of making an impact.' Or they might have been saying '. . . and I've never found anything he's said remotely funny!'

In the end, I put them on a very high shelf in the spare bedroom – yeah, let them intimidate our guests! How do you like that . . . Mum!

The others, the various comedy awards and my Golden Rose of Montreux* are all in a storage box in the loft. I'm not really the trophy room type. Maybe that's about me struggling to come to terms with my success – or maybe it's just that most of them look like they were designed by the guy who runs Timpsons.

---

* Actually the end broke off my Golden Rose of Montreux. Now, there's a shit awards ceremony – and you have to go all the way to Switzerland for it!

One for the grandchildren – me with
Anton Dec and Declan McAnt.

CHAPTER 21
THAT'S ALL FROM ME . . .

'As one door closes, another one opens – but that's second-hand cars for you.'

We made over a hundred episodes of *TV Burp*, and to be honest, most of it is a bit of a blur. One particular show does stand out though.

For the 2010 Christmas special, I had the idea that we'd get Shane MacGowan of The Pogues on to sing his Christmas hit 'Fairytale of New York' to a staffer dressed as a beluga whale – the whale would 'sing' the Kirsty MacColl part as a series of whale-like squeaks.*

'You're having a laugh, aren't you?' groaned Spencer, rolling his eyes. 'There's no way he's going to say yes to that!'

He had a point. This *was* the show that Lionel Blair had turned down – at that time, the world's most bookable act. 'I'm fed up with people taking the piss,' he'd told his agent, which I thought was refreshingly honest.

Even Basil Brush's agent had said no, saying it was 'not the sort of show that Basil wishes to be associated with'. Well, Brush has always been a bit 'up' himself, if you ask me.

Unfortunately, it was one of those weeks where nothing much else in the show leant itself to a closing number.

'OK,' I said. 'If Shane won't do it, I'll do it dressed as him.' This was

---

* I'm sure there was a perfectly good reason for this, but I can't for the life of me remember what it was!

always a bit of a shoddy fallback position as far as I was concerned – largely because it just signalled that we hadn't been able to get hold of whoever it was the joke was about, and from a practical point of view it meant me having to be involved in the song, which we always recorded first thing after lunch. By then the novelty of dressing up and putting wigs on had slightly worn off, and I much preferred walking in at the end and signing off with 'That's all from us. Goodnight!'

So Spencer put the call in. Poor Spencer – he'd had to make all sorts of bizarre requests to agents over his time as producer of the nation's top sideways look at the week's TV. I once came in with a clip from *Nick Baker's Weird Creatures* – remember Nick Baker? We characterised him as the world's most inept naturalist; each episode, it seemed he'd set off to find the eponymous weird creature – and find something else instead. Nick is a lovely bloke – we had him on the show a couple of times and he was happy to play along with it. Just as well really, as we would have done it anyway!

The clip I'd found featured Nick in the British Museum next to a stuffed shrew mounted on a circular piece of brown moss. I was suggesting that the moss looked like the top of Sir Trevor McDonald's head.

'What we do,' I said, having shown everyone the clip at the writers' meeting, 'is we get Trevor McDonald in, we tuck him under my desk with just the top of his head showing. Mounted on his head is a similar stuffed shrew to the one in the clip. Then at my signal, he pops up and says "I'm Trevor McDonald, and here is the shrews!"'

I have to say it was a beautiful gag – not only did it have a bizarre visual set-up, it had two punchlines – the surprise reveal of Sir Trev, and then the shrews/news gag. If it had been a mouse, that would still have made it in – but a shrew? Come on!

It was the sort of gag that when I came up with it, it made me want to take the rest of the day off.*

What I loved about Spencer was that even though he knew he might well look a bit of a prat making that call, he could see what a great gag it was, and I knew he would do whatever he could to make it happen.

Here's how that phone call went:

SPENCER: I'd like to book Sir Trevor McDonald.

SIR TREVOR MCDONALD'S AGENT: Well, just so you know, Sir Trevor is a serious journalist, a much loved national treasure and very rarely appears on light-entertainment shows. So, it would have to be something that is in keeping with his reputation. What is it you'd like him to do?

SPENCER: We'd like him to hide under a desk for five minutes with a stuffed shrew on his head and then pop up and say, 'Here is the ten o'clock shrews.'

SIR TREVOR MCDONALD'S AGENT: I am certainly not going to ask Sir Trevor McDonald to do that!

So that lovely gag never made it to air.

Back to Shane MacGowan, and his agent explained to Spencer that Shane got a huge number of requests every Christmas to sing his Christmas hit and that he always turned them down. *But* he knew he was a fan of *TV Burp* – so he'd ask him.

Much to everyone's surprise, he said yes.

His fee was five hundred quid cash to the bloke who was with him and a bottle of vodka for Shane.

---

* I couldn't because I had an *Emmerdale* Omnibus to watch and two episodes of *Celebrity Coach Trip*.

We rehearsed the show as usual and broke for lunch. Shane was due at about half past two and we were all very excited to meet him.

At three o'clock, Spencer ambled onto the studio floor, which I knew spelled trouble because usually he was up in the gallery with a can of Fanta and a big bag of Monster Munch.

'Shane MacGowan's agent just called,' he said. 'Shane is unconscious in his hotel room – so we need to revert to plan B – you'll need to sing the song.'

Bugger! I thought, bitterly disappointed.

Then Spencer's phone rang again.

'OK . . . thanks for letting me know,' said Spencer.

'That was Shane's agent again. Apparently Shane's woken up, they've filled him with coffee and he's in a taxi on his way – so we'll stick to plan A.'

When poor Shane did turn up, he looked like a ghost – the Ghost of Christmas 1988, in fact.

Wearing a long black leather coat like Herr Flick from *'Allo 'Allo,* he stood swaying in front of us clutching a litre bottle of White Lightning in each hand.

I joked afterwards that it was the one time we had someone in the studio who was more pissed than the director.[*]

'Who's going to get those out of his hands?' whispered Spencer. We were all paranoid that having got him to the studio, something might upset him and he might suddenly bolt. The director, bless him,

---

[*] That was a little unfair – I had a long running joke with the director Peter Orton that he was an alcoholic because he used to like to have a glass of white wine with his lunch. The fact is he was brilliant both before and after lunch. It was Peter who, amongst other things, would shoot those little sketches where we recreated a little corner of the *EastEnders* or *Corrie* set so that when they went out you couldn't see the join between the clip and the sketch.

introduced himself to Shane and gently prised the bottles from his hands. Maybe MacGowan recognised a fellow traveller,[*] but he let go of the booze. Game on!

The intro to the song started up, and when Shane sang, something happened to him – he was transformed. He sounded exactly the same as the record. We were all held in rapture – it was really quite beautiful. Even the bits where the runner dressed as the beluga whale squeaked his responses had a forlorn quality. At the end, I walked over and did my sign-off. Shane cackled, then whacked the whale on the head with the microphone – a punk to the last! We got it in one take.

When I told my kids I was giving up *TV Burp*, to my surprise, they cheered and started dancing round the room.

'Yaaaay!' they cried.

'Woah!' I said, a little confused. 'I thought you liked the show?'

'We do, but you're just so grumpy when you're working on it!' said the fourteen-year-old. She was right – for the months that I was putting the show together, although I was physically at home, in my head I was somewhere else.

I might as well have been on tour.

I'm extremely grateful to that show – it bought me a house and made me a household name. Part of the title sequence was included in the opening ceremony of the London Olympics and it opened a lot of doors for me, but watching eight hours of TV a day for six months of the year was no way to live.

The last series was a particularly tough one for me. The pressure of delivering a weekly show had started to get to me, and it didn't help that I'd left my agent the year before. He also ran the production company that made the show and now he was threatening to sue me.

---

[*] I know, sorry, there I go again, implying that our director had a drink problem – he absolutely didn't.

Well, to be fair, I sued him first.

I sued him, then he sued me, then I counter-sued him, by which time we'd both had enough, so we settled out of court.

At one point, I figured I might be able to ease the blow if I could find a successor, another comic to take over the *TV Burp* 'franchise'. An Anton Du Beke to my Dale Winton. The idea came to me during my lunch break at one of the *TV Burp* recordings.

Yes! I thought! *That's my ticket out of here!*

I knew I couldn't try and fob off the producers with someone who was on their way up, no, I had to offer up someone blue-chip, an M&S not a Saniflo – someone with real star power. The biggest comedy star in the country who I also had the mobile phone number of was Peter Kay.

I mean I know Peter a bit but we're not regular mates; we've had a couple of long phone calls but that's about it. We'd had a really good chat about the business – it's what comics do when they get together. He'd just finished that massive tour of arena gigs and was a little annoyed that the tabloids had reported him making twenty million quid off it – 'It was a lot more than that!' he whined. Peter's got his head screwed on; he's very canny with his dough and a smart business man. There was a gag going round at the time that he'd struck such a hard deal with the Manchester Arena that he was getting a cut of the car park!

He also told me how he'd got a discount with a helicopter company to ferry him back and forth from his home in Bolton.

'Most nights I'm back by half past ten and having my tea in front of the telly!' he chuckled. 'By bedtime, I've almost forgotten I've done a gig!'

He was talking, of course, about a gig in front of twenty-one thousand people!

He likes his telly, does Peter, and more importantly I knew he was a fan of *TV Burp*.

'What can I do you for?' said Peter – OK, maybe he didn't say that. I'm aware that's how a southerner thinks someone from Bolton answers the phone. He probably said, 'What are you up to?'

Pretty quickly, he was singing the praises of *TV Burp*, which was nice, but I didn't have long and so I cut to the chase.

'I'm looking for someone to take it over, Peter, and wondered whether you'd be up for it?'

There was a pause, and then.

'Oh no, no, I couldn't do that. No, no, that's your show, no one else could do it.'

I made a half-hearted effort to convince him, but I knew I was wasting my time – he had bigger fish to fry.

Disappointed, I said goodbye.

As I headed back to the studio, who should be heading towards me but Micky Flanagan – he was recording *8 Out Of 10 Cats* in the studio next door. I knew Micky a bit from my days in the clubs. He was a couple of years behind me but I remember being on the bill with him and I also remember thinking, to my great shame, that he wasn't 'all that'. I thought of him as a really great, funny bloke in person, but his act . . . I dunno . . . for me there was something missing.

Then I got siphoned off the circuit and started doing TV shows and I hardly ever saw him. Then one night I caught his set on *Live From The Apollo*.

Oh, it's Micky! I thought, *I wonder what he's up to . . .* He was brilliant, just great – daring, cheeky and outrageous, getting away with stuff that no one else could have done, with that twinkle and winning smile of his. There's nothing more thrilling than seeing a comedian on top of their game. I'm not sure the material had changed that much, but what made the difference was that he'd discovered his comic voice.

''ello, Aitch!' he said with a grin. OK, I've done it again – I'm projecting my middle-class Kent idea of how a cockney speaks.

'Hi, Harry!' he said, twanging his braces and adjusting his pearly jacket.

'Me and the wife love *TV Burp*!' he said.

'Well, it's interesting you should say that, Micky . . .' I said, seizing my chance. 'How would you like to take it over!'

'Yes, please!' he said without a second's hesitation. 'I'd love to!'

Bingo! I could see it now – 'Micky Flanagan's *TV Burp*!' Yes! I'd landed one of the hottest properties in comedy to take over the show – this was a slam dunk!

Unfortunately, what Micky forgot to tell me was that he'd just signed an exclusive deal with Channel 4.

Never mind.

I still think it could have been great though.

The last ever recording of *Burp* was a strangely moving affair – for those of us involved in it, anyway. We got Wagbo back and the Knitted Character, Amanda Lamb and the real Heather from *EastEnders**, Cheryl Fergison. We all sang Adele's big hit at the time, 'Someone Like You'.

A lot of the team had tears in their eyes as I signed off, but not me! It felt like a huge weight was being lifted off my shoulders. I can only compare it to how I felt when I gave up medicine. I jumped in the car to take me home, pulled my headphones on and half expected to hear Eric Burdon.

---

* We could never get anyone from *EastEnders* to come on the show because of the blood feud over the clip permissions, but through a perfect bit of timing, the character of Heather had been murdered the week before. Cheryl being out of the show meant she was free to join us. I'd been so rude about her I was amazed she agreed, but she was a great sport. She popped up from under my desk looking angry. I said, 'If you're Heather, then who's she?' And we cut to Steve Benham sitting on the sofa eating a box of chocolates.

Spencer Millman

From: Claire
Sent: 25 November 2008 11:09
To: Spencer Millman
Subject: FW: Harry Hill TV Burp

O MY GOD!

xxxxc

From: Wendy
Sent: 24 November 2008 18:59
To: ITV Viewer Services
Subject: Harry Hill TV Burp

For the attention of Harry Hill. As an ex doctor you might be interested in that my grandsom laughed so much at your TV Burp programme that he had to be rushed to hospital with a torn hole in his pleural membrane and has to be kept quiet for 6 weeks while it closes up. This means that he is banned from watching your programme for some time. Sometimes you can be too funny!.

Get well soon! The best review I ever got.

The two most common questions I get asked when I meet people for the first time are 'Have you lost weight?' (It's common knowledge that TV adds a few pounds.) I normally reply, 'Yes, I'm very ill.' That tends to shut them up.

The other is 'When are you bringing back *TV Burp*?'

Even now, all these years later, I still get asked maybe twice a week.

So the answer to those two questions – in advance, just in case we do bump into each other are: One, no, I've put it on. And two, no, I'm not.

Reviving *TV Burp* would be like when the Beatles reassembled after John died and recorded 'Free As A Bird'. Don't get me wrong, I love that song, but it's no 'I Am The Walrus', is it? Let's be honest, it's not even 'Why Don't We Do It In The Road'.

But maybe it would be fun to unpack what *TV Burp* would be like today, if we were to risk completely trashing its reputation.

What would be in it?

The Crown? Yup, we could have some fun with that.

Tiger King – yup that's going in!

The Masked Singer, for sure.

Naked Attraction? I think so.

So, there's no shortage of stuff ripe for a 'sideways look'. Could it ever live up to those glory days? Not with me behind the desk, not any more. Let some other sucker do it.

CHAPTER 22
MASTER OF ONE

'Why is it only Tudor buildings that we mock?'

At the height of *TV Burp*, someone had the bright idea that I ought to front a prank show. Let's be clear, the only prank show I ever liked was *Candid Camera* – and that was when I was about five. After that, I always felt that they were rather mean-spirited. But they reckoned there was a gap in the market and that I was the one who was going to bring the prank show, kicking and screaming, into the twenty-first century.

Quite why I went along with it, I have no idea, but sure enough, the production company hired a couple of producers who knew how to make one, and work started on *What Are The Chances Of That Happening*.

One of the pranks involved me hiding in the boot of an office worker's car and waiting for him to open it – at which point, I was to sit up and say, 'What are the chances of that happening?', climb out of the boot and walk off. I duly got into the boot – I can't remember how we gained access to his car; it must have been set up by a relative, because I'm pretty sure we didn't force the lock. I was lying there for, I don't know, forty minutes? No sign of the driver.

The producer opened the boot to let some air in and then closed it again, locking me back in for another wait. Another twenty minutes went by. Still no sign of the driver. So, I'd been in the boot of this man's car for an hour now – the time it took to record virtually a whole episode of *TV Burp* and we'd recorded precisely nothing of any use.

In the end, someone was sent off to find the bloke who's car I was lying in to tell him to get down to the car park and open the boot of his car.

So the bloke came down, but, of course, he suspected something was up. He opened the boot and looked in – and I looked back at him, and he rolled his eyes and tutted and looked generally pissed off.

'What are the chances of that happening?' I said wanly.

'Oh, for fuck's sake . . .' he sighed. Then I got out of the boot of his car and wandered off.

Ha bloody ha!

Another prank was getting a member of the public to hold onto a dog on a lead. I would then approach dressed as a police officer and accuse them of not picking up some dog muck that we had planted. After I'd made various legal threats, I was to remove my wig, moustache and policeman's helmet to reveal myself as Saturday teatime favourite Mr Harry Hill – at which point, presumably, me and the member of the public would collapse in a big heap of laughter on the grass.

So they randomly picked an elderly man, who in a very public-spirited way held onto the dog on its lead. Then I walked in and started accusing him of letting his dog foul the footpath.

He became quite upset quite quickly, so I whipped off the disguise and looked at him with a forced grin. He looked back at me with a panic-stricken expression on his face. 'Who are you and why are you dressed like a policeman?' he said. 'I don't understand what's happening to me!'

I explained that I was Harry Hill and that we were filming him for a TV show.

To which he replied, 'Why?'

Which to be honest I still struggle to find an answer for.

There was one very funny scene though – involving the very

talented improvisor Katy Wix. A family had set up their dad to think he was being filmed for a reality TV show where he was being helped to get fit by a personal trainer played by Katy. I played the director of the shoot – in a blond wig, styled into dreadlocks, and a pair of wire-rimmed glasses.

'Right, get down on the floor!' barked Katy at the man in his own front room. He duly lay on the carpet. 'Now do twenty press-ups!' she shouted, and he started to do twenty press-ups. Unfortunately, I was laughing so hard the footage was unusable.

Weirdly, ITV liked the pilot, but I said I wanted nothing more to do with it. The last I heard, they were trying to get it off the ground with Christine Bleakley hosting it.

If you're reading this, Christine, don't get into that boot!

The only job I ever got fired from was as a DJ for Capital Radio. Yeah, I know, me as a DJ? I couldn't really see it either. I got hired by the same person who hired me to host *Top of the Pops* ('Ladies and gentlemen, always engaging . . . it's Skunk Anansie!'). There was a rumour that I had an 'encyclopaedic knowledge' of popular music. I'm not sure where that came from, as I've got an incredibly idiosyncratic knowledge of music. Just glancing at the stuff I've been listening to recently on Spotify I see Daft Punk, Black Midi, John Lennon and Charles Aznavour – doesn't sound very Capital FM, does it?

I took the job because it was around the time that *Burp* was starting off and I kept being told that the show was going to be 'cancelled'.

The money was pretty good, the drag was it was live on a Sunday lunchtime.

I'd never DJ'd before and had always shied away from anything live, as I don't consider ad-libbing one of my strengths.

'Don't worry,' said the person hiring me, 'We'll get you in and train you up!'

Kill me now! Looks like I'm really enjoying my time as an authorised representative of Capital Radio plc, don't it?

So one morning, when one of the studios was quiet, I was booked in to do a dummy run. The Capital building is right on Leicester Square – a great location. I arrived with absolutely no idea of what I was going to say or do and took my seat in front of the microphone with the technician opposite who would be operating the equipment.

'Just relax and say whatever you want!' said my new boss.

'Good morning, this is Harry Hill, and I'm going to be your DJ for the next hour!' I barked. Then my mind went completely blank. I looked down at the playlist that I'd been handed and introduced 'Ignition' by R. Kelly.

As I watched the track playing down, I started to panic – I still couldn't think of a single thing to say. In desperation, I stared out of the window and saw the Aberdeen Steak House across the other side of the square.

'What a lovely day it is today!' I said – even though there was some light drizzle. 'I'm looking out over Leicester Square and I can see the

Aberdeen Museum Of Steak! What's your favourite steak? Why not call me and let me know?' Then I nodded to the technician, and he cued up 'Bring Me To Life', by Evanescence.

On it went like that – me stumbling around helplessly, trying to engage with an imaginary audience.

'You probably just need to come up with some ideas for games and stuff,' said my new boss. 'And when you're live, people will be phoning in, so you can have some banter with them. I'm not worried.'

Well, he should have been! I certainly was.

They thought it might be a good idea for me to sit in for a bit with Chris Tarrant who was their breakfast host, so I did that one morning.* He didn't have a technician – he was flicking all the buttons and sliders himself, playing the deck like a musical instrument. Because he was in control, he could time perfectly when he brought in sound effects and jingles and tracks. It was a virtuoso performance.

'Any tips?' I said to him as I left.

'Just enjoy it,' he said.

It was too late for that.

The question I really wanted to ask was, 'Is it too late to get out of it?'

Every time I thought about being sat in front of that microphone, my mind would freeze. I decided I didn't just need to write a few ideas down and improvise around them, I needed to write a script.

So that's what I did. Every week for three months, I turned up on a Sunday with a script – barely a single word was ad-libbed. I wrote gags and games and routines. I decided to call the show *Funch* – a cross between Fun and Lunch.

I took a car horn in and pretended it was a pet seal. I'd do surveys outside in Leicester Square on things like an international arms trading conference that was going on that weekend. I'd ask people

---

* No, I didn't ask him why he hadn't laughed once at *An Audience With Harry Hill*.

– who were mainly foreign tourists – things like 'What's your favourite gun?' You know, real Sunday-lunchtime fun! I'd get hold of the audio from interviews that various pop stars had done with the other DJs, cut the DJ out, and put my voice in instead and edit them to make them look ridiculous. It was a helluva lot of work! Plus, it took up a big chunk of my Sunday and meant that I missed Sunday lunch every week, which is a particular favourite of mine and such a big part of family life.

I had a weekly quiz, 'Funch Family Tag', which required a couple of members of the same family handing each other the phone, taking it in turns to answer dumb questions like 'Name the double act. One was fat, the other thin and together they entertained the nation all through the eighties.'

The person on the other end of the phone answered, 'Little and Large?'

'No!' I said. 'The correct answer is Carol Vorderman's legs!'

The problem I had was that no one was phoning in.

I mean no one. I had to get friends to do it and pretend to be listeners.

The budget didn't run to any decent prizes, so as long as it was a friend, I would just make the prizes up – knowing that I'd never have to pay them out. In this way, Steve Brown 'won' a thousand pounds, his son won 'every CD in the top-forty chart' and my mum won a two-week stay in a donkey sanctuary in Somerset.

Then one Friday, I was in the building, running a couple of jingles past the technician, when I bumped into the new boss. The old one, the one that had hired me, had fallen on his sword shortly after I'd arrived.*

---

* This is a familiar pattern in my career. A new person in the job is a fan, they hire me, then leave the job. The new person isn't a fan. The show gets cancelled shortly after.

'Oh, Harry! I'm glad I've seen you,' he said. 'I've been listening to your show . . .'

'What do you think?' I asked, not really wanting to know the answer.

'Mmm.' He pondered for a moment. 'Is there any way you can make it more eighteen-to-twenty-four-female friendly?'

I was more than a little startled by this suggestion.

'I'm a forty-year-old man!' I said. 'How would I know what eighteen-to twenty-four-year-old girls want to hear?'

He nodded and suggested I tried playing 'two songs back-to-back.'

I suppose I should have taken that as a signal that all was not well, but I pressed on.

A couple of weeks later, I bumped into him again.

'We need to have a chat,' he said. So we sat down at a table in Capital's large open-plan office.

'Now,' he began, 'We've done some market research on your show . . .'

Uh-oh!

'Now, some people absolutely love it.'

'That's good!' I said with a slight feeling of relief, although I sensed that wasn't the whole story.

'But our crucial eighteen-to-twenty-four-year-old-female target audience hate it!'

'Hate' seemed like a strong word for a fairly innocuous couple of hours of silliness, but I took it on the chin!

'Which is why I'd like this Sunday's show to be your last,' he said, leaning back in his chair.

It took a moment to dawn on me that I was being fired.

Even though I wasn't enjoying doing the show, I didn't like the idea of being given the boot either!

'Well . . .' I said. 'If you think I'm going to come in on Sunday, you can forget it!'

I swung my Adidas sports bag across my shoulder and flounced off.

After that I vowed to never do anything just for the money – especially if it meant missing your roast beef and Yorkshire pud.

CHAPTER 23
BABY, LOOK AT ME . . .

'My sister overdosed on Night Nurse and woke up a fully qualified nurse – but only at night.'

Not long ago, my sixteen-year-old daughter, in a moment of pique, shouted at me, 'You're not even famous any more!'

Which made me smile.

It was designed to wound me, of course, like only a teenage daughter can, but to be honest I took a sort of perverse satisfaction from it.

I haven't taken particularly well to being what she might call 'famous'.

I've always been a fairly private person; I've never invited the press or a camera crew into the house or paraded my kids in front of the world for cash. I don't go to openings, I don't go on panel shows.* You won't ever see me in the jungle or splashing about in the *Big Brother* hot tub. I rarely even go on celebrity versions of quiz shows like *The Chase* or *Catchphrase* – even though there's not a bad living to be made from ploughing that particular furrow.

You wouldn't believe some of the shows I've been offered and turned down.

The World's Most Dangerous Roads was a no. I dunno, but I just didn't fancy getting run over in a foreign country.

Celebrity Show Jumping? Sounds like a sure-fire way to end up in a neck brace.

---

* Except *8 Out of 10 Cats Does Countdown* but that's one of the few times I got to see my old friend Sean Lock.

Strictly . . .? I'm very happily married, thank you!

It goes back to Brucie again. He gave me a couple of really good bits of advice – the first was, 'Don't go on other people's shows – only go on your own show!'

That came back to bite him on the bum when his agent phoned and asked me to go on a one-off special Bruce was doing. 'Any reason why you don't fancy it?' he asked. 'Yeah,' I said. 'Tell Bruce he told me not to!'

Bruce's other nugget was prompted by me telling him how unhappy I was with a show I'd been involved with.

'Don't worry about the show you've just done,' he said. 'Worry about the show you're going to do next!'

And the last little tip, which I've always tried to follow, was, 'When you finish a show, don't hang around to see what people think of it – go on holiday!'

That's some of the best advice I've ever had.

Initially, being recognised in the street was quite good fun – people asked me for autographs, and I'd sign 'Best Wishes, Harry Hill' and really take my time over it! Sometimes I'd add a little drawing of myself and occasionally even one of the person asking for the autograph – I'd chat to them, ask them where they were from, invite them on holiday and generally get to know them.

By the time *TV Burp* was at its zenith, I started to get a bit paranoid. I was snapped 'off duty' a couple of times with the kids, and not long after those photos appeared in some magazine or other, I was in the park and spotted a photographer. As he saw me, he appeared to dart behind a tree. I assumed he was paparazzi – looking for exclusive photos of me walking my two fox terriers Albert and Ruby. He walked briskly off, and paranoid as I was, I gave chase.

He started to walk more quickly and so did I.

In my mind, he was trying to get away from me.

He disappeared round a corner and when I caught up with him, he was crouched, focusing his camera at something on the ground – clearly a ruse to shake me off.

'Got any nice photos today?' I asked him sarcastically.

'Er, yes . . . got a few,' he said. He seemed to be nervous that his quarry had challenged him.

'Anything you want to show me?' I said with a cold look in my eye that I normally reserve for traffic wardens.

'Er . . . OK,' he said and started to scroll through his pictures on the screen on the back of his camera.

There was one of a crocus, several more of ducks, a couple of the sun reflected in the pond. There were none of the Saturday teatime favourite, Harry Hill. I felt like a complete twat.

'I like to take photos of nature,' he said enthusiastically.

'Great!' I said, furiously backtracking. 'They're really good, by the way!'

'Thanks for taking an interest,' he said, smiling. 'I really appreciate it.'

And I skulked off.

It gets worse.

One afternoon, I went to get into my car and saw that the windscreen had been shattered and that in the middle of it – right over the driver's seat – there was a bullet hole.

I immediately ducked, and keeping low, ran back to the house.

'Someone's trying to kill me!' I panted to Mrs H.

'What are you talking about?' she said with characteristic sympathy.

'Someone has taken a potshot at the car!'

'Where?' she said, rolling her eyes.

'It's not safe to go out there!' I said, pulling the curtains shut, a growing feeling of panic rising inside me. 'They could still be out there!'

She told me that if I genuinely thought that someone had fired a gun at the car, I ought to call the police.

So, I dialled 999.

I don't know whether you've ever called the emergency services, but as soon as I was put through I felt like a complete time-waster. Really, you should only call them if someone is at risk or a crime is in progress – this 'assassination attempt' had 'cold case' written all over it.

In the end, I was given the number of the local police station and I called them and got through to a rather weary police officer.

'Hello,' I said. 'There's a gunshot wound to my car windscreen.'

'A wound?' he said rather testily.

'Not a wound, sorry,' I corrected myself. 'A hole. It looks like someone has fired a gun at my car, like maybe it's a warning shot or something.'

'Did you hear a gunshot?'

'Er . . . no . . .' I said – this was the first time I'd considered that. If someone had fired a gun, how come neither me nor Mrs H had heard it go off?

'Maybe they used a silencer . . .?' I offered, pressing into play all the knowledge of contract killings that I'd garnered from watching *Heartbeat*, *The Bill* and *Midsomer Murders*.

'Hmm . . . Well, we're very busy,' he said.

That's when I pulled out my trump card.

'It's Harry Hill!' I said, even though as you know, it's not my real name. 'I only mention it because of what happened to Jill Dando!'

Around six months earlier the *Crimewatch* presenter Jill Dando had been cruelly gunned down on her doorstep by a mystery assailant, who presumably was still at large.

What I now appeared to be postulating was that this same gunman had a 'hit list' of top TV personalities that he was working down – and that number two on that list very probably was me. Quite what the gunman's criteria was remains a mystery – who was third on that list? Keith Chegwin? Timmy Mallett? I'm cringing in embarrassment as I think about it, but the idea of some celebrity assassin was enough to pique the interest of the police officer on the other end of the line. Careers have been built on less!

'Hmm, well the earliest I could get someone to you would be later tonight,' he said.

The rest of my evening was spent trying to work out who I had upset enough for them to resort to hiring a contract killer. Could it be the controller of Channel 4? I mean the ratings for *The Harry Hill Show* hadn't been brilliant, but murder seemed like a rather extreme response . . . Could it have been the heckler who'd threatened me with a bottle that time outside the Hackney Empire? Had he finally managed to track me down? As I drilled down into it, the list of potential arch-enemies seemed endless – I had no idea I was so unpopular!

There was a knock on the door shortly before midnight – and when I opened it, standing there was a very big policeman with his helmet under his arm.

'Come in,' I said. 'Thanks for popping round.'

He looked like he was about eight feet tall standing in my front room.

'Now, I take it that's your Austin A30 out front?' he said, getting straight to the point.

I nodded.

'Well, I took a look at your windscreen, and first thing's first – that is *not* a bullet hole.'

'Thank God!' I said, swooning with relief and making a mental note to send round a box of Celebrations to the local constabulary the next day.

'No, it's probably been caused by a stone being flicked up by a car or kicked up by some kids.'

It seemed I was going to see Christmas after all.

'However, looking at the car . . .' he continued, '. . . I see your tax disc is out of date. Which is an offence. So, if you want to avoid a fine I suggest you get that sorted out straightway.'

'Yes, Officer.' I said meekly, seeing him to the door.

I'd gone from being victim to perpetrator in two easy minutes.

There are benefits to being well known, of course, but I'm not sure I've seen my fair share of them yet.

I've heard of celebrities being given cars and watches and holidays and all sorts – but not this one! Maybe they think a short-sighted bald man in a big collar isn't going to boost sales? Even when *Burp* was sponsored by Hula Hoops, I didn't get so much as a free packet! The best it got was when I was walking along London's Southbank with the kids one hot, sunny day. We passed an ice-cream van – which was charging £3.50 for a 99. I know, right? Three fifty? For a 99? Utter rip off! I mean, there are times when you just have to make a stand.

The kids begged me, but I stood firm.

'I'm not paying that!' I shouted at them – in my mind's eye, I was Rosa Parks on that bus!

''ello 'arry!' came a voice from inside the ice-cream van. 'Any chance of a selfie?'

Now he was really pushing it!

'If you let me 'ave a selfie, I'll give you and the kids free ice creams!'

Needless to say he got his selfie – and I don't think my kids have ever looked up to me more.

Having a famous name is supposed to get you a good table in a restaurant, but using mine always made me feel embarrassed and a bit desperate. I once wanted to book a table for two at top restaurant The Ivy at very short notice – a forgotten Valentine's day or something – so, I needed to try every tool at my disposal.

'Hello, it's Harry Hill here. Any chance of a table for tomorrow night, please?'

'Hang on, I'll go and check . . .' said the maître d'. A few moments later, he was back.

'Who did you say it was?' he asked.

'Harry Hill!' I proclaimed.

'Hang on . . .' He went away again.

'No,' he said on his return.

CHAPTER 24
CHICKEN BOMB

'I like to go to a Tesco Express and take as long as I would in a normal Tesco – don't tell me how fast to shop!'

I had long harboured the desire to make a movie. I have a pile of screenplays that I've written that so far have never seen the light of day. I have one about a hugely successful trader on Wall Street – who just happens to be a giant soft toy. If that's not to your taste, how about the story of a farmer and his wife who have what they think is a rat infestation, but turns out to be Rod Stewart? No? Maybe I can tickle your fancy with *Dog Thief!* The story of a man who steals dogs in an attempt to find the reincarnation of his childhood pooch that was his only rewarding relationship growing up. Not sure? OK, how about *The Postman*? Which tells the story of an alcoholic postman who sees a furry creature that asks him for a lift to see The Bay City Rollers live in Glasgow and who, in the course of their road trip, helps him to put his life back on the straight and narrow?

OK, final one, and I know you're going to like this one – how about *Jalan,* the tale of an eighty-five-year-old lady who has a baby that is a strange Mr Blobby-like character as a sort of modern-day twist on the Frankenstein story? If Martin Scorsese or Steven Spielberg are reading this, then do please get in touch.

OK, so I can't write what you might call straightforward Richard Curtis style romcoms. I wish I could – but I can't. So, whilst I haven't *yet* been able to raise funds to make those ideas into films, I was able to get someone to back *The Harry Hill Movie*.

It was, I must say, one of the most exciting things I have ever been involved in.

I had in mind that it should be a silly road trip, with the plot, such as it was, serving to connect up a series of funny set pieces. I wasn't sure you were able to do that, then someone pointed me in the direction of *Pee-Wee's Big Adventure* – and yes, there was a precedent! That film is a series of big gags connected by the dumb idea that Pee-Wee's trying to find his stolen bike.

That film was, of course, directed by the brilliant Tim Burton – who bizarrely I'd met around the time I was putting my movie together.

My new agent* had arranged for me to present an award at the Empire Film Awards – an annual beanfeast at a top London hotel for film-industry types. He figured it might connect me up with a few movie moguls.

Having given the award, I was standing around at a loose end, studying Simon Pegg's hairline and remembering why I don't usually go to awards ceremonies, when I heard someone call my name.

I turned to see Helena Bonham Carter making a beeline straight for me. I'd never met HBC, before, so I was more than a little surprised that she even knew who I was.

'Harry! Me, Tim and the kids love your shows!' she gushed. 'It's one of the few times we all sit round watching TV together!'

'How wonderful,' I spluttered – I've never found praise very easy to take face to face. Then I looked across the room and heading towards my new friend Helena and I was her then-hubby Tim Burton – he waved at me and I waved back.

He shook me warmly by the hand and asked whether they could have a selfie with me for their kids. I mean come on! Could it get any better than that?!

Yes! Yes, it could!

---

* Fanfare, please! I like Bob Monkhouse's line about his agent – 'He was always there when he needed me!' Nuff said.

Gary Oldman then joins us. 'Hello, Harry!' he says and the four of us – Me, Tim effing Burton, Helena Bonham Carter and Gary frigging Oldman – stand chatting.

Everybody in the room was looking at me like, 'Who the f*** is he?!'

Part of the reason I got funding for my film was because of the huge success of *The Inbetweeners Movie,* which had pulled in some forty million quid at the box office.

Money talks, and suddenly people were more open to the idea of British comedy movies.

Me and producer Robert Jones put together a top notch cast – Julie Walters played my nan, Johnny Vegas provided the voice of Abu the Hamster, Sheridan Smith played the love interest. We even got our own Inbetweener Simon Bird on board to play a baddie, and Matt Lucas played my evil twin brother Otto. I'd met Matt at the Chuckle Club years earlier when he was just eighteen. I could see he was fantastically talented and asked him to be in some short films I was making for BBC2 – he said he'd love to but was heading off to Bristol to study drama. The next time I saw him, he was dressed as a baby, playing the drums for Vic Reeves!

The plot, such that it was, saw me living with my nan and my hamster Abu (Abu Hamster – get it? I'm not sure how many people did!)

The movie kicks off with a high-speed chase on disability vehicles, followed by a gun fight with some chickens, which is interrupted by Abu being violently sick.

I end up on a road trip to Blackpool, pursued by Otto, and on the way we meet indie band The Magic Numbers, who were running a bed-and-breakfast. I have a brush with a species of sub-aquatic shell people – one of whom I fall in love with. The whole thing culminated in a fight on top of Blackpool Tower and ended up in the shell people's cave singing the Candi Staton hit 'You've Got The Love'.

I thought it was fantastic!

I was aware that like all my stuff, it wouldn't be to everyone's taste, but I didn't wait to find out! The morning after the premier, with Bruce Forsythe's words ringing in my ears ('Go on holiday!'), me and the family flew to Barbados to spend Christmas in the sun. I deliberately didn't scan the web for reviews – after all, there wasn't much I could do about it at that stage. After a week or so, I relented and checked my inbox – there was a very sweet email from Matt Lucas saying that he'd enjoyed working with me and that he'd had lots of nice messages from people saying they'd enjoyed the film. One sentence worried me though – 'I know a few of the press have been a bit dour.'

Hmm . . . I know Matt is such a kind person that for him to even mention poor press probably meant it was worse than he was letting on. So I emailed Robert Jones with one simple question: *How bad is it?*

To which he replied:

Put it this way, it ain't gonna be making the critics' top ten any time soon.

When you're that close to something, it's sometimes difficult to be genuinely discerning about its qualities. I started to worry that in my enthusiasm to get the film made, I had indeed delivered a turkey. So when I got back from Barbs, I toddled down to the Vue cinema on Fulham Road, pulled my hat down as far as it would go and bought a ticket to my own movie. I have to say I still loved it . . . and so did the other eight people in the cinema!

In retrospect, I'm not sure what the press were expecting from a Harry Hill film. I remember asking the editor after he'd done a first cut if it was any good.

'It's good,' he replied, 'but it ain't *Chinatown*!'

So much fun. Robert Jones (third from left), Steve Bendelack (third from right) and me on the set of *The Harry Hill Movie*. (Photographer unknown)

CHAPTER 25
JOURNEY TO A DREAM

'I donated a scanner to the local hospital. Well, I say scanner – it can also be used as a printer.'

On the face of it, Simon Cowell and I are very different people. You probably wouldn't sit us next to each other at a wedding, or even on *Celebrity Coach Trip*.

He rides around in a chauffeur-driven Rolls-Royce and holidays on fancy yachts with Philip Green, Sinitta and Amanda Holden. He courts publicity, and he's self-consciously acquisitive, whereas I . . . well I think we know each other well enough by now for you to know that I am . . . less . . . so . . .

However, it turns out that the one thing we do have in common is that neither of us like musicals.

So how did me and him find ourselves putting one on at the London Palladium?

It was 2011 – cast your minds back, please!

TV Burp was riding high. *X Factor* was in its absolute pomp – the top of the Saturday telly tree. The tabloids were full of it, and it was the show on everybody's lips. It was the year after One Direction had finished third and I'd been having a laugh on *TV Burp* with another *X Factor* contestant, a rather unkempt looking Brazilian gentleman called Wagner – I'd created Wagbo, a cross between him and another contestant Mary Byrne, who worked on the till at Tesco.

'Born of Mary of Ireland and of Wagner of Brazil, the mutant ninja Wagbo!'*

He would turn up on shows like *This Morning* or *Lorraine*, kiss the host, shout, 'Wagbo!' and run off.

I loved the Wagbo years – we hired a short actor called Kevin O'Leary to play him in a long blonde fright wig and black dress. I'd only planned it as a one-off, but liked it so much I kept writing him in.

When the show won a British Comedy Award that same year, I didn't want to go (see my earlier opinion on awards ceremonies), so I sent Wagbo to pick it up for me. He ran up to the podium, picked up the award, shouted, 'Wagbo!' and ran off as I laughed like a drain from the safety of my armchair.

TV Burp at that time was on just before *The X Factor*. Simon and his team were fans and used to watch it whilst they were in make-up, and they'd always been very generous about letting us use clips – he recognised that it was better to be seen as in on the gag than sniping from the sidelines.

It may surprise you to learn that I was a genuine fan of *The X Factor* too. It was essential viewing in our house – don't forget I had three young girls at the time. The year before, I'd taken them to see a live recording of the show and much to their excitement they'd met One Direction, Louis, Cheryl and the gang.

---

* The other *TV Burp* writers really didn't like Wagbo. After his first couple of outings, they told me there had been a bit of a backlash against him on social media and that people were complaining that there weren't enough funny clips on the show. I didn't care! I loved Wagbo like a son! Besides, if there had been enough funny clips to fill a show, I wouldn't have had to invent Wagbo! I was leant on to kill him off, and he died in a hail of bullets – fired by the Knitted Character. The following series, I had the idea that Wagbo hadn't died and that instead he'd mated on his deathbed with the Knitted Character and produced a Wagbo/Knitted hybrid called 'Knickbo'!

'We're not doing Knickbo!' growled Spencer.

I would watch it with Mrs H and the kids with a pad of paper on my lap – jotting down ideas for *Burp*. By then I was usually a bit drunk, to be honest, because by seven thirty on a Saturday night, I'd finished the script for the following week's *Burp* and dispatched it to Spencer, so I felt like I'd earnt a drink.

That year, I was sitting, a little tipsy, in front of the final of *The X Factor* with my children, watching as Little Mix lifted the big prize. I reflected on the fact that I'd watched every single episode of the show from when it had first started seven years earlier, and I thought to myself, *How can I turn this huge amount of useless knowledge into some kind of higher art, or better still . . . money!*

Then as the confetti cannons went off on screen and Little Mix wept with excitement, it hit me like a thunderbolt.

'That's it!' I cried, staggering to my feet and reaching for another can of Stella. 'My fortune lies not in a weekly TV show that takes a sideways look at the week's TV but in writing *The X Factor* musical!'

I quickly googled *The X Factor* and found out that some version of it went out in eighty-four different countries all over the world! We could open a show in London! Broadway! Moscow! Warsaw! Hong Kong! Berlin! Copenhagen! 'We're going to be rich, children!' I said, tossing them the Argos catalogue and telling them to choose whatever they fancied.

OK, I'm exaggerating – but I did think that a musical set in the world of *The X Factor* stood a good chance of being fun, popular and lucrative.[*]

My first mission was to get in touch with Simon Cowell to give him the good news, so the next day I phoned the controller of ITV, Peter Fincham.

'I'm in the bath!' he said. So I explained my idea and asked him how I could get in touch with Simon.

---

[*] One out of three ain't bad!

'I'll hand you over to him now!' he replied. I'm kidding, of course! Peter wasn't really in the bath with Simon Cowell – but they *were* close! He told me that he was seeing Simon later that day. 'I'll sound him out,' he said.

The next day I got a text message: *I talked to Simon, he's really keen to meet up.*

'Yes!' I cried, punching the air. Can you imagine how exciting that felt? I was coming to London! *Wait a minute,* I thought, *I am in London!*

Then it dawned on me – I would need someone to write funny, catchy songs, and preferably someone who'd written a musical before.

So, I called Steve Brown.

I'd met Steve years earlier when I'd needed someone to play keyboards for me on my stand-up tour. My old friend Matt was long retired from showbiz – living in the shadow of the South Downs with his lovely wife Jane.

Richard Thomas (who wrote *Jerry Springer: The Opera*) had helped me out a couple of times, but he was too busy working for Frank Skinner. The tour was fast approaching and I needed music! So I met Steve at The Agent's office for a sort of job interview.

That day, Steve was surly and non-committal and acted like he was there under sufferance. I hired him on the spot!

He is now one of my best friends, and I talk to him three or four times a week.

He's very unusual. Not only does he have a wonderful ear for a catchy tune, he's also very funny and writes good gags. He wrote a lot of the songs for the original *Spitting Image* and briefly had his own satirical song spot on *Newsnight* during the eighties.

Steve's ten years older than me and hails originally from Bromley in Kent. In fact, he'd played on stage at the Three Tuns Pub in Beckenham with David Bowie when he was a would-be teenage pop star.

Most people know him as the on-screen musical director, Glenn Ponder, in Steve Coogan's *Knowing Me, Knowing You.*

He'd drifted into writing songs and theme tunes for TV like *They Think It's All Over . . .* and the 'Wonky Donkey' jingle for Ant and Dec. He also discovered singer-songwriters Rumer and Laura Mvula and produced their first albums for them, but his heart, as it turns out, is in musicals.

He wrote *Spend, Spend, Spend,* the story of the pools winner Viv Nicholson, which won an *Evening Standard* award for best new musical and which also prompted a letter from his great hero Stephen Sondheim, who wrote that Steve had written 'possibly the first great British musical'.

Great credentials for my project, right?

Better credentials, in fact, than mine.

I phoned Steve without delay.

'Steve, I've had a great idea, and one that's going to make us both very rich – *X Factor: the Musical!*'

There was a long silence on the other end of the line.

To be fair, Steve, like a lot of musicians, wasn't a fan of *The X Factor,* and he'd been promised vast wealth by a TV comic before when he'd worked for Brian Conley.

'You're gonna be a multimillionaire!' Brian had told him. 'Because you're not just Steve Brown, musical director now – you're Steve Brown, *Brian Conley's* musical director!'

Last time I checked, those multimillions still hadn't showed up.

'Yeah, maybe, let's meet up,' said Steve warily.

So we met up, and I explained how I thought it could work. His main concern was the style of the music.

Talking it through, we realised that the songs should sound like the sort of songs they sang every week on *X Factor.* Pop songs. Once he'd got his head around that, he was on board and I arranged for us to meet the big cheese himself: Simon Cowell.

It turns out that Simon's right-hand man was Nigel Hall* who I'd first met in 1999 when he was the producer of *Stars in Their Eyes*, so I knew him a bit and also knew he was up for a laugh.

When we got to the Sony building just off Kensington High Street where Simon has his office, Nigel explained that Simon was 'running a bit late'.

We were given a cup of tea and a copy of *Heat* magazine and we waited. Twenty minutes later, he came back to us.

'Good news, Simon has left home, and he's now in the car on the Westway.'

Ten minutes later . . .

'Simon is fifteen minutes away, he's at Shepherd's Bush roundabout.'

Twenty minutes later . . .

'Simon is in the road and walking towards the building!'

Then . . .

'Simon is in the lift!'

Then . . .

'Simon's coming up the corridor!'

Then the door to the office opened and Nigel said, 'It's Simon!'

As the cigarette smoke cleared like some bizarre episode of *Stars In Their Eyes* – there he was in the doorway.

I don't know whether you've met Simon Cowell before, but it's an odd thing. He's smaller than you think and he has no feet. His trousers appear to be glued to the soles of his shoes so that his feet remain invisible.

I was once in a dressing room with him, getting ready for a photoshoot to promote the musical. I commented on his nice suit and asked him where it was from.

'I have to have them made, Harry,' he said. 'I'm a very odd shape.'

---

* Global Head of Television – to give him his full title.

His face? Well, his face is a bit like an impressionist painting. You know Monet's lily pond, which looked one way if he painted it in the morning and completely different if he painted it in the evening? So it was with Simon's face. Sometimes it looked like he'd surfaced suddenly from a mile underwater, like his head had suddenly decompressed. Sometimes it was like looking into a dark void, at others it appeared as the face of a young girl, and occasionally, I swear I looked at Simon Cowell's face and saw my own face reflected back at me.

What he does have is an amazing stillness and weird charisma that I've never experienced before or since. I know, right? He's just got this thing where, when you're with him, you feel like anything is possible.

I actually came away from that first meeting wondering whether I might be falling in love with him.

'What's this about?' he said, easing himself into one of the beige leather sofas in his beige-leather-lined office.

'It's about Harry's idea for the *X Factor* musical, Simon, remember?' prompted Nigel.

Steve and I then talked in general terms about how the show wouldn't just be taking the mickey out of *The X Factor*, it would also be a celebration of it.

'Much as we do on *TV Burp*,' I said.*

At the end of the meeting, Simon nodded, sat back on his sofa, and said the magic words.

'It's yes from me!'

Me and Steve tumbled out onto the pavement shortly after and looked at each other aghast.

---

* That was always the way we got out of any trouble on *TV Burp* – we'd tell whoever we were trying to wrangle permission to use clips from that it was 'a celebration' of their show – when really, nine times out of ten, it was just a straightforward 'takedown'.

'Shit!' said Steve. 'We're going to have to write the bloody thing now!'

My first job was to do some research. I started watching musicals. Most of the musicals I'd seen up until that point I'd found over-sentimental, schmaltzy and usually forty-five minutes too long.

I watched *The Rocky Horror Show*, which I liked, and me and Steve went to see *Shrek* and *Sweeney Todd*. We even went to see the Spice Girls musical, *Viva Forever* – well, the first half anyway.* My wife once got home from the shops and walked in on me watching *Chicago* at half past eleven in the morning and expressed concern that I might be gay.†

At that first meeting, Simon had told us that he'd recently banned two words from being used on the show – 'journey' as in, 'It's been a fantastic journey and I don't want it to end!' and 'dream' as in, 'This is my dream, Simon! I've had it all my life!'

So we decided that Steve would write a song called, 'I'm Dreaming Of A Journey On My Journey To A Dream'.

The plot of the show was pretty straightforward. It was about a poor girl, Chenice, who lived in a caravan with her grandfather, who was on an iron lung in an ITV black spot so that they'd never heard of *The X Factor*. The pair were visited by a young plumber, Max – the love interest – who explains to the grandfather that he is a frustrated singer-songwriter and has entered *The X Factor*. The grandfather, hearing this, explains that Chenice has a great singing voice and realises that this might be their ticket out of poverty! Unfortunately,

---

* Steve's favourite thing is to book tickets for a musical and simultaneously book a table at a restaurant for dinner at nine o'clock – because usually he doesn't make it through to the second half.
† I know it's a horrible homophobic cliché to suggest that it's only gay men who like musicals and I've castigated Mrs H for her prejudice.

when Max plugs in his power tools he inadvertently unplugs the iron lung and the grandad perishes clutching *The X Factor* entry forms to his chest.

I'm glad you're laughing.

There was also a talking dog called Barlow and a hunchback called Trevor Modo, who Simon rejects from the competition and who then disappears off into the rafters of the theatre.*

To cut a long story short, Chenice wins *The X Factor*, the hunchback is revealed as the son of Andrew Lloyd Webber, and Simon unzips his outer skin to reveal that he is in fact an alien who's been sent to earth because his 'planet has run out of money'. Then a UFO flies down, Simon the alien gets into it and disappears off into the vast expanse of space.

Like I said, a pretty straightforward musical-theatre story.

Having bashed out a synopsis, a date was set for Steve and me to go back to meet with Simon and his team, where we'd talk him through it. He would then decide whether he wanted to go ahead with it or whether it would be destined to become another one of my doomed projects.

'This is just the story, Simon,' I said at that second meeting. 'It's not all the jokes that we're going to have in the show and it's not all the music and songs either. It's funny, yes, but don't expect the whole shebang.'

I'd heard that he had a rather short attention span, so I'd paid a graphic artist to do some story boards – so that he'd have something to look at.

So, with Simon, Nigel and their team sitting comfortably, I took a deep breath and began.

---

* That was one of my favourite bits. Trevor was played by the comic Charlie Baker, and his song/rap 'I'm Better Than That' was the most scathing number in the whole show.

'She lives in a caravan . . . grandad on an iron lung . . . plumber . . . grandad dies . . . hunchback, etc.'

I looked over at Simon and he was laughing like an idiot – I mean really laughing – slapping-his-thigh-throwing-back-his-head laughing. So was Nigel. They all were! I looked across at Steve. We were both thinking, *We've got this in the bag!*

'Chenice then sings a duet with Max,' I said and Simon looked at me and he said, 'Yeah, but it can't be a duet . . .'

'. . . Er . . .' I said, not quite understanding his objection.

So, he repeated it.

'It can't be a duet,' and he was now looking at me with his void look, the look that says, 'Cross me if you dare.'

'Of course it's not a duet! Ha ha!' I said with a nervous laugh, thinking *There's no way I wanted to blow it over a silly detail like who's singing what, particularly at such an early stage.* So I moved on to the next bit – but I was thinking, *Bit weird, what was all that about?*

I think, in retrospect, it was about Simon flexing his muscles.

I got to the end, and it was time for Steve to play us his song.

'I'm dreaming of a journey on my journey to a dream . . .' At this point Simon put his arms in the air – like he just didn't care – waving them back and forth, and Nigel and the team joined in. I'm not kidding! He then started singing along.

He was laughing and singing and at the end, he applauded and turned to Steve and said, 'That's great, Steve, I really like it, but you should change key a couple of times at the end.'

To which Steve replied, 'No.'

Suddenly, the atmosphere changed. Gone was the sunny, upbeat bonhomie and in blew an arctic frost.

'It could do with a key change,' repeated Simon.

'I don't think so,' said Steve dismissively.

'This is very much a work in progress, Simon!' I interjected thinking, *We need to get out of here before the whole thing goes tits up.*

'We can sort all that out when we know better what the show is . . . What do you think, then? Are we on?'

Simon looked at Steve, hesitated, then turned back to me and smiled that gleaming white smile that startles small mammals at night.

'I'm giving this the green light!' he said.

'What's the next stage?' said Nigel.

'Money!' I replied.

The next day I was on a train travelling down to Devon to see my brother whistling 'There's No Business Like Show Business', feeling awfully smug about my new career as a librettist when I got a phone call – it was Nigel.

'Well done, yesterday!' he said breezily.

'Thanks, Nigel. It really couldn't have gone better, could it?'

'Ah, well, that's why I called. How important is Steve?'

Uh-oh! I thought, *Here we go!* This is the showbiz I know – it's never straightforward plain sailing, getting what you want all the way. It's like the song says – one day it's all on, the next it's all over.

'Well, Nigel . . .' I said. 'We sort of come as a team . . . It's a musical, so we need someone to write the songs, and I'm confident that Steve really is the best person for that job.'

'Well, he can't argue with Simon,' he snapped. 'Otherwise it's going to be a very short relationship!'

'He didn't really *argue* with Simon,' I reasoned. 'It was more a frank exchange of views . . .'

'Believe me, baby, that's as close to an argument that Simon's been for ten years.'

'OK, leave it with me.' I sighed.

I phoned Steve and explained the situation.

'No one argues with Simon, apparently,' I said.

'Listen, mate,' he replied, a bit of his Bromley heritage creeping into his voice. 'I've had fights with all sorts of people over the years and they usually come round in the end . . .'

'That's just it, Steve!' I said, a little too forcefully for a packed train carriage. 'You can't have a fight with Simon Cowell!'

'All right, here's what I'll do.' He sighed. 'I'll write the songs – if he doesn't like them he can get his own people in.'

I called Nigel back with Steve's offer, who talked to Simon, and it was all smoothed over.

Steve did write the songs and neither of us ever heard anything other than positive things about them from Castle Cowell.

No endeavour in show business is more collaborative than a musical. You need a really good team – and on the face of it, we had one. Sean Foley was directing – he was very much the comedy director *de jour*, having had big hits in the West End with *The Ladykillers* and *Perfect Nonsense*. We had the hotshot designer Es Devlin* who'd had huge success designing big touring shows for bands like U2, Adele and Mika. Our choreographer was to be Kate Prince – the founder of the hip hop dance troupe ZooNation. It was nothing short of a dream team.

We assembled a cast, workshopped it for a week or so, rewriting the whole time, and then the moment came for us to perform it in a stripped-down way, in the basement of the Soho Theatre in Wardour Street for Simon, his entourage and all the West End theatre owners and their representatives, with a view to securing Simon's permission to press on with the project – and crucially, a venue to stage it in.

Just before the show was due to start, we got a series of phone calls.

'Simon's running late, Simon's on Oxford Street, Simon's round the corner . . . Simon's in the building . . .'

---

* Interestingly, if you look on her website, she's expunged all mention of her work on *I Can't Sing*! Success has many parents, but failure is an orphan.

Eventually Simon arrived with Nigel, Amanda Holden and Sinitta in tow. The rest of the audience were producers, promoters and theatre owners – really hard bitten, 'Nothing impresses us!' types. Your quintessential 'tough crowd'. The last time any of these guys laughed was when one of their rival's shows was cancelled.

I deliberately positioned myself away from Simon so I couldn't see his face, just in case he was hating it. The show started and, unbelievably, it couldn't have gone better – everyone was laughing hysterically from the off.

In the interval, the bloke from Andrew Lloyd Webber's company came up to me and Steve and said, 'Tell me you'll take the Palladium!'

The show finished to a standing ovation – unheard of in that kind of workshop situation and in front of that sort of crowd. Smelling success, Simon sprang to his feet, ran up onto the stage and said, 'I'm backing this 110%!'

We were off!

The producers accepted the offer of the Palladium which, after all, only seats a mere 2400 people, and we set to work trying to find our Simon.

Who would you cast in the role of Simon Cowell if you had your dream option? Bearing in mind that Simon had the power of veto over it, so in other words it had to be someone younger than him and better looking.

After countless auditions it turned out that there are basically only three people who are the right age, who look a bit like him, who can sing and dance and who can be funny. At that time one of them was in *Charlie and the Chocolate Factory*, so he was out of the picture; one of them was working on Andrew Lloyd Webber's new musical; and the third one was Michael Ball and he, at that time anyway, was apparently 'too fat'.

'We haven't got time to get him into shape!' said one of the producers. 'We haven't got the resources to follow Michael Ball around steering him out of Greggs!'

Then someone suggested Nigel Harman.

'What? Dennis from *EastEnders*?' I said.

Actually me and Steve had seen him in the first half of *Shrek* and he was by far the funniest thing in it. It turned out that before *Easties* came knocking his background was in musical theatre – he could sing, he could tap dance and everything! He was slim and handsome too! Bingo!

So Nigel got the part.

The role of Chenice went to the Oscar-nominated, but then unknown Cynthia Erivo.

For the rest of the cast, we didn't want a load of perfect-looking people; we wanted people of all different shapes and sizes – the sort of people who don't usually get cast in musicals.

When Simon came to a rehearsal and saw the bunch we'd assembled, we got a message back saying that he thought the cast were 'a bit weird-looking', to which Steve replied drolly 'Hasn't he ever watched *The X Factor*?'

A couple of weeks before the press launch, it was revealed that Simon had got his new girlfriend, Lauren, pregnant. Naughty Simon!

It was a huge story in the tabloids and guaranteed a big turnout for the launch. It was here that I first met Andrew Lloyd Webber. He was mumbling and I could only catch the odd word, so I staged an intervention.

'How's it going with your show?' I asked.

At that time he was working on *Stephen Ward,* his short-lived musical about John Profumo's osteopath.

'Oh, it's really good!' he said, brightening. 'We've got a song in it called "What the Fuck's Going On!"'

To which I replied, 'That's what you should have called the show, mate!'

His face fell, and he looked like he was going to burst into tears, so I made my excuses and left.

I know this all sounds like gratuitous name-dropping, but I'm trying to give you an impression of the kind of people I was rubbing shoulders with at that point! I've got Simon Cowell to my left, I've got Sinitta to my right, Andrew Lloyd Webber's in the room and as if it couldn't get any better, who's this? It's only the face of Belvita Breakfast Biscuits herself . . . Lisa Snowdon! For some reason Simon had requested that she host the launch.

The idea was to prompt people into picking up the phone to book tickets.

Unfortunately, that didn't really happen. Hardly anyone bought any tickets. A lot of people came to see it, but I'm yet to meet anyone who paid for the privilege.

In the meantime, they were preparing the London Palladium for the arrival of our show. So, Steve, Sean and I were invited to a site visit. We walked up the front steps and had our photo taken with a big poster advertising the musical with our names on it. Inside, there were hundreds of people welding, sawing and painting.

'We'll never fill it!' I joked as we stood at the back of the dress circle, looking at all those empty seats.

'I give it six weeks!'

A couple of weeks later, we moved from the rehearsal room near London Bridge into the Palladium and got ready to start the previews. Now, if you don't know, the preview stage is where you get about a month to do the show in front of a live audience in the theatre to iron out any problems. There's a gentleman's agreement that during that time no press will review it.

The first preview is, of course, very exciting. It's the first time you've really seen it performed in front of a crowd. So, as the orchestra struck up, me, Steve and Sean slunk in and stood at the back of the stalls.

Then we heard it – laughter!

They were actually laughing.

I felt tears welling up in my eyes and at that point I realised I had become what I most despised – a luvvie! I had fallen in love with musical theatre. I looked across at Steve and Sean and they both had big, juicy tears rolling down their cheeks. It was a great first half, only spoilt by the interval, which was an hour long.

It turned out that they'd packed so much scenery into the Palladium that the backstage area was now like a Rubik's cube – you had to move everything to get to the thing you needed and that took an hour. That wasn't the longest interval though; two days later it was twenty-four hours long because something broke and we had to send the audience home after the first half.

The next day, a skip turned up outside and they just started throwing stuff out. Great big lumps of scenery.

It worked though. We got the interval down to twenty-five minutes!

Ironing out those sorts of teething problems are exactly what the previews were for, but suddenly the press started reporting that it was a 'troubled musical'. I sensed that the knives were out for us.

Steve, Sean and I developed a daily ritual. We'd meet in the bar next door to the Palladium, have a few drinks and go and watch the preview, then we'd meet up afterwards for a few more drinks. I hadn't drunk so much booze since my med school days! We'd make notes during the show and we'd cut it down and improve it.

Over that month, it got increasingly tighter and funnier and better. Then, ten days before we were due to open, we got the royal visit: Simon turned up to see how his money was being spent.

The show was always so much funnier when he was in the crowd and it was a huge treat for the audience. He'd arrive a little late and sit somewhere near the front so everyone could see him as he took his seat. The whole place would erupt in uproar as they tried to grab selfies . . . which was all great publicity for the show.

The next day, I received an email from Simon via Nigel (I wasn't allowed to have his email address), which on the whole was very positive. He's got a very good eye for lighting and production, but he did have some issues with the plot . . .

'I feel that my character is at times made to look like a bit of an idiot,' it said.

Uh-oh! I thought. *It's taken him eighteen months, but the penny's finally dropped!*

He went on . . .

'. . . The suggestion that I am the hunchback's father is ridiculous!'

Yes, sorry, I should have explained – the one plot point that we'd been told to change if we wanted the Palladium was the bit that suggested the hunchback's dad was Andrew Lloyd Webber. So with a flourish of the playwright's pen, I'd simply changed it to Simon.

The email concluded with: 'Overall I was very happy but we need to rein it in.'

'What do we do?' said Sean.

With ten days till opening night there just wasn't much time to do anything.

'Ignore it!' I said.

Which is exactly what we did.

So to the opening night, and what a star-studded night it was. We had Louis Walsh, Terry Wogan, Ronnie Corbett, David Walliams, Cilla Black, Philip Green, Jimmy Carr . . . Union J (Waddya mean who?), Sinitta, Amanda Holden (who appeared inexplicably to have forgotten to wear her trousers). I know! What a weird bunch!

**Manning the box office. Steve Brown and
I on the steps of the Palladium.**

The Palladium was packed,* the cast were on fantastic form – all the little worries that we'd had about various parts of the show suddenly disappeared. In short, it couldn't have gone better and received a huge standing ovation.†

The next day we had some really great reviews – OK, there were one or two sniffy ones. If truth be told, the literati didn't really want to like it; the very idea of 'X Factor: the Musical' and Simon Cowell got up some people's noses. The *Sunday Telegraph*'s theatre critic refused to review it because he claimed 'it isn't a musical.'‡

* The only other time that it was that full was six weeks later when it closed!
† Actually that's a given at a first night – even if the show stinks.
‡ What a stuck-up prick!

I caught the music critic Paul Morley on BBC2 harping on about how 'Simon Cowell wants to own the culture'. As far as I could see, it was just plain snobbery. Besides, it wasn't Simon who wanted to own the culture – it was me!

Despite these few dissenters, it felt like we might have got away with it.

Ticket sales were slow, but I was doing my bit – I was going two or three times a week! Steve and I had said that we needed an office at the Palladium because we might need to do last-minute rewrites, so we had our own dressing room there – where before the show I would leave my coat.

Basically, I was doing a lot of what I believe is called 'flouncing about'. Suddenly, I thought I was Noel Coward. 'I've got a hit show at the London Palladium, doncha know!'

The staff of the theatre, who all seemed to genuinely love the show, greeted me like I owned the place. I even got a discount on the Yorkie man-sized chocolate buttons that they sold out front. Normally £3.50, I was getting them for £3! Does it get any better than that? Steve and I would go to the bar before the show and we would go to the bar after – high on success, booze and buttons. Sir Ian 'Gandalf' McKellen turned up one night, Rowan Atkinson another! We were on our way – we were going to be rich!

Four weeks after opening night, I was in a cab on my way home after a matinee (Yes, I was even doing matinees!) and I noticed a missed call from the producer.

I called her straight back. 'Oh, hi, Rebecca!' I said breezily. Then as a joke added, 'I thought we'd get longer than four weeks, ha ha ha!'

To which she replied, 'How did you know?'

I heard a low grunting noise that sounded like a wounded animal, then I realised it was coming from me.

'Noooooooo!' I groaned.

And that was it.

The following night the producers, Steve, Sean and I all turned up to break the news to the cast and crew as they came off.

They were the people who suffered most, this bunch of very special and talented people. They were all signed up for a year and all they got was two weeks' notice. I know it's not quite the same as the pit closing in a mining town, but it's as close as us luvvies get to it.

There was a moment in the show where the grandad, who'd died in the first half (the one who'd been on an iron lung, remember?), came back as an angel, swinging across the stage on a wire.

'God loves this show!' he'd say.

On the last night, I changed it.

'God loves this show, but even he couldn't make it run!' he wailed to a massive laugh.

Steve and I didn't really make any big money out of it but we didn't lose any either.

We did both get a souvenir onesie, some really good new friends and I had the most fun I've ever had on a project. I can't wait to do it again!

Why did it fail? Probably because we took on too large a venue. I found out later that no one in the history of the Palladium had ever launched a new musical there. What we should have done is started small and toured the provinces, like all the other shows do!

I do have another theory though. Nigel had said early on in the process that 'We've got to get Simon's jeans right.' So Simon donated a pair of his actual jeans for the costume designer to 'work from'. After she'd finished with them, I sweet-talked her into giving them to me. I cut them up into one inch squares, mounted them on a piece of card, framed them and gave them out as first-night presents to the cast. *A genuine piece of Simon Cowell's trousers*, it said. *Believed to have healing and aphrodisiac properties. Touch it for luck!*

So clearly, someone forgot to touch it.

**Eat my shorts – Simon's trousers on my kitchen
floor about to be shredded as souvenirs.**

CHAPTER 26
TONIGHT, MATTHEW . . .

'I can't sleep. I bought a second-hand memory foam mattress and it's remembering someone else.'

Like a lot of students in the late eighties, I'd often watch *Stars In Their Eyes* on a Saturday night before going out to enjoy some proper entertainment. We'd all sit round our student digs watching it, and I promise you I don't know anyone who watched it in any other way than with their tongue firmly in their cheek.

We watched it *ironically*, laughing *at* it rather than with it. This is no reflection on the costume and make-up teams – I'm afraid there's just no way that you can make a plumber from Bolton look like Neil Diamond. As the head make-up designer on the show was once heard to exclaim, 'These are hands, not wands!'

When they asked me if I'd like to sing on the celebrity version – which for me was even more naff than the civilian version – I jumped at the chance.

But it wasn't quite in the bag, they wanted me to audition.

At the time, George Michael's song 'Outside' was in the charts and had a great video set in a blinged-up gents' toilet, complete with disco balls, revolving urinals and Village People-style LAPD cops. I thought I could have some fun with it – so I auditioned with that song, as George.

I met the executive producer Nigel Hall (Yes, the same Nigel I'd later be working with on *I Can't Sing!*) at a rehearsal room in Covent Garden, along with the show's musical director Ray Monk at the piano, and off I went. 'Let's go outside . . .' I sang in a voice that was two parts John Inman to one part Danny La Rue. He stopped me before I got to the chorus.

'No, no, I'm not getting it!' he said. 'Listen, Harry, we'd love to have you on the show. Is there anyone else you can do?'

At the time I had a bit of a party piece doing The Smiths' frontman Morrissey, easy to do – you just adopt a Mancunian accent and sing through your nose.

Ray struck up 'This Charming Man' and I did perhaps Britain's worst Morrissey impression.

'That's it!' cried Nigel, jumping to his feet. 'I love it! No one's ever done Morrissey before!'

They wanted two minutes of 'This Charming Man' and a week or so later I got a cassette through the post with a guide track on one side with Ray singing, and on the other an instrumental version for me to practise to.

Within a couple of days, Mrs H banned me from singing it in the house, so I'd have it on my Sony Walkman and practise it whilst I was walking the dog.

I can't tell you how relaxed I was about it – I just saw the whole thing as a bit of a laugh.

Until the day of the show.

Sharing *my* episode was Denise Welch as Petula Clark, the Channel 4 newsreader Kirsty Young as Peggy Lee, Ben Freeman from *Emmerdale* as Robbie Williams and Michelle Collins as Chrissie Hynde.

It was only after I'd done my first dress rehearsal that I realised that everybody was taking the whole thing incredibly seriously.

As I walked back through the smoky doorway for a pow-wow with the producer, one of the guys operating the doors[*] looked at me, rolled his eyes and said witheringly, 'Good luck with that, mate!'

---

[*] Spoiler alert! They're not automatic doors at all, it's just two hairy stagehands moving a couple of heavy bits of painted MDF.

Backstage, Nigel was in a bit of a spin.

'It doesn't sound anything like Morrissey!' he exclaimed 'We'd better get the vocal coach in!'

The vocal coach duly turned up and got me to sing my two minutes for her. By now I had a lump in my throat and was wondering whether it was too late to back out of it. 'I'm sorry,' she said, 'But Nigel's right, it doesn't sound anything like the tape!'

'What tape?' I said.

'This tape!' she said, holding up the guide track.

'That's not Morrissey!' I spluttered. 'That's Ray Bloody Monk!'

Down in the make-up department I met the formidable Gloria, who informed me that she'd had a wig made specially, which she duly glued to my bald head. I looked in the mirror. I looked more like Christopher Lee in *The Devil Rides Out*. 'It's too far forward!' I said, 'Morrissey's got a receding hairline!'

'Well, that's not clear from the photo the researcher faxed me!' she said and showed me a fax that was such high contrast it looked like a Victorian etching – you couldn't make out any of the detail whatsoever.

'Trust me, it should be more like this,' I said, sliding it back on my forehead.

No one seemed to have ever heard of The Smiths or Morrissey – which was weird because we were filming it for Granada, which was based a stone's throw from the Salford Lads Club.

The deal was that we got to keep the outfit after we were done. As I slipped on the see-through chiffon blouse, bead necklace, eighties baggy jeans and a pair of Doc Martens shoes – all topped off with a pair of specs and a hearing aid – I started to wish I'd gone as someone a bit more glamorous – Elvis or something – because I suspected that if I turned up anywhere in that lot, I'd get wolf-whistled.

By this time, I was starting to get nervous.

Not as nervous as some of the other star guests, though.

'You heard about Denise?' said Michelle Collins as I bumped into her in the corridor. 'She's being sick in the toilets!'

The whole thing is a bit of a blur, to be honest. We had been told that if we cocked it up the first time, we'd get one more attempt.

As I stepped up to the smoky doorway, the same operator who'd put his two pennies in at the rehearsal, looked me up and down and audibly tutted.

'You're next, mate,' said the floor manager.

'Smoke going in!' a voice barked over the intercom, and the narrow space behind the doors filled with smoke, and I started to choke.

Then I heard Mr Kelly say the immortal words, 'Singing live, Harry Hill is Morrissey!'

'Good luck, mate,' said my friend the door operator. 'You're gonna need it!'

The doors opened and I stumbled out like someone trapped in a burning building – but in 1983.

'A punctured bicycle on a hillside desolate!' I croaked, swinging a bunch of gladioli round my head and occasionally checking my hearing aid hadn't fallen out.

It seemed to be going pretty well, and so I started to relax and then missed out a whole verse and chorus, finishing a minute early.

As the music kept going, I just danced. I danced and I whirled the gladioli about. A minute felt like two weeks.

'Go again on that!' came Nigel's voice through the floor manager's headphones.

Back up to the smoky doorway I was marched, and had to do the whole thing again. Between the two takes, they got what they were looking for.

'How do you feel?' beamed Matthew Kelly through his beard.

'Stupid!' is what I wanted to say.

In the end, Kirsty Young won. I swear she packed the audience with mates.

Years later, when ITV approached me to take over Matthew Kelly's job and host it, it seemed to me it could be a lot of fun. Before I agreed, I thought I'd better remind myself of how it worked and took a look at some of those original shows. I'm afraid that what I saw was pretty much unwatchable. The pace was incredibly slow, everything seemed to take forever – the contestants sang for a full two minutes – which doesn't sound long but can seem like a lifetime on TV.

Apparently, the reason they always put the music act on last on chat shows is because people just reach for the remote and turn over – or worse, turn off. And that's with the real stars singing, if people got an itchy finger watching Tina Turner singing 'Steamy Windows', they're probably going to get one watching a middle-aged mum from Middlesbrough singing it.

For me, the fun of the show was the build-up and the reveal – in other words, do they look or sound like the person they're supposed to be doing?

Nine times out of ten, the honest answer to that question I'm afraid was not much.

By 2014, the prize seemed a bit ropey too, when we had *X Factor* and *Britain's Got Talent* offering recording contracts and huge cash prizes, the idea that any of our 'star guests' could make a career out of singing as Kenny Rogers in pubs just seemed a bit silly.

If you look back at the Matthew Kelly years, pretty much all he does is introduce the guests, ask them a couple of standard questions like 'When did you become a fan of this person?', 'What will it mean to you if you win?' type of shtick, then he intros the guest who comes on and sings, then he puts his arm around them and says, 'How do you feel?' Then he points out that they would have made their nan or other dead relative very proud. 'See you after the break.'

That's not to denigrate what he did, but you know, the show didn't depend on MK's ready wit or interview skills.

I just felt, rightly or wrongly* that I needed to add some laughs to try to make the show more entertaining by larding on a whole extra layer of irony.

I also insisted that we get some acts that some of the younger audience might actually be aware of – Rihanna, Beyoncé, John Legend, Eminem. There'd been this long gap since the previous series and one of the attractions of hosting the show to me was that there was a huge bunch of singers and musicians that *Stars In Their Eyes* hadn't touched.

The producers told me 'do what you want with it' and to 'sprinkle your magic dust'. That phrase. It usually means, 'We haven't got a clue what to do with it and can you help us out, please?'

So, I said we needed to cut the songs down to a minute, that we couldn't do straight videos of the contestants at home or work because that's what *X Factor* and all the other shows were doing and that we should try to make our videos funny.

Pretty quickly, it became clear that the production team was divided into two camps – one that thought I was doing exactly the right thing with the show, slightly sending it up and acknowledging that times had changed.

Then there was the other camp who thought that I was meddling in things I didn't understand and was committing a heinous crime against light entertainment.

'What about the little old lady in Bolton?' was a familiar refrain from one of the producers. 'She's not gonna know who Rihanna is!' And 'You can't get members of the public to do lines or tell jokes!'

I just thought that was rather patronising. It's always a big mistake to underestimate your audience. Sure, you can give them what they've always had, but why not try something different? Why not take a risk? I mean, what's the worst thing that can happen?

* Wrongly, as it turned out!

The answer to that depends on which camp you fall into.

Hands up, the pilot was terrible.

We recorded it at Elstree Studios and the audience queue looked like the queue for Lourdes. It was a far cry from the young trendy crowd we got for *TV Burp*. They didn't laugh at my jokes – a lot of them didn't even seem to know who I was.

I felt rather badly let down when I saw the list of acts – all the old faces were back! Dolly Parton, Tina Turner, even Neil Diamond for crying out loud! Even worse, Matthew Kelly cast such a long shadow that the contestants kept calling me Matthew!*

The eggiest bit was after the guests had stopped singing and I had to do the 'How do you feel?' bit and tell them how well they'd done. A lot of the time I didn't think they had done that well! My *TV Burp* persona would have taken the piss, but there was no way I could do that, not to real punters. So I tried to fake it – I felt awkward and it showed.

I got home that night and Mrs H asked me how it had gone.

'We're screwed!' I said, and once again I was trying to work out if it was too late to back out of it.

I hardly slept a wink that night lying there in a cold sweat, trying to work out what I could do to turn it round.

A couple of days later I got the first cut of the pilot – I was just so bad in it! Usually when I watch myself back, I laugh a lot – what can I tell you, I like me!

Watching this, I didn't laugh once – I cried a couple of times, but didn't laugh!

They'd cut all the laughs out of it in an effort to fit it all in to an hour. I'd do a gag and they'd cut straight off me to a wide shot of the weird-looking crowd, which just killed the laugh stone dead!

---

* It was also kind of confusing for me because, as we now know, Matthew is my real name.

Sometimes, not always, but sometimes you need to stay with the comic to see his reaction and just hear the laugh.

It's a delicate flower, comedy, and the way it's cut can make the difference between something working or not. I went into the edit, sat with the editor and helped him recut it. The pace improved and suddenly a lot of the laughs were there.* Crucially, everyone now agreed with me on one thing – we needed to cut the songs right down.

In any event, all the contestants were great fun – they produced some really funny videos and seemed to enjoy the challenge of delivering lines.

I really loved the running gag we had with Jenna Boyd† dressed as Adele looking for her baby, and one of the funniest things I've ever been involved in was watching her smash up a grand piano with an axe whilst singing, 'Someone Like You'.

The audience weren't as keen, though!

I didn't read the reviews, but I was aware of them and I know the ratings tanked after week one.

I'm not sure what the specific gripe was, but I think it was more or less that I was hogging the show and tampering with a national institution.

The truth is you don't need a comedian to host *Stars In Their Eyes*, you need Matthew Kelly, or Cat Deeley or Dermot O'Leary! You need someone with a light touch who's willing to take a back seat.

I think we all know that's not me!

I learnt an important lesson, though. If I'm offered a show these days I think, *what can I add to this that isn't already there?*

If the answer isn't *laughs*, we should probably all move on.

---

* Particularly after we'd dubbed them on!
† Who I'd met on *I Can't Sing!*

CHAPTER 27
ALIEN FUN

'Hitler was a bad man. Winston Churchill was a good man. But if you're in a hot air balloon with Hitler and Churchill and you're losing altitude, the one you throw out is Churchill because he's the fat one.'

Let's face it, since I waved goodbye to *TV Burp* in 2011, I haven't managed to find a telly format that's as popular with you lot as it has been with me.

There, I've said it, it's out there.

That hasn't stopped me trying, though.

After my brief forays into movies, musical theatre, and, er . . . killing off *Stars In Their Eyes*, I figured I ought to get a proper job.

Sky One had wanted to work with me ever since I'd given up *TV Burp*, and commissioned an idea I had for a spoof cookery series. Out of all the TV stuff I've done, *Harry Hill's Tea Time* is the show that I loved doing most. It's just a shame that pretty much no one ever saw it! That's the problem of selling a show to Sky One!

People's viewing habits have loosened up a lot, particularly since the various lockdowns, but it certainly wasn't the case in 2014 when I took the Murdoch shilling.

I can't really complain – I just wanted to make that show so badly that I was prepared to make it 'just for me'.

The idea was basically a cookery show where all the recipes were pretty much inedible. So for instance, we had a seven-shoe roast – a child's shoe inside Janette Krankie's shoe, inside . . . Until finally the whole lot was placed inside a very large shoe indeed – that of Fiona

284

Bruce. Each shoe was coated in margarine first to 'keep the dish moist'. The theory was that if you cook anything for long enough, eventually it becomes tender enough to eat.

It involved a lot of visual gags, slapstick and general mucking about, which I thought would appeal to kids and families alike.

The show was built around a celebrity guest who I would interview at the same time as teaching them how to cook. So whilst I was rubbing margarine into a size-nine shoe, they'd be doing it too, and I'd be taking them back over their career by showing them carefully selected clips of their shows that I'd take out of context, just as I had on *TV Burp*.

So for instance, when we had *Dragons' Den* star Deborah Meaden, who famously runs a series of caravan parks in the West Country, on the show, our task was to make a trifle in the back of a caravan as it was travelling at speed along the M5 – cue a lot of mess.

When Martin Kemp came on, we got him making a Spandau-Sagne – a lasagne made with sheets of pasta cut to look like the members of Spandau Ballet. That episode featured a voice-activated fridge – when you opened the fridge door, you shouted what you needed and it got thrown at you from inside the fridge.* Big lumps of cheese, tomatoes and, of course, a large jet of milk.

Most of the guests, knowing the tone of the show, were happy to go along with it – even Sir Trevor McDonald (yes, in an uncharacteristic moment of madness, he'd agreed to help me out – I can only assume his agent was on holiday or had developed a gambling habit and needed the money)! We had found a clip of him talking about camel sausages in the Middle East, so I introduced him to The Camilla Parker Bowles Sausage Dispenser, a machine with a

---

* The assistant producer, Hannah – who was easily the smallest person on the team – was crouched inside the fridge throwing cheese and salad at Martin Kemp. Nice work if you can get it.

picture of the duchess on the front that Sir Trev loaded a camel's hump into. When I pressed a button, a sausage flew out of her mouth and into his.

The only guest who didn't seem at all pleased to be on the show was Jason Donovan. He became rather tight-lipped when I played clips of him in the Australian soap *Neighbours,* which had made his name – it seemed he wasn't yet ready to laugh at his past. Unfortunately, that was the only reason we'd booked him! That episode introduced the viewers to Slurpy the bush kangaroo – a wine-tasting marsupial who got so drunk tasting the wine that he ended up in the liquidiser.* Like I say, it was the maddest, most fun show I've ever been involved with.

We had King Gary himself, Tom Davis, as regular character Egg Wallace, dressed as a giant egg – or we did until the costume proved so heavy it did his back in and for the second series we had to get someone else.† One of my favourite moments was him rapping with a puppet dressed as Kanye West on his head as comic Holly Burn, dressed as Kim Kardashian, doled out soup from a tureen to Gok Wan.

I live for moments like that!

At the end of each show, The Delia Smiths (three ladies dressed as Delia Smith circa 1974) would sing us out with a number by The Smiths. I'd then drag someone up from the audience and get them to join us for the meal we'd 'cooked'. I'd then yell, 'It's Sausage Time!' and a twenty-foot-long helium-filled sausage was released into the audience as the meal descended into a food fight.

---

* Poor Jason! I'll never forget standing next to him as he watched grim-faced and muttering four-letter words as a long pre-recorded sketch was played into the studio where I appeared dressed as him in a spoof of his *Neighbours* marriage to Kylie Minogue. The final straw came when I lifted Kylie's veil to reveal Slurpy the wine-tasting kangaroo. For a moment, I thought he was going to walk!
† The brilliant Paul Putner.

I was trying to bring back the sort of controlled chaos of the anarchic ITV children's show *Tiswas* that I felt had been lacking from TV for a long time. That food fight was such good fun. I remember we had Emilia Fox as our main guest and brought on Samantha Fox as her long-lost sister. Now to a gentleman of my age, Sam Fox has a particular resonance – if you know what I mean. Sam really got into the food fight – at one point she was sitting on my chest smashing custard pies into my face and laughing hysterically as The Delia Smiths sang 'Big Mouth Strikes Again'. It's at times like that, that I think, *If the young me could see the old me, he'd be so proud!*

The Delia Smiths.

If *TV Burp* was my Beatles, then I guess *Alien Fun Capsule* was my Paul McCartney and Wings.

The idea was to try to re-invent the panel show. No one had tried that for a while, not since Vic and Bob's *Shooting Stars*, so I figured I was in with a chance.

If you didn't catch it – and don't worry, you're not alone – it consisted of me wrangling two teams of two celebrities, who I'd gently take the piss out of by showing them clips of themselves taken out of context. It felt like some of the good bits from *Burp* and some of the more accessible bits of *Tea Time*.

Originally, I planned to call it 'Is This Funny?' But it was pointed out fairly early on that there was a danger that the critics might just write a one-word review – *No!*

The idea was to have two teams of comedians – and to reduce the amount of work I had to do, it would be up to them to bring in the stuff that they found funny. It could be a clip they'd seen on YouTube or a humorously shaped vegetable or the lady in the dry cleaners with a funny laugh – that sort of thing. It seemed like a good way to get a few new funny faces onto ITV too – as they have a rather narrow roster of talent. Basically if it hasn't got Phillip Schofield, Holly Willoughby, Ant and Dec, Bradley Walsh or Stephen Mulhern in it, you can forget it!*

We would then discuss what the comics had brought in – giving us all a chance to be funny – then I would award points according to the audience's reaction. Thinking about it, does anyone else think that's a much better idea for a show than the one we ended up with?!

Well, let me tell you why *Is This Funny?* didn't work . . .

We booked a fringe venue in North London and booked some comics – some good ones too, some of my favourites.

When they turned up, virtually none of them had done their homework – in other words they hadn't bothered to bring anything in that was funny.

Right! We thought, maybe it would work if *we* provided the funny stuff – the vegetables, the clips . . . the newsagents? So we booked another venue and some more comics and tried again – this time, they didn't bother looking at the stuff we'd sent them. We got

---

* Looking at that list, it's a bit 'white' too, isn't it?

schoolboy excuses back like – 'Sorry I couldn't open the file' or 'Sorry the speakers on my laptop weren't working'.

They were funny nights, though – I particularly remember Nick Helm attempting to get a greased up turkey into a microwave.

So we ditched that and made it a mix of celebs and comics – but as we didn't ever get much out of the comics, we settled mainly on celebs.

Before we got into the studio, I got *Burp* survivors Dan Maier and Paul Hawksbee to help me find some funny clips of the guests from shows they'd appeared in. Then I wrote a pretty tight script.

At the recordings, I kept getting told to give the celebs plenty of room to react – because they might say something funny or I might react to something they said with a funny ad-lib. So initially, I left lots of gaps. The truth was, the guests hardly ever said anything funny, and the show was taking three hours to record.

In the edit, we'd cut out all the ad-libs, leaving us pretty much with my original script!

In other words, the script was funny enough on its own. So, after the first series I put my foot down, motored through it and shaved an hour off the time we had to spend in the studio.

The first series was a bit patchy, but I felt the second and third were consistently funny and as good, in places, as some of the best bits of that *TV Burp* that everyone bangs on about!

Where else could you see the fertility expert Lord Robert Winston, Anita Rani, Gaynor Faye and myself dressed as Cannon and Ball singing with the real Cannon and Ball?

Or an item called 'Chipolata or Regular Sausage' where I shoved sausages through a hole in a box on Des O'Connor's head? Or Sir Tom Courtenay, Alison Hammond, Les Dennis and Martine McCutcheon singing her hit 'This Is My Moment' accompanied by the George Formby Society? Or indeed, Pat Butcher burping the words to the Nat King Cole hit 'L.O.V.E'?

Exactly!

The best thing about it for me was that every week, without fail, I'd get a phone call after it had gone out from my great hero Barry Cryer congratulating me on 'bringing silly back'.

Barry wasn't exactly alone, but the ratings never really hit the sort of heights you need to justify that Saturday teatime slot.

One of the problems with it was that no one could ever get the name right. 'I love that *Alien Time Capsule*' they'd say or 'I really don't get *Alien Fun Box*!'

By series three, ITV had clearly got cold feet and moved it to the summer months – the light-entertainment graveyard. No one watches TV in the summer – they go outside and eat sausages and have arguments!

So we quietly moved on.

Listen, I wasn't sorry to see it go, I was never entirely comfortable around all those celebs – I always felt that I had to look after them. 'Hello, Judith Chalmers! Has someone got you a drink? Alison Hammond! How's your dressing room?'

That feeling is perhaps best illustrated by an incident with one of our guests from the first series who I shall call Brian. Brian's a fine actor but like a lot of actors, he's slightly out of his depth in light entertainment, where he's required to be a version of 'himself'.

During the rehearsal, I got a message through from the producer that Brian was not happy to hit himself over the head with a metal tray. Would I please talk to him?

Maybe that needs a bit of explanation.

The sketch I was trying to cajole Brian into taking part in was a reworked version of one of the great variety acts of yesteryear, Bob Blackman's 'Mule Train'. Bob would come on and sing the Frankie Laine hit 'Mule Train' whilst hitting himself over the head with a metal tray. It sounds unlikely, but check it out on YouTube – it's absolutely hilarious.

Jimmy Tarbuck once told me that he was on the bill with Bob Blackman during a summer season, and one night he asked Jim to watch the act as he had a 'new bit'. Jimmy stood in the wings and watched as Bob started the song as usual – whacking himself over the head with a tin tray. Then halfway through, he jumped off the stage and whacked a member of the audience over the head with the tray instead. That was the new bit! Unfortunately for Bob, the man in the front row took exception to this assault, stood up, and punched him in the face.

We had a stack of trays and the other guests were happy to whack themselves over the head with them in the name of entertainment, but Brian wasn't.

'Get Brian a softer tray!' I barked at Chloe in the art department. She brought me the entire stack and one by one I tried them out, hitting myself over the head with them until I found one that was of the required softness. The truth is, they were all exactly the same.

'Try that one, Brian!' I said, offering him a tray I'd carefully auditioned.

He bashed himself gingerly over the head and agreed that one would be fine and he took part in the sketch, but what a palaver.

With *TV Burp*, we were able to improve it quietly out of the glare of Saturday teatime – but because of that big hit, I can't really do that any more. Every new show I'm involved in appears with a big fanfare and naturally, is compared to my one big hit. I'm not complaining! In many ways, with my act, I was lucky to have one!

If they'd asked me back to do more *Alien Time Boxes* – or whatever it was called – I'd probably have felt duty-bound to do it, so I like to look at it this way – by axing it, ITV saved me a lot of hassle! Three series and move on! That's my motto!

CHAPTER 28
NATIONAL SERVICE

'The poppy had special significance for my grandad because between the years 1939 and '45, he was . . . a heroin addict.'

Meet Dave, the last caveman . . .

A little while ago I had the idea to develop a live show that relied purely on visual comedy. I figured that if I could come up with an idea that required no language, it could travel all around the world without any need for translation.

After much thought, I based it at a time before man had developed language – and called it *The Last Caveman*.

I wrote a script and took it out to a few West End producers who might like to invest in my new groundbreaking idea.

They found it surprisingly difficult to get their heads round! To be fair, a silent comedy doesn't read particularly well on paper, particularly if you're used to reading dialogue and putting on revivals of *Blithe Spirit*.

It requires a certain amount of imagination to see where the laughs will fall.

Originally I'd planned to cast great visual comics in the lead roles but the message I kept getting back was that I'd have to be in it for it to sell any tickets.

So with no one reaching for their cheque book, I thought to myself, *Why don't I just try it out like I would if I was building up my stand-up act?*

Which is how I found myself aged fifty-five years old, dressed in a caveman fur, a Max Wall wig and false teeth, emerging from behind a cardboard rock in front of forty people in a small room at the Battersea Arts Centre.

I'd made the rock myself from the cardboard box that our new TV had come in. I'd also made a papier mâché bear costume and various other props. I got a couple of my favourite physical comics to help me out – Holly Burn, playing my love interest cave woman, and Paul F Taylor, playing the bear.

I had about forty minutes of loosely related visual gags and business, and for the first ten minutes the audience stared at me like I had gone completely mad. They seemed to be thinking, *When is he going to stop doing this, put on his big collar and do his usual shtick!*

I had that now familiar cold sweat dripping from under my wig and down the back of my neck and was once again wondering what on earth had possessed me to do it.

But!

Gradually, once they started to get a handle on what the show was, they started to laugh. As the cast and I sat downing pints in the bar afterwards, we realised that we'd got enough laughs to make it worth trying it again.

Over the next few weeks, I re-wrote and refined it, I adapted the bear costume so that it was now a dinosaur and got five dates booked in at fringe theatres – knowing that at the end of those dates, I'd have a clear idea of whether it was worth pursuing properly. The first night of that little run at a community theatre in Surbiton surprised all of us.

The audience got it from the start and laughed all the way through. It almost went *too* well – like the audience were drunk or off their faces on meow-meow! I was thrilled and very, very excited! I couldn't wait to refine it further and run it again on the following Monday.

Unfortunately on that day, as I was loading the papier mâché dinosaur into the car, I got a phone call from my daughter's school asking me to come and pick her up because she had developed a 'persistent cough'.

That's right, you guessed it, the coronavirus had arrived.

In any event, she didn't have Covid, but naturally I felt we all needed to self-isolate and I reluctantly cancelled the remaining *Caveman* shows. The next day, Boris told everyone to 'avoid going to theatres' and by the end of the week, the nation was in its first full lockdown and show business had come to a grinding halt.

Faced with months of no live gigs, what was I going to do?

I've always kept my name on the medical register, mainly for nostalgic reasons. All it involves is paying a yearly subscription – and up until relatively recently, being on the register meant you could still write prescriptions. That came in handy more than once – I'd write the local teenagers up for heroin.

Of course not!

No, very rarely I'd write myself a prescription for antibiotics or something if I had tonsillitis. All that disappeared when something called 'accreditation' appeared – and you had to prove you were up to speed with all the latest treatments and protocols, which seems a bit unfair!

I was then listed on the register as retired.

When the coronavirus pandemic reared its ugly red-pronged head, I got an email from the General Medical Council asking me whether I'd be interested in 'returning to work'. Remember this is some thirty years after I'd last wielded a stethoscope professionally.

As the vaccination programme in this country has gotten under-way and we found our way out of repeated lockdowns, it's been easy to forget the sense of panic and fear of the unknown of March 2020 when we entered that first one.

There was a genuine concern that the hospitals might be overrun and that people would be dying gasping in the streets, which resulted in the building of the huge Nightingale Excel Hospital over in East London.

As I contemplated the GMC's request, my thoughts went back to my grandad Theophilus Botting, who joined up the day that the Second World War kicked off. He subsequently spent five years away from home fighting in the Middle East at the battle of El Alamein, then liberating Italy on his way home.*

I decided it was my turn to step up. I also thought it was probably the only way I was going to get a round of applause on a Thursday night.

So, one evening after a few gin and tonics, I clicked on the email and filled out the form.

As soon as I pressed 'SEND', I started to panic. I'd felt out of my depth when I'd been doing it every day – how would I feel thirty

---

* He'd managed a tailor's shop in civilian life and described the war as some of the best days of his life.

years later? I checked my inbox regularly over the next couple of days and breathed a tentative sigh of relief when no one got back to me.

I started to relax. *There must be thousands of doctors better qualified than me*, I thought, but just like Grandpa Theo I'd offered my services to the nation. I'd done the right thing.

Then I got a phone call.

'Hello, Dr Hall, it's Sharon here from the London Workforce Hub, and I'd like to talk to you about your return to work!'

I did what any brave patriot who has been called to serve their country would do – I furiously started to backtrack.

'Hello, Sharon, I don't want to waste your time but just so you know it's thirty years since I practised and I'm sure there are lots of other . . .'

'No, that's not a problem,' Sharon interjected breezily.

'No? Oh. OK.'

'So let's just run down a few questions . . .' she said as if she was sending someone out to service the fridge. 'What was your specialty?'

'Ah!' I said. 'That might be a problem, you see, I only worked for two years . . .'

'Well, what was your last post?'

'I was a physician . . .'

'So, what sort of cases would you be dealing with? Emergencies?'

'Well . . . yes . . .'

'Respiratory problems?'

'Well, yes . . . but—'

'Great, that's just the sort of expertise we're looking for!'

As the conversation went on, I felt a rising sense of panic.

'In theory, when could you start work?'

'Well . . . I'm not sure . . .' I faltered. The fact was, show business had been cancelled and I was very much at a loose end.

'Well, are you working at the moment?'

'Er . . . no . . .' I confessed.

'So, in theory you could start pretty much immediately?'

'I . . . suppose so,' I said – it was starting to feel like something out of a Franz Kafka novel.

'OK. Dr Hall, could you start on Monday at the Nightingale Excel Hospital in Stratford?'

I nearly fell off my chair.

'No!' I barked in desperation.

'No?' said Sharon, a little taken aback.

'Well, that is I'm in South London, so it would be very difficult for me to get to . . .' I flannelled.

'So you would prefer a South London hospital?'

'Yes, I mean, no . . . I mean, whatever you think, Sharon!'

By then, I was half expecting the doorbell to ring, to be bundled into a taxi and delivered back to St George's where my medical career had started.

'Right, now to make sure you are who you say you are,' said Sharon 'I'm going to FaceTime you. If you could hold up your passport, I can verify your identity.'

This was my last hope! Surely, if Sharon saw my face, she'd recognise me as the floppy collared host of *Alien Fun* thingy and we'd both collapse in a heap of laughter at the very idea of me being let loose on sick people again!

'Imagine waking up on a ventilator and seeing my face, Sharon!' I'd laugh, and Sharon would laugh too, and I'd offer her free tickets to my next show and agree to fast-track her nephew on to *Junior Bake Off*, we'd agree to forget all about me ever being a doctor again, and we'd part friends.

It's a testament to my current standing in the showbiz firmament that Sharon – who it turns out is a lady in her mid-sixties and who, from what I saw, cuts her own hair – failed to spot everyone's favourite absurdist comedian.*

I cursed my lockdown beard and waited to be informed of my new post.

Fortunately, in the time it took for my application to be processed, the programme of social distancing, frantic handwashing and mask-wearing had paid off, and a second peak in mortality – which would have been caused by me joining the fray – was averted.

The fact is, you don't really want to be treated by someone who only became a doctor in the first place because he liked playing with matches and who is not so much focused on your medical condition as on his next gag.

As lockdown followed lockdown, I tried a few 'Zoom gigs', which were initially quite good fun – more for the novelty than for anything else. Most of the time, I felt a bit silly standing in the spare room shouting at my laptop. I talked to a couple of comics who had tried drive-in gigs. Bill Bailey described the experience as 'like performing to a bunch of people who are waiting to get on the Cross-Channel ferry', so I passed on that opportunity. I talked to one comic who'd had to take up a job delivering for Iceland to make ends meet and who figured he may never gig again.

It all looked rather bleak.

I didn't get back on stage for fifteen months – the longest I've gone without a gig since my days with The Hall Brothers.

My first one back was at the Moth Club, an ex-servicemen's members' club in the heart of Hackney. I was nervous. *Can I still do it?* I wondered. Would I just be so rusty that it would be literally like starting again?

---

* It's a snap judgement, I know, but from what I saw, I suspect Sharon is more likely to be found most evenings, curled up on the sofa with a Hilary Mantel.

As my name was announced and I heard the audience applause, it just kicked in, like one of Pavlov's dogs. The crowd seemed so pleased to see me, and believe me, the feeling was mutual.

It was like coming home and although the audience were socially distanced and the numbers had been heavily restricted, it was thrilling. That night, I think we were all reminded of what we'd been missing out on. It was as if life in lockdown had been in black and white and suddenly it was all back in colour.

As I drove home at around midnight, passing people coming out of pubs and restaurants and generally hanging out, my mind was buzzing with possibilities, ways of improving the new gags plus ideas for others. It was like meeting up with an old friend I hadn't seen for a while, and I recognised it as that same feeling I'd had as I was driving back to Southampton General Hospital from my first open spot at the Comedy Store all those years ago.

'I remember, this is how it feels!' I said aloud to no one in particular.

I don't care what it says on my birth certificate, when I'm on stage I'm still that same twenty-six-year-old dreamer who ran away from the steady job and joined the circus.

I've been busy, haven't I? If you ever bought a ticket to one of my shows or tuned in, I have to tell you that it has always meant a lot. Sometimes I've thrilled you (The Badger Parade?), sometimes I've even made you proud (*TV Burp* sweeping the board at the BAFTAs?), no doubt sometimes I've disappointed you (*Stars In Their Eyes*?), and other times I've just confused you (a musical about *The X Factor*?). And I'm afraid to say, that's not going to change any time soon!

But that's what you like about me, right? I'm the idiot who's prepared to stick my neck out and make a complete fool of myself in the hope of getting a lousy laugh.

Why did I become a comic?

Was it, as Mrs H has postulated in the past, that I didn't get enough attention as a kid and I'm trying to make up for it?

It doesn't feel like that to me. I suspect the real reason is much more pedestrian.

I was lucky enough to be born with a modicum of talent. When I used it, I liked the feeling it gave me, so I did it again. Then every time I did it, I got a little better at it and the feeling got better, so I kept doing it.

I fear it might be as simple and as boring as that.

There's no real point in looking back. The fun is hurtling towards the next thing.

After all, life is short.

ACKNOWLEDGEMENTS

This book is very much a product of the global corona virus pandemic. If I hadn't been stuck indoors for weeks on end with nothing to do but plan the next toilet roll raid, I'd never have got round to writing it. So a big thank you to COVID 19.

In addition, I'd also like to thank my editors Myfanwy Moore and Izzy Everington at Hodder Studio.

None of what you might call 'my career so far' would have been possible without the support and gentle sarcasm of my other half Magda 'What book?' Archer and our kids Kitty, Winnie and Freddie so they must be top of the list with my mum Jan and the wider Hall family bubbling just under.

Over the years I've been helped by hundreds of people – too many to list, but here's a few. Adam Starkey , Ex Hall Brother Robert Mills, Sam Hullah, Steve Brown and Mark Allis (AKA The Caterers), Al Murray, Stewart Lee, Steve Bowditch, Stephen Taylor, Phil McIntyre, Ed Smith, Bobby Bragg, James Gill, Peter Fincham, Claudia Rosencrantz, Spencer Millman, Peter Orton, Geri Dowd, Harry Banks, Nikki Startup, Chloe Brown, Steve Nayler, Nick Linford, Andrew Jobbins, Chris Thornton, Richard Easter, Hugo Young, Paul Lyon-Maris, Giacomo Palazzo, Paul Stephens, Steve Bendelack, Robert Jones, Nigel Green, Sean Foley, Mob Dar, Alan Thorpe, Danielle Lux, Murray Bolland, Nigel Hall. I owe a huge debt to fellow TV Burp survivors Brenda Gilhooly, Daniel Maier, David Quantick and Paul Hawksbee.

I've lost a few over the years; my old school friend (and SCI Executive) Patrick Crawley, TV Director Robin Nash, song and dance man Ronné Coyles and my old partners in crime Matt Bradstock-Smith and Burt Kwouk. I miss them all.

During the final stages of putting this book together I got the sad news that Sean Lock had died. Although he'd been ill for a while it was still an awful shock and I'm afraid I just couldn't bring myself to put him into the past tense. So in my book he's still alive and just as wise, funny and brilliant as ever.

ASCENT of MONEY /
1. Words for money ✓

SCORPION KING
1. Mirror on Rock. Barber ✓
2. Earnings key event in scorpions life ✓

~~December~~

(BG) EMMNDILE ✓
1. Whats this — letter. ✓
2. Edna thorough fold — madge re-folds .✓

~~DANGERMEN~~ diving   THE DEVIL'S WHORE
1. Lap dancing — ankles revealing ✓
2. Its lost London is lost ✓

ROSE SHRAGER
1. couldn't get out door   ?

2. HOUSE GEST
1. I can't find toilet paper. ✓

2. LAST MILLIONAIRRE
1. Laughing at naked idea

200 DAYS
1. Penguin first date ✓

DOCTORS
.. You're all the same! — Driving
                    P.M.T.

Bentley
~~Mercedes~~ dealer ✓

UNDERDOG
1. There are 6 .... (mistak
2. Have 2 left feet. ✓

— emergency stop ✓
— you've passed .
— Drives me home